ECONOMIC COMMISSION FOR EUROPE

Geneva

Financing Global Climate Change Mitigation

ECE ENERGY SERIES No. 37

UNITED NATIONS

New York and Geneva, 2010

NOTE

The designations employed and the presentation of the material in this publication do not imply the expression of any opinion whatsoever on the part of the Secretariat of the United Nations concerning the legal status of any country, territory, city or area, or of its authorities, or concerning the delimitation of its frontiers or boundaries.

Mention of any firm, licensed process or commercial products does not imply endorsement by the United Nations.

ECE/ENERGY/81

UNITED NATIONS PUBLICATION

Sales No. E.10.II.E.1
ISBN 978-92-1-117017-7
ISSN 1014-7225

no loan
UN2
E/ECE/ENERGY/81

Foreword

Climate change is widely recognized as the most fundamental and defining challenge of our generation. The average temperature of the earth's surface has risen by 0.74°C since the late 1800s and it is projected to increase by up to 4° C by the year 2100 in absence of an internationally agreed comprehensive set of obligations for climate change mitigation and adaptation and mechanism of their implementation. Even if the minimum predicted increase takes place, it will be larger than any century-long trend in the last 10,000 years. Consequences for environment and sustainable development would be immense, with heavy impact on human habitat, economic and social growth and achievement of the UN's Millenium Development Goals (MDGs) and other internationally agreed development objectives.

Energy efficiency is among the most effective method of mitigating climate change. This has been upheld by the United Nations Regional Commissions that support, among others, energy efficiency market formation and facilitate the identification and development of bankable investment projects for climate change mitigation. The review of financing mechanisms can be relevant when considering new carbon market instruments. The UN Regional Commissions aim at spreading the knowledge of and stimulating discussion on models and best practices for replication with due adaptation under proper market conditions. The goal is to combine technical assistance in the design and implementation of investment projects, advice on policy and institutional reforms and direct links with investment funds in order to establish mechanisms able to fast-track the development of self-sustained markets for energy efficiency and renewable energy and to facilitate compliance with future legally binding reduction targets for greenhouse gasses (GHGs).

Energy efficiency, in particular, provides a win-win solution to combine climate change mitigation with energy security concerns. A more rational use of energy allows energy-importing countries to reduce their dependence on sometimes unsafe global supplies and to mitigate the adverse economic effects of excessive imports. On the other hand, energy exporters benefit from more efficient production and domestic consumption of energy as new resources for export are made available.

Some economists argue that closing the 'energy efficiency gap' will not cost the global economy very much. It may come free. For those of you who have been working in this field for the last few years, you know that self-financing climate change mitigation will not be easy. Indeed, the Global Energy Efficiency 21 Project – based on the experience of the UNECE Energy Efficiency 21 Programme – is aimed at promoting an investment climate in which cost-effective energy efficiency and renewable energy investment projects can be developed and financed through the support of the UN Regional Commissions.

This publication is the result of work conducted by all five UN Regional Commissions (Economic Commission for Europe (ECE), Economic and Social Commission for Asia and the Pacific (ESCAP), Economic Commission for Latin America and the Caribbean (ECLAC), Economic Commission for Africa (ECA) and Economic and Social Commission for Western Asia (ESCWA)) in the context of the Global Energy Efficiency 21 (GEE21) Project, launched in December 2008 by the ECE.

Addressing the challenges identified in this publication will require a strengthened cooperation between all UN Regional Commissions in order to provide a global forum for exchange of information and a hub of capacity building services, as suggested by the UN System Chief Executives Board. A renewed commitment at the regional level to assist in the design, implementation and evaluation of projects is also necessary and the Regional Commissions can effectively take advantage of their close links with local governments, national institutions and the private sector developed in over 60 years of broadly based intergovernmental dialogue on a wide-ranging set of economic and social issues. All this means a joint effort which considers the close correlation between policy reforms and the development of bankable projects and it goes to the core of energy efficiency market formation in the carbon intensive energy economies.

It is our pleasure to bring to your attention this publication on *Financing Global Climate Change Mitigation*.

Jan Kubis
Executive Secretary
UNITED NATIONS ECONOMIC COMMISSION FOR EUROPE

Noeleen Heyzer
Executive Secretary
UNITED NATIONS ECONOMIC AND SOCIAL COMMISSION FOR ASIA AND THE PACIFIC

Alicia Bárcena
Executive Secretary
UNITED NATIONS ECONOMIC COMMISSION FOR LATIN AMERICA AND THE CARIBBEAN

Abdoulie Janneh
Executive Secretary
UNITED NATIONS ECONOMIC COMMISSION FOR AFRICA

Bader Al-Dafa
Executive Secretary
UNITED NATIONS ECONOMIC AND SOCIAL COMMISSION FOR WESTERN ASIA

Contents

LIST OF FIGURES

LIST OF BOXES

ACRONYMS

AAU:	Assigned Amount Unit
ACPC:	African Climate Policy Centre
ADB:	Asian Development Bank
AFD:	Agence Française de Développement
AFDB:	African Development Bank
AFREC:	African Energy Commission
ALBA:	Bolivarian Alternative for the Americas
APCTT:	Asia Pacific Centre for the Transfer of Technology
APEC:	Asia-Pacific Economic Cooperation
ASEAN:	Association of South-East Asian Nations
AU:	African Union
BEC:	Biomass Energy Conservation

BEEF:	Bulgarian Energy Efficiency Fund
CAPP:	Central African Power Pool
CCS:	Carbon Capture and Storage
CDM:	Clean Development Mechanism
CEE:	Central and Eastern Europe
CER:	Certified Emission Reduction
CIF:	Climate Investment Funds
CFI:	Commercial Financial Institutions
COMELEC:	Comité Maghrebin de l'Electricité
CTF:	Clean Technology Fund
COMESA:	Common Market for Eastern and Southern Africa
COP:	Conference of Parties
CSD:	Committee on Sustainable Development
CSI:	California Solar Initiative
DFI:	Development Finance Institutions
DSM:	Demand-side Management
EAPP:	East African Power Pool
EBRD:	European Bank for Reconstruction and Development
EC:	European Commission
ECCAS:	Economic Community of Central African States
ECA:	Economic Commission for Africa
ECE:	Economic Commission for Europe
ECLAC:	Economic Commission for Latin America and the Caribbean
ECOWAS:	Economic Community of West African States
ECSEE:	Energy Community South East Europe Treaty
EEREA:	Energy Efficiency and Related Environmental Aspects
EIB:	European Investment Bank
ESCAP:	Economic and Social Commission for Asia and the Pacific
ESCWA:	Economic and Social Commission for Western Asia
EE:	Energy Efficiency
EEI:	Energy Efficiency Initiatives
EMC:	Energy Management Company
ERU:	Emission Reduction Unit
ESCO:	Energy Service Company
ETS:	(EU) Emission Trading Scheme
EU:	European Union
EUA:	European Union Allowance
EurAsEC:	Eurasian Economic Community
FIRST:	(Berkeley) Financing Initiative for Removable and Solar Technology
GEF:	Global Environmental Facility
G8:	Group of Eight
GHG:	Greenhouse Gas
GTZ:	Gesellschaft für Technische Zusammenarbeit
IAEA:	International Atomic Energy Agency
IDB:	Inter-American Development Bank
IEA:	International Energy Agency
IET:	International Emission Trading

IFC:	International Finance Corporation
IPCC:	Intergovernmental Panel on Climate Change
IPP:	Independent Power Producer
IRENA:	International Renewable Energy Agency
JI:	Joint Implementation
JRC:	(EU) Joint Research Centre
KfW:	Kreditanstalt für Wiederaufbau
LAS:	League of Arab States
MDGs:	Millennium Development Goals
MERCOSUR:	Southern Common Market
MIT:	Massachusetts Institute of Technology
NDRC:	National Development and Reform Commission (China)
NEPAD:	New Partnership for Africa's Development
ODA:	Overseas Development Assistance
OECD:	Organization for Economic Cooperation and Development
OLADE:	Latin American Energy Organization
OPEC:	Organization of Petroleum Exporting Countries
PPA:	Power Purchase Agreement
PCG:	Partial Credit Guarantee
PRG:	Partial Risk Guarantee
PROSOL:	Moroccan Solar Water Heating (SWH) Loan/Leasing Facility
R&D:	Research and Development
RCC:	Regional Cooperation Council
RCM:	Regional Coordination Meeting
RE:	Renewable Energy
REC:	Regional Economic Community
RISOE:	(UNEP) Centre on Energy, Climate and Sustainable Development
RSA:	Republic of South Africa
SAARC:	South Asian Association for Regional Cooperation
SADC:	Southern African Development Community
SAPP:	Southern African Power Pool
SBFF:	Small Business Financing Facility
SCI:	Strategic Climate Fund
SED:	(ECE) Sustainable Energy Division
SECCI:	(IDB) Sustainable Energy and Climate Change Initiative
SECI:	Southeast European Co-operative Initiative
SEFI:	Sustainable Energy Finance Initiative
SEI:	(EBRD) Sustainable Energy Initiative
SME:	Small and Medium Entreprise
SPECA:	Special Programme of Economies of Central Asia
SPV:	Special Purpose Vehicle
SSA:	Sub-Saharan Africa
SWH:	Solar Water Heater
TA:	Technical Assistance
TPES:	Total Primary Energy Supply
TPPPA:	Third-Party Power Purchase Agreement
UMA:	Maghreb Arab Union

UNASUR: Union of South American Nations
UNDESA: United Nations Department of Economic and Social Affairs
UNDP: United Nations Development Programme
UNEP: United Nations Environmental Programme
UNF: United Nations Foundation
UNFCCC: United Nations Framework Convention on Climate Change
UNFIP: United National Fund for International Partnerships
UNFPA: United Nations Population Fund
UNIDO: United Nations Industrial Development Organisation
WAPP: West African Power Pool
WB: World Bank
WEC: World Energy Council
WEO: World Energy Outlook
WIR: World Investment Report
WSSD: World Summit on Sustainable Development
WWF: World Wildlife Fund

ABBREVIATIONS

bn: billion
bcm: billion cubic metres
CO_2:   carbon dioxide
Gt: gigatonnes
GW: gigawatt
GWh: gigawatt-hour
kt: kilotonnes
KW: kilowatt
KWh: kilowatt-hour
mln: million
Mt: million tonnes
MW: megawatt
MWh: megawatt-hour
p.a.:   per annum
ppm: part per million
t: metric tonne
toe: tonne of oil equivalent

Preface

This report is one of the first outputs of the Global Energy Efficiency 21 (GEE21) project, launched by the United Nations Economic Commission for Europe (ECE) in December 2008 at COP-14 in Poznan (Poland). The GEE21 project is designed to develop a more systematic exchange of experience on capacity building, policy reforms and investment project finance among countries of the other regions of the world through their UN Regional Commissions in order to promote self-financing energy efficiency improvements that raise economic productivity, diminish fuel poverty and reduce environmental air pollution such as greenhouse gas emissions. The GEE21 project stems from the positive experience in the ECE region of the Energy Efficiency 21 (EE21) programme, in particular of the project Financing Energy Efficiency Investments for Climate Change Mitigation (FEEI), mainly financed by extrabudgetary funds from the Fond Français pour l'Environnement Mondial (FFEM), the UNEP/Global Environmental Facility (GEF/UNEP), the United Nations Foundation (UNF/ UNFIP) and the European Business Congress (EBC). The GEE21 project also relies on additional funding from the government of the Russian Federation.

Financing Global Climate Change Mitigation specifically aims at providing an appraisal of the energy efficiency situation worldwide and giving guidance on further action. It is meant to have strong practical implications for practitioners who operate in the field of sustainable energy and energy efficiency financing as well as for policymakers willing to enhance energy efficiency and renewable energy investments. The former will find references to a wide array of financing mechanisms and preliminary information on local contexts, while the latter will be given an overview of the instruments available and the economic and institutional conditions promoting their success.

An additional goal of this report is to draw attention to the practice of energy efficiency as a powerful tool not only to fight climate change, but also to promote sustainable development and reduce poverty. Indeed, unlike other mitigation strategies, improvements in efficiency reduce emissions while diminishing energy costs and natural resource depletion. The efficient use of energy can thus be a milestone for a wider strategy on the achievement of the MDGs and the objectives of the World Summit on Sustainable Development (WSSD), so that the perennial strain among development, population and resources is finally broken or at least loosened. In order to do so, however, policymakers need to be aware that suitable regulatory regimes and correct incentive structures are fundamental to the delivery of sustained self-financing energy efficiency. From now to 2012, tremendous efforts must be undertaken to negotiate an effective and equitable way to restructure the rules of the game so that every economic activity fully bears the costs of its negative environmental externalities and takes into account the discount rate of resources in an inter-generational perspective.

For further information, please contact:

Gianluca Sambucini (Secretary of the Committee on Sustainable Energy)

United Nations Economic Commission for Europe
Palais des Nations, CH-1211 Geneva, Switzerland

Tel: +41 (0)22 917 11 75 – Fax: +41 (0)22 917 00 38
gianluca.sambucini@unece.org
www.unece.org/energy/

Acknowledgements

The volume was prepared by Gianluca Sambucini, Andrea Bonzanni and Brinda Wachs (ECE) with inputs from each of the UN Regional Commissions. The regional overviews have been drafted by Andrea Bonzanni (ECE), Kohji Iwakami and Kelly Anne Hayden (ESCAP), Manlio Coviello and Claudio Carpio (ECLAC), Pancrace Niyimbona, Joe Atta-Mensah and Nancy Kgengwenyan (ECA), Anhar Hegazi, Walid Al-Deghaili and Ziad Jaber (ESCWA).

Jacquelin Ligot (Senior Consultant for the UNECE Secretariat) has contributed with the survey of the 22 financing mechanisms, the drafting of chapters 1-4 and annexes I-III as well as with a review of the entire publication.

This work has been published in the context of UN-Energy, the United Nations inter-agency framework mechanism on energy. UN-Energy was established in 2004 to help ensure system-wide coherence in the implementation of the WSSD's energy-related decisions. The group maintains an overview of major ongoing initiatives within the UN and focuses on substantive and collaborative actions both in regard to policy development in the energy area and its implementation. All of the five UN Regional Commissions are active members of the group, whose membership amounts to 20 UN agencies, programmes and organizations. Currently, UN-Energy is chaired by Mr. Kandeh Yumkella, Director-General, United Nations Industrial Development Organization (UNIDO). The ECE and the contributors are grateful to the UNIDO colleagues within UN-Energy for their valuable feedback on an earlier draft of this report.

The editors are also thankful to Laura Cozzi (International Energy Agency), who has provided useful data on abatement targets and investment needs, used in chapter 1.

Executive summary

Carbon abatement scenarios assign to energy efficiency (EE) and renewable energy (RE) a predominant role in climate change mitigation. This will require massive investments and the mobilisation of substantial new financial resources. Against this backdrop, it is useful to review existing mechanisms that channel funds to EERE projects and understand the success factors in designing EERE financing mechanisms. This is the purpose of the first part (chapters 1-4) of *Financing Global Climate Change Mitigation – Sources of Financing Energy Efficiency and Renewable Energy Investments*.

After an overview of the forecasts on abatement needs, the investment levels necessary to achieve these targets and the important differences in financing between EE and RE, Chapter 2 seeks to provide a summary of 22 selected EERE financing mechanisms and an assessment of the relevance of the carbon market for EERE financing. The chapter does not aim to rank or assess their quality. The lack of systematic evaluations of EERE financing mechanisms means that energy experts and policy makers are deprived of the intellectual foundation needed to assess their effectiveness and worth.

Chapter 3 discusses Technical Assistance, looking at why it is needed, how it is funded, and how it could be better targeted and accessed.

Chapter 4 highlights ingredients for success, starting with the appropriateness and fit to the local institutional environment.

The volume then provides a review of the technical, economic and regulatory conditions in each region and a summary of main activities undertaken by national governments and international institutions, with a particular regard to the work of the UN Regional Commissions (chapters 5-9).

The *Economic Commission for Europe (ECE)*, whose members range from the least to the most energy efficient countries in the world, stresses the importance of international cooperation on policy reform, capacity building, technology transfer and investment. Its members' experience in promoting EE, the positive results of the still ongoing effort to reduce the east-west energy divide and its synergies with local authorities and the private sector make the ECE a successful model of regional intergovernmental cooperation for the delivery of EE improvements.

The *Economic and Social Commission for Asia and the Pacific (ESCAP)*, working to make the dramatic growth of some of its members possible for the whole region and sustainable over time, pushes for a new "virtuous" paradigm of development and inserts EE into the broader context of the attainment of the MDGs and poverty reduction. While recommending policy reforms, ESCAP looks with optimism to the attractiveness of the region to investors and to the EE programmes launched by some of its members.

The *Economic Commission for Latin America and the Caribbean (ECLAC)* analyses the energy and economic situation in the region over the last few decades and states that, despite significant structural changes in the use of sources and their sectoral distribution, improvements in energy efficiency and the levels of emissions have not been satisfactory. Nonetheless, numerous programmes implemented at the national level by several countries, as well as the trend toward closer regional integration and activities promoted by ECLAC, make Latin America and the Caribbean among the most active regions of the world in the promotion of energy efficiency and renewable energy sources.

The *Economic Commission for Africa (ECA)* points out that, despite the region's extremely low level of energy consumption and the challenge to make energy available while addressing economic development needs, a more rational use of energy is needed to guarantee sustained access to the millions of Africans still without electricity, to maximise the benefits from its vast natural resources and to prevent irreversible environmental deterioration. ECA underlines the lack of an effective regulatory framework and, except in isolated cases, the inadequacy of the local economies to generate or attract investment. A positive trend is seen, however, in the establishment of several regional economic groupings and supranational power pools.

The *Economic and Social Commission for Western Asia (ESCWA)* shows how the global impact of climate change and its consequences suffered by some of its members make EE and other mitigation measures necessary even in countries with vast conventional energy resources. The case studies presented are also proof of how well-designed regulation and financing mechanisms can attract significant investment and achieve results.

The publication contains four annexes. The first three focus on financing and outline respectively the building blocks for EERE financing, the main public finance mechanisms for climate change mitigation and the sources of financing available from development finance institutions (DFIs). The fourth annex is a compilation of the main EE legislation in national regulatory frameworks.

1. Energy efficiency and renewable energies (EERE) for climate change mitigation

The purpose of this chapter is to give an overview of the energy efficiency (EE) and renewable energy (RE) environment, including the differences between EE and RE, their respective roles in climate mitigation, and projected costs and investment requirements for mitigation.

1.1. Role of EERE in achieving climate change mitigation goals

There is a wide international consensus on the central role that energy efficiency and renewable energy can play in achieving defined carbon abatement goals. The International Energy Agency's (IEA) "BLUE" scenario, the most aggressive emission reduction scenario to the 2050 horizon elaborated as part of its first "Energy Technology Perspectives" at the request of the G8 and released in 2008, explores the least-cost solutions to achieve the most ambitious scenario of the Intergovernmental Panel on Climate Change (IPCC) of keeping temperature increases below $2.4C_0$ (this seems to be consistent with CO_2 concentrations in the atmosphere of 450ppm, although opinion is still mixed). According to this scenario, energy-related emissions would need to be halved by 2050 compared to their 2005 levels (from 27 to $14GtCO_2$), implying staggering emission cuts of $48GtCO_2$ compared to the baseline scenario ($62GtCO_2$ in 2050). End-use efficiency accounts for 36% to 44% of all reductions in BLUE and renewables account for 21% (46% of the electricity mix in 2050). These two options (i.e. end-use efficiency and renewables) thus account for the bulk of reductions in BLUE.

Similarly, in a recent presentation, IEA Executive Director Nobuo Tanaka estimated that EE and RE (including biofuels) could account for respectively 54% and 23% of the necessary abatement effort by 2030 in the 450ppm scenario[1].

McKinsey, the international management consulting firm, confirm these conclusions with regard to the potential role of EE (or "energy productivity"[2]) in achieving carbon saving targets[3]. McKinsey estimates that $170bn p.a. could be invested from now until 2020 in energy productivity opportunities yielding an average internal rate of return (IRR) of 17%. These investments, equivalent to respectively 1.6% and 0.4% of global fixed investment and global GDP today, could cut the projected growth of energy demand from 2.2% p.a. to 0.7%, generating savings ramping up to $900bn by 2020, and delivering up to half of the emission abatement required in 2020 to cap the long-term concentration of greenhouse gases in the atmosphere at 450ppm. Not least, this would avoid investment in energy infrastructure that would otherwise be needed to keep pace with accelerating demand. The IEA, in its 2006 World Energy Outlook, estimated that on average an additional $1 spent on efficiency in electrical equipment and appliances avoids more than $2 in investment in electricity supply.

1.2. Current and projected financing flows for carbon mitigation

1.2.1. Current investment flows

In "Global Trends in Sustainable Energy Investment 2008"[4], an annual review of investment trends in the sustainable energy sector co-produced with New Energy Finance, the United Nations Environment Programme (UNEP, under its Sustainable Energy Finance Initiative (SEFI): www.sefi.unep.org) estimates overall global investment in sustainable energy at $155bn in 2008[5]. This figure, compared to the $33bn in 2004 (that is, an annual average growth of 45%), well reflects the clean energy boom of the last few years.

Asset finance –the focus of this survey– reached about $116bn (including small-scale projects). This is equivalent to about 9% of global energy infrastructure investment and 1% of global fixed asset investment. Wind was the leading sector in 2008, accounting for 48%, followed by solar (22%), biofuels (15%), and biomass and waste (7%). An important limitation of this annual review is that the financing of EE projects hardly features at all, as these numbers exclude investment by governments and public financing institutions and those financed from companies' own cash flow.

Europe and industrialised countries maintained the lion's share of asset finance, with close to $50bn and $82bn respectively. This was due to supportive policies in many European countries, as well as an investor base that is comfortable with financing RE projects and more intense competition for deals.

However, the share of developing countries continued to increase, reaching 31% in 2008, with $36.6bn, almost 20 times the 2004 level of $1.8bn. China attracted almost 50% of that share, more than the combined shares of South America (despite the strong performance of Brazil, in particular in sugar cane ethanol), the Middle East and Africa.

1.2.2. Projected investment flows

Estimates of future investment needs to meet climate mitigation targets vary widely. This is because they use different methodologies, they are not focusing on all sectors (the main focus is usually on the power sector) and they do not necessarily take into account the avoided investments in power capacity expansion due to EE (see Table 1.1 below).

Prominent among such estimates was the 2007 report by the United Nations Framework Convention on Climate Change (UNFCCC) on "Investment and financial flows to address climate change"[6]. The aim of the UNFCCC secretariat was to quantify the amount of additional investments necessary to reduce emissions by 25% below 2000 levels by 2030 (from 38.9 to 29.1GtCO2-equ). Under its reference scenario, GHG emissions would total 61.5GtCO2-equ in 2030. The report estimated that the necessary average annual additional investments to reach the target amount to $200-210bn (see third row of table 1.1). This would only represent 1.1-1.7% of the estimated total global investment in 2030. The 2008 "update" to this report[7], while leaving unchanged the emission abatement projections, revised however upwards by 170% its estimate of the additional necessary investments, "mainly due to higher project costs", and concluded that "any future agreement to enhance mitigation needs to encompass a variety of funding sources and delivery mechanisms that address GHG mitigation from all sectors in all countries, and also foster development and transfer of mitigation technology".

Clearly, this is an area where more work is needed so that at least a sound methodology can be agreed upon. Negotiations on equitable burden sharing arrangements between industrialised and developing countries need to be based on robust numbers on the real cost of climate mitigation.

Table 1.1: Some global estimates of costs and investment requirements for mitigation

Study	Estimate	Basis
World Bank Group, Clean Energy Framework, 04/2006	$30bn p.a. for power sector in developing countries	Investment estimate, assuming stabilization at 450ppm, on top of $160bn p.a. for electricity supply in developing countries over 2010–30, of which currently only half is financed
Stern Review, 11/2006	$1,000bn p.a.	Annual global macroeconomic cost; central estimate by 2050, consistent with stabilization at 550ppm; represents 1% of global GDP by 2050, ranging from net gains of 1% global GDP to reduction of 3.5%
UNFCCC, 08/2007	$200-210bn p.a.	Estimate of annual global investment and financial flows by 2030, broadly consistent with stabilization at 550ppm
IPCC, 11/2007	5.5% to -1% (gain) reduction in global GDP	Estimate of annual macroeconomic costs to global GDP, ranging from 3% to small increase by 2030 and from 5.5% to 1% gain by 2050 for targets between 445 to 710ppm
OECD Environmental Outlook to 2030, 05/2008	$350-3,000bn p.a.	Annual global macroeconomic cost, central estimate, consistent with stabilisation at 450ppm; represents a 0.5% loss to global GDP by 2030 and 2.5% by 2050 or an average 0.1% slow down of growth
IEA, Energy Technology Perspectives (ETP) 2008, 06/2008	$400-1,100bn p.a. for energy sector	Global cumulative additional investment needs between now and 2050 for energy sector estimated at $17 trillion, or 0.4% of global GDP (~550ppm) and $45trillion, or 1.15% of global GDP (~450ppm)
IEA, World Energy Outlook 2009, 10/2009	$250bn p.a. from 2010 to 2020; $936bn p.a. from 2021 to 2030	Investment estimates for end-use and power plants efficiency (57 to 65%), plus investments in alternative sources (renewables, biofuels, nuclear and CCS)

Source: World Bank (2008), Annex 2 of "Development and climate change: a strategic framework for the World Bank Group" and World Energy Outlook 2009.

Box 1.1: Investment estimation in the World Energy Outlook 2009

One of the most recent forecasts on the investment needs to achieve reduction targets is IEA's "450" scenario, released in the World Energy Outlook 2009. This scenario is an attempt to compute the investment needed to stabilize the concentration of greenhouse gases in the atmosphere to a level around 450ppm of CO_2-equivalent, widely regarded as the necessary level to limit the probability of a global average temperature increase in excess of 2°C to 50%. According to the IEA's estimation, global energy-related CO_2 will peak at 30.9Gt just before 2020 and decline thereafter to 26.4Gt in 2030, an amount 2.4Gt below the 2007 level and 13.8Gt below that in the "Reference" scenario (that is, assuming absence of policy change).

In line with most other forecasts, end-use energy efficiency investments account for about 70% of total investment in 2020 and for almost 60% in 2030. Increased use of renewable energies (mostly for power generation and heat) accounts for 19% in 2020 and 24% in 2030. Biofuels, nuclear and carbon capture and storage (CCS) represent smaller yet growing over time shares. Over 45% of these costs have to be borne by the "OECD Plus" countries (roughly corresponding to the ECE region), although their share of total abatement burden is foreseen to decrease over time.

The IEA notes that additional investments need to be weighed against the benefits they generate. Notably, fuel savings over the lifetime of the capital stocks are estimated to be more than twice as large the additional investment needed in the transport, industry and building sector. Further, oil and gas import bills would reduce by 50% compared to the "Reference" scenario for all major energy importers. Finally, additional long-term savings are realized through the reduced spending to curb air pollution, which is estimated at $240bn worldwide in 2007 and set to rise by over 250% in the "Reference" scenario.

1.3. Differences between EE and RE

Energy efficiency and renewable energy are often lumped together on account of their common and important role in climate mitigation. Yet, investment in EE and RE differ in a number of important respects. Table 1.2 highlights the most salient of these differences.

Key differences pertain to the purpose, nature and size of the investment, the awareness, skills and motivation of the sponsors, the nature of financial benefits, project risks, as well as financing methods and sources. The implication from a financing point of view is that, even when RE investments are small or medium scale, the financier of these projects will need to deploy different skills and approaches to appraise and finance these two types of investments. This has consequences for capacity building needs and the design of financing mechanisms.

Table 1.2: Main differences between investment in energy efficiency and renewable energy

	Energy Efficiency	Renewable Energy
Purpose of investment relative to project proponent's main business	Ancillary	Core
Nature of investment	Mostly retrofit, or part of capacity expansion	Mostly greenfield
Size of investment	Mostly small and medium scale	Can be large in some technologies (e.g. wind, CSP)
Nature of project proponent	Going concern	Usually a SPV
Awareness of project proponent to potential project benefits	Can be low	High
Skills and motivation of project proponent to undertake project	Can be weak and low (SMEs)	Strong, high (professional developers or utilities)
Nature of financial benefits arising from projects	Energy savings and other cost reductions stemming from productivity improvements (if any)	Power (and/or heat) sales, or avoided purchase of power and/or heat (if captive use)
Risks (other than technical)	Output of underlying industrial/commercial activity	Intermittency of RE resource (wind, hydro) Off-taker's creditworthiness Adverse changes in regulatory framework (e.g. feed-in tariffs relative to wholesale power price)
Financing method	Corporate (balance sheet) finance (unless an ESCO provides off-balance sheet financing)	Can be project finance if project is big enough
Financing source	Mostly debt (unless project involves an SPV, e.g. to create own generation sources)	Usually debt and equity

Source: J. Ligot.

Some of these differences in approach are worth elaborating:

(i) Project finance (non- or limited-recourse financing) is seldom encountered in EE financing. It is not just any debt financing of a project, rather it typically combines three features:

   a. The construction (most frequently green-field) of a discrete piece of physical asset(s) that provides services for which a user fee can be charged, such as a toll, water or electricity charges. Often operation of the project asset(s) is the object of a legal or natural monopoly conferred to the operator through a concession or equivalent contract generally awarded through some transparent and competitive process (e.g. a motorway, an airport, a power plant). In the field of EERE, concessions or equivalents are rare, because saving energy or producing RE are not natural monopolies, although large wind farms are typically financed on a project finance basis.

   b. The project asset(s) and its revenues are "ring-fenced" in a special purpose vehicle (SPV), which seeks to maximize its leverage or gearing (debt to equity ratio) in order to limit the capital outlay and risk to shareholders. The 2008 credit crunch has led the pendulum to swing back in the other direction, with banks now requiring a much larger infusion of equity, especially in emerging markets, increasing loan margins and reducing loan tenors[8].

   c. The debt financing extended to the SPV is without or with only limited recourse to the project sponsor/investors/operators. The project revenues are the primary source of loan repayment and the project asset(s) the main security for the loan. If the project fails and the SPV defaults on its debt service obligations, the lender has no recourse to the SPV owner(s).

Because of these characteristics, the legal documentation of project finance transactions is complex (as is risk allocation between the parties to the deal) and transaction costs high. As a result, project finance is generally not suitable to EE projects, unless the EE project entails the construction of an asset with a dedicated revenue stream, e.g. a cogeneration plant. In this case, the pre-requisites for project finance can be met, if the facility is large enough. However, EE projects are usually small and it is tricky to segregate and ring-fence "project revenues" which accrue from savings and productivity improvements.

(ii) EE financing requires an assessment of the product market in which the project proponent operates and of its distinct risks, whereas for RE is sufficient to know the technology specification and the electricity market.

The appraisal of grid-connected RE projects requires an assessment of the electricity market (and regulatory framework, in particular feed-in tariffs), of the terms of the off-take contract between the project proponent (typically an SPV) and the creditworthiness of the off-taker. Bankers draw significant comfort from the existence of feed-in tariffs (special, guaranteed prices for electricity from renewables and an obligation for distributors or single buyers to purchase it at this price). This relative simplicity and the attractive level of feed-in tariffs explain the boom of wind (and now solar) energy in many parts of the world. At least 63 countries, states or provinces have enacted feed-in tariffs, and this trend is expected to continue[9]. Even South Africa has now generous feed-in tariffs although its electricity prices remain among the lowest in the world.

EE projects, being implemented by a wide variety of project proponents in the public, industrial or commercial sectors, call for an assessment of the product market in which the project proponent operates (e.g. steel, cement, textiles, etc). The main risk of EE projects is neither technical nor linked to the energy market, but mainly concerns whether the project proponent is competitive in its main product market and whether this market is growing, flat, or shrinking. A practical implication is that the appraisal of such projects cannot be done by a single unit or team, unlike for RE projects. This also explains why banks have been historically uncomfortable with these projects, as they do not fit neatly their conventional structure organized around "sectors" or "products" (the long-held view that a cost saving is not a real revenue is another source of reticence).

2. Selected mechanisms and sources of financing

The purpose of this chapter is to provide a survey of mechanisms and sources of financing for energy efficiency (EE) and renewable energy (RE) investments for climate change mitigation. Given its scope, this survey can only be considered an introduction to the subject.

2.1 Relevance of financing mechanisms

Although figures on the order of magnitude of that effort are still hazy (see chapter 1 and table 1.1 above), the need for massive scaling up of EE and RE (EERE) investments presented in the previous session will require a gigantic effort. Proposals for new financial resources are being discussed among the parties to the UNFCCC[10]. It is essential that these additional resources be channelled in the most efficient and effective fashion. In this context, a survey of existing mechanisms and sources of financing for EERE investments, highlighting their merits and disadvantages as well as success factors and conditions of replicability, can make a worthwhile contribution to a well-directed effort to scale up resources for climate change mitigation.

2.2. Main EERE financing mechanisms

This section presents a selection of 22 from a vast and diverse array of EERE financing mechanisms[11]. This report focuses on the financing of small to medium scale projects.

Sixteen of these mechanisms target developing countries or countries in transition; five are global or regional in scope; five provide equity/quasi-equity; 13 debt, five guarantees and one pure grant. Four involve Energy Service Companies (ESCOs) and four energy utilities; five schemes target households; 16 involve private financial intermediaries; six public or not-for-profit. Most rely on some form of public financial support. Carbon finance is also reviewed, although it is less a mechanism than a source.

There are several ways to classify these mechanisms, such as by nature of financial instrument (e.g. debt, equity, etc.), by type of beneficiary, by nature of the public subsidy element it contains, etc. The approach chosen here is to focus on the key issue or barrier that these mechanisms were predominantly designed to address in the targeted geography. The list of these mechanisms is shown in Table 2.1.

Table 2.1: List of 22 EERE financing mechanisms surveyed

Main issue addressed	Name of mechanism	Targeted geography
Closing the equity gap: Dedicated private equity funds (3 schemes)	European RE Fund LP (Platina Partners) EnerCap Power Fund LP GEEREF	EU * CEE * Developing countries *
Closing the debt-equity gap: Dedicated subordinated debt funds (2)	FIDEME CAREC	France Central America *
Supporting a nascent ESCO industry (3)	1st Energy Conservation Programme UkrEsco Bulgarian ESCO Fund	China Ukraine Bulgaria
Using utilities or municipalities as relays in the financial intermediation chain (5)	EmPower New York PROSOL TPPPA for Solar PV CHUEE Berkeley FIRST	USA Tunisia USA China USA
Financing energy access (off-grid communities in rural areas) with micro-finance (1)	Grameen Shakti	Bangladesh
Mitigating risks of local lenders: Guarantees (2)	USAID Development Credit Authority 2nd Energy Conservation Programme	Developing countries * China
Remedying the inability or unwillingness of CFIs to finance EERE projects: Special Purpose Financing Vehicles or Windows (3)	BEEF IREDA Carbon Trust	Bulgaria India UK
Dedicated DFI EE/RE credit lines to local CFIs (3)	EE Revolving Fund EBRD SEFF AFD Climate credit line	Thailand Countries in transition China

Source: J. Ligot.

NB: the asterisk * refers to multi-country schemes.

The main generic barriers to investments in EERE projects are summarized in table 2.2 below, which also shows how the 22 mechanisms are tackling these barriers. In several cases, programme designers were trying to solve more than a single issue and mechanisms are thus listed under more than one heading. This means that the ultimate sources of funding (e.g. Global Environment Facility (GEF), international financial institution (IFI) loans, taxes, etc.) are not discussed as such, but only listed in connection with the mechanisms they support. It is clear from the table that some of the main barriers, such as low energy prices, are beyond the reach of a financing mechanism and can only be tackled by policy reform. This point is further discussed in chapter 4.

Table 2.2: How EERE financing mechanisms address generic barriers to EERE investments

Barrier / Issues	Solutions provided by financing mechanisms	Examples (the lead country and number under which the mechanism is surveyed below in parenthesis)
(1) Low or distorted fossil energy prices		
a. Low energy utility tariffs	Investment subsidy	PROSOL (Tunisia) (10) BEERECL (Bulgaria) (21)
b. Other subsidies to production/ consumption of fossil fuels	Concessional funding (interest rate below market, long grace period and tenor)	AFD (China) (22) Thailand REEF (Thailand) (20)
(2) High cost vs. alternatives, e.g. SWH	Investment subsidy	Empower New York (USA) (9) PROSOL (10) BEERECL (21)
	Concessional funding (interest rate below market, long grace period and tenor)	Grameen Shakti (Bangladesh) (14) AFD (22)
	Long-term lease coupled with tax credits	TPPPA for solar PV systems (USA) (11)

Barrier / Issues	Solutions provided by financing mechanisms	Examples (the lead country and number under which the mechanism is surveyed below in parenthesis)
(3) Lack of domestic sources of capital and/or inappropriate terms		
a. Long-term debt	State or DFI-funded credit line to local banks	EERECL (21) (Thailand) REEF (Thailand) (20)
b. Equity	Dedicated equity funds	Platina Partners (Western Europe) (1), EnerCap (Central Europe) (2), GEEREF (global) (3)
c. Quasi-equity	Dedicated quasi-equity funds	FIDEME (France) (4), CAREC (Central America) (5)
	New funding institution or new funding window	BgEEF (Bulgaria) (17), IREDA (India) (16), Carbon Trust (UK) (19)
	Micro-finance	Grameen Shakti (Bangladesh) (14)
(4) High perceived risks by banks	Partial Loan Guarantees	CHUEE (China) (12), USAID guarantee (global) (15), Energy Conservation Programme II (China) (16)
	Integrate loan payments into utility bills	PROSOLAR (10),
	Integrate loan payments in local taxes	BerkeleyFirst (USA) (13)
	New funding institution	BgEEF (17), IREDA (16), Carbon Trust (19)
(5) Weak project development, appraisal and technical assessment capacity	TA for capacity building	BEERECL (21), CHUEE (China) (12), AFD (22)
	Dedicated banks	BgEEF (17), IREDA (India) (16)
	Using utilities as a hub	CHUEE (China) (12)
(6) High transaction costs	TA for project preparation	BEERECL (21), AFD Tunisia (22)
(7) Lack of awareness, information	Campaigns Website Free energy audits	BEERECL (21)
	Using utilities as a hub	CHUEE (China) (12)
(8) Lack of EE project developers such as ESCOs	Help create new ESCOs or strengthen existing ones	Energy Conservation Programme I (China) (6), UkrEsco (Ukraine) (7), Enemona (Bulgaria)(8)

Source: J. Ligot.

2.2.1. Closing the equity gap: Dedicated private equity funds

Equity is required to finance projects undertaken through a special purpose vehicle such as an Independent Power Producer (IPP) project, or an ESCO. Unless the sponsor is a large company or utility, this equity is generally supplied by private equity funds. Until last year, the share of equity funding in the project capital structure could be as low as 15-20% in the most developed markets. The financial and economic crisis has led to the deleveraging of project capital structures and therefore a higher proportion of equity is now required. This section showcases three types of funds dedicated to sustainable energy: a purely private fund operating in the most mature and secure market (Platina); a private equity fund operating in countries in transition where some perceived (mostly regulatory) risks warrant the comfort brought by public investors (IFIs) (EnerCap) and a public fund comprised of funds investing "patient" equity in dedicated EERE funds in emerging markets (GEEREF).

1. Europe - European Renewable Energy Fund 1 LP (Platina Partners)						
Launched	Amount	Target end-users	Technical Assistance	Subsidy	Donor/DFI financing	Website
2008	€75mln (target €250mln)	RE	No	No	No	www.platinapartners.com

Platina manages and advises funds, investing both in buyout and RE opportunities. It is currently managing four funds investing in renewable energy projects. Its latest fund, EREF, (€75mln raised to date) will invest primarily in businesses that own renewable energy generation assets in order to aggregate between 500MW and 700MW of electrical generation capacity. It is expected that €30mln of the fund will be reserved to secure and finance a pipeline of projects still in their development phase in order to boost the fund's returns.

EREF investment focus is on European RE projects and companies involved at all stages from development through operation. The firm typically commits €1-3mln at the development stage and up to €50mln of equity in the construction and operational stages of projects using proven technologies such as wind, biomass and solar.

This is a purely private equity fund invested in mature technologies of developed countries (Western Europe), and hence there is no need for technical assistance. Noteworthy, however, is this fund's ability to take development risk (i.e. all pre-commissioning risks).

2. Central and Eastern Europe - EnerCap Power Fund LP						
Launched	Amount	Target end-users	Technical Assistance	Subsidy	Donor/DFI financing	Website
2007	€100mln	RE + co-generation	No	No	Yes: EBRD, EIB (equity investments)	www.enercap.com

EnerCap is a private equity fund targeting primarily RE projects in the new member states of the European Union (EU). In those countries (central Europe and the Baltic states for the most part), the renewable energy market remains underdeveloped compared to that of the older member states. However, these countries will need to meet RE targets and are in the process of developing regulatory support systems, such as feed-in tariffs. These factors, and the resulting need to provide comfort to private investors, explain why two DFIs (notably, the European Bank for Reconstruction and Development (EBRD) and the European Investment Bank (EIB)), both invested in the fund.

3. Global - Global Energy Efficiency and Renewable Energy Fund (EC)						
Launched	Amount	Target end-users	Technical Assistance	Subsidy	Donor/DFI financing	Website
2007	€110mln (target €200mln)	EE, RE	Not apparent	Yes: subordinated equity	Yes: EC (€80mln grant)	www.eif.org/about/geeref.htm

Launched by the European Commission (EC) in 2008, the Global Energy Efficiency and Renewable Energy Fund (GEEREF) is comprised of funds aimed at promoting clean energy investments in developing countries and economies in transition (except EU members or "accession" countries). GEEREF primarily invests (between 10% if no less than €2mln, and 50% if no more than €20mln) in RE and sustainable energy infrastructure funds. With other partners, it can also co-invest in selected projects. The focus is mainly on sub-investments in equity (or quasi-equity) below €10mln. The European Commission,

Germany and Norway have committed about €110m to the GEEREF over the period 2007-2011. The EIB Group is the fund manager.

Once fundraising is completed, GEEREF would be a public private partnership where public investors' shares are subordinated to those held by private investors, with a "waterfall" mechanism whereby, once the fund is liquidated, the latter will receive their investment plus a certain return before any other distribution to public shareholders. This scheme has been effective in mobilizing capital for new asset classes in developing countries, especially in those regions where perceived risks are a high hurdle to private capital mobilization. GEEREF makes its own investments in sub-funds on a *pari passu* basis with co-investors and on commercial terms, but GEEREF funding is nonetheless an attractive proposition as there is often a lack of equity investment available through the market for EERE projects in the regions where these sub-funds operate. GEEREF made its first investment in 2007 in an Indian fund with further investments expected in Southern Africa and China (PRC).

2.2.2. Closing the debt-equity gap: Dedicated subordinated debt funds

4. France - FIDEME (ADEME) [COMPLETED]						
Launched	Amount	Target end-users	Technical Assistance	Subsidy	Donor/DFI financing	Website
2002	€45mln	RE, waste to energy	No	ADEME's €15mln contribution is not remunerated and "repaid" after that of private investors	Yes, ADEME (subordinated equity)	N/A (project is completed)

FIDEME was set up by French investment bank Natixis in partnership with the Agence de l'Environnement et de la Maîtrise de l'Energie de la France (ADEME), the French public agency for energy efficiency, at a time when raising equity capital in France for RE projects such as wind farms was difficult. In this €45mln fund, ADEME invested €15mln in shares that are not remunerated and subordinated to those of private investors. FIDEME is thus able to take more risk to help small companies finance their projects. FIDEME provides mezzanine debt financing to RE projects through the subscription of convertible bonds issued by the project companies. Thanks to FIDEME financing and its subordinate position, sponsors obtain the complementary funds they require to close the financing of their projects. Furthermore, the FIDEME security package has a second security rank compared to the banks' first-ranking pledge. As a result, FIDEME plays an essential part in ensuring that a successful project finance structure is achieved by accepting risks considered unacceptable by banks.

FIDEME is now fully invested. It has financed 27 projects, worth over €320m, and has contributed to the creation of 300MW of new capacity, a third of which was in wind power from 2004 to 2006. In addition, FIDEME had an important demonstration effect for the financial community, as it was seen as an attractive instrument to overcome difficulties in accessing equity faced by certain developers, which in turn limited their ability to raise senior debt for projects that can generally sustain a high leverage (debt to equity ratio). Natixis is in the process of raising a second similar fund, Euro-Fideme 2.

5. Central America - Renewable Energy and Cleaner Production Facility (CAREC) (IADB)						
Launched	Amount	Target end-users	Technical Assistance	Subsidy	Donor/DFI financing	Website
2006	$20mln	EE, RE	Not apparent	IADB	IADB	www.eandcocapital.com/en_usa/carec.html

The Central American Renewable Energy and Cleaner Production Facility ("CAREC") is a $20mln, innovative mezzanine and debt financing facility developed and managed by E+Co Capital, a subsidiary of E+Co, a global not-for-profit, public purpose investment company, with financial ($5.5mln) and institutional support from the Multilateral Investment Fund of the Inter-American Development Bank (IADB).

CAREC invests in proven RE technologies, EE and cleaner production projects with small and medium-sized enterprises in the seven countries of the Central American region (Belize, Costa Rica, El Salvador, Guatemala, Honduras, Nicaragua and Panama). CAREC is not a private equity fund, but it is intentionally structured to utilize mezzanine-financing mechanisms such as subordinated debt, convertible debt, preferred shares and other quasi-equity instruments.

2.2.3 Supporting a nascent ESCO industry

Energy Service Companies (ESCOs) are a key component of a dynamic EE market. They provide diagnostics, technical solutions, procurement and implementation services and they can also finance projects. Few countries have managed to spawn a flourishing ESCO market, due to a number of well-documented barriers. This section provides examples of programmes that aimed to kick-start an ESCO industry (through, e.g. pilot ESCOs in China, a state-owned ESCO in Ukraine) or to support the growth of an existing ESCO by facilitating its access to finance (Bulgaria).

6. China - Energy Conservation Programme (Phase I, IBRD/GEF)						
Launched	Amount	Target end-users	Technical Assistance	Subsidy	Donor/DFI financing	Website
2008	$26mln	EE	Yes	Yes, GEF grants	Yes, IBRD	N/A

Initiated in 1998 by the World Bank and strongly supported by the Chinese government, the China Energy Conservation Programme helped create from scratch an ESCO industry in China. The project supported the establishment of three new pilot ESCOs (or Energy Management Companies (EMCs) as they are called in China), as well as their efforts to adapt and develop Energy Performance Contracting (EPC) in the Chinese market. The project included (i) $5mln of GEF grant support to each company for development of initial projects and (ii) $21mln of IBRD loan funds, on-lent to the companies, for scaling up their business. These full-service, shared savings ESCOs (or EMCs) were specially formed for the project in the Liaoning and Shandong Provinces and Beijing Municipality, with shareholders consisting mainly of other publicly owned companies. A major TA program for the new ESCOs and funding for a few initial pilot projects was financed by the EC, which gave the programme a very important jump-start.

The three pilot ESCOs have been successful in delivering energy savings and emission reductions and in showing that the ESCO model and EPC mechanism (using much simpler EPC contracts than in the US) can be successfully and profitably implemented in

China. New ESCOs have entered the market as a result. Investments by ESCOs soared between 2004 and 2008 from $94mln to $1.49bn[12].

Phase II of the Energy Conservation Programme was approved in 2002 with the objective of scaling up China's ESCO industry nationwide. The project includes (i) a major EMC loan guarantee program backstopped with GEF funds and (ii) training, technical assistance, and policy development support for the emerging ESCO industry through EMCA, China's newly formed EMC association.

7. Ukraine - UkrEsco (EBRD/EC)						
Launched	Amount	Target end-users	Technical Assistance	Subsidy	Donor/DFI financing	Website
1998	$20mln (new $20mln in 2005)	EE in industry	Yes	Yes, sovereign loan	Yes, EBRD (senior loan)	http://www.ukresco.com/en/

UkrEsco, a majority state-owned company, was set up in 1998 by a joint initiative of the EBRD, Ukraine and the European Union's (EU) TACIS Programme. Ukraine's economy is highly energy-intensive and there was no ESCO industry. One way to establish an industry was to create a pilot ESCO, which would have a strong demonstration impact across the country through its projects. Since its establishment, the company has successfully expanded into a full-service provider, implementing projects across a wide spectrum of industries and technologies. The original EBRD sovereign loan of $20mln was supplemented by a new $20mln EBRD loan in 2005 and UkrEsco is slated for privatisation.

8. Bulgaria - Bulgarian ESCO Fund / Enemona (EBRD)						
Launched	Amount	Target end-users	Technical Assistance	Subsidy	Donor/DFI financing	Website
2008	€7mln (EBRD loan)	EE	Not apparent	No	Yes, EBRD (senior loan)	www.eesf.biz (in Bulgarian)

The Bulgarian ESCO Fund, Energetics and Energy Savings Fund SPV (EESF) is a special purpose company listed on the Bulgarian Stock Exchange which finances the energy services business of Enemona AD, a construction and engineering group and majority shareholder of the fund. Typically the fund has supported energy efficiency projects in kindergartens, schools, hospitals and other public buildings.

In 2008, the EBRD extended to the fund a €7mln loan providing Enemona with the long-term capital it needed to expand its ESCO business in Bulgaria. The proceeds are used to purchase receivables from EPCs carried out by Enemona. Since its establishment in 2006, EESF has purchased receivables under more than 20 EPCs. This financing technique, known as forfeiting, enables Enemona to provide off balance sheet finance to its clients without burdening its own balance sheet.

Enemona is one of the first Bulgarian ESCOs and among the pioneers implementing an EPC with guaranteed results in municipal buildings.

2.2.4. Using utilities or municipalities as relays in the financial intermediation chain

As they directly interface with most energy users (in grid-connected areas), energy utilities can be a suitable intermediary for the delivery of EE and/or RE equipment, services, training and financing to end-beneficiaries, as the example of the China Utility-based Energy Efficiency Programme" (CHUEE) illustrates below. Utilities and municipalities can also provide finance and/or credit enhancement since both have strong legal powers to enforce payment, as examples from Tunisia (SWH) and the USA (EmPower New York, BerkeleyFirst) show. Another example from the USA showcases the innovative adaptation of Power Purchase Agreements to the financing of solar photovoltaic systems.

9. USA - EmPower New York™						
Launched	Amount	Target end-users	Technical Assistance	Subsidy	Donor/DFI financing	Website
2004	n/a	EE for low-income household	Yes	Yes (cross-subsidy from electricity user to lower-income users)	No	www.getenergysmart.org/LowIncome/EmPower.aspx

EmPower New York[SM] is a utility Demand Side Management (DSM) scheme targeting lower-income utility customers, which is part of NewYork Energy $mart™, a series of programmes aimed at lowering electricity costs through EE and funded by a System Benefits Charge (SBC) paid by electric distribution customers. EmPower's focus is on cost-effective electric reduction measures, particularly lighting and refrigerator replacements, as well as other cost-effective home performance strategies such as insulation and health and safety measures. On-site energy use education provides customers with additional strategies for managing their energy costs. Investments are undertaken at no cost to the eligible household. The New York State Energy Research and Development Authority (NYSERDA), a public benefit corporation, administers the SBC funds and programmes. Implementation has been outsourced to Honeywell International.

10. Tunisia - PROSOL (UNEP/ANME)						
Launched	Amount	Target end-users	Technical Assistance	Subsidy	Donor/DFI financing	Website
2005	$9mln p.a.	SWHs for households	Yes	Yes, UNEP (concessional loan) Italy and ANME (grant)	Yes, UNEP, ANME, Italy	www.anme.nat.tn/index.asp?pId=259

To encourage the adoption of SWH (SWHs), whose high cost relative to alternatives was a significant barrier, the PROSOL project relies on two incentives: an upfront cash grant from the Tunisia National Agency for Energy Conservation (ANME) paid directly to eligible installers and a (initially concessional) 5-year loan granted by the UNEP Mediterranean Renewable Energies Programme (MEDREP) and subsequently by local CFIs to the installers, effectively serviced by the customers via their electricity bill issued by the Tunisian Electrical Power Company (STEG). The scheme has been successful (about 118,000 m² of SWH installed). Its main advantage lies in the fact that payment through the utility bill reduces risk of credit default (STEG can cut off supply in case of default) and lowers collection costs. The customer now legally carries the debt whereas in the earlier version of PROSOL the installer was the legal debtor. The programme was extended in 2007 to the tertiary sector.

11. USA - Third Party Power Purchase Agreement (TPPPA) for solar PV systems						
Launched	Amount	Target end-users	Technical Assistance	Subsidy	Donor/DFI financing	Website
2004	n/a	Solar PV systems for households	No	Grants and tax rebates	Federal Government, State	http://us.sunpowercorp.com/business/products-services/services/financing.php http://www.sunrunhome.com/learn_about_solar/solar_power_purchase_agreement/

Third-party ownership using a power purchase agreement (PPA) is rapidly becoming the primary model for financing large solar photovoltaic (PV) systems in the commercial and public sectors in the US. It is also beginning to emerge for residential customers. Under the TPPPA model, a third party designs, builds, owns, operates and maintains the solar systems and sells back solar-generated electricity to the end-user. This model removes the burden of upfront costs from the end-user, and also allows the solar contractor, who has significantly greater expertise than the end-user, to assume the responsibility for system installation and maintenance. Tax credits and accelerated depreciation for the solar systems help drive down their cost, as well as reducing the electricity price charged to the end user. US companies SunEdison and SunPower are two leading TPPPA proponents. SunEdison first used the model in 2004 on a commercial installation, and has since installed 34MW of systems for commercial users financed via TPPPAs (or Solar Power Services Agreements (SPSAs) as SunEdison calls them). Companies like Walmart, Whole Foods, Safeway, Staples and Macy's use solar PPAs, for example. Also in the US, SunRun has pioneered the model for residential customers.

12. China - "China Utility-based Energy Efficiency Programme" (CHUEE)(IFC/GEF)						
Launched	Amount	Target end-users	Technical Assistance	Subsidy	Donor/DFI financing	Website
2006	$146.9mln	EE, all end-users	Yes, GEF/ Finland/ Norway	Yes, GEF ($16.5mln)	Risk-sharing with 3 CFIs	www.ifc.org/chuee chuee@ifc.org

IFC/GEF's CHUEE programme (see also box 6.2) is a rare example of a package of risk-sharing facilities (benefiting three banks: Shangia Pudong Development Bank, Industrial Bank and Bank of Beijing), technical assistance and advisory services to multiple partners including ESCOs, equipment suppliers and also utilities. Utilities, gas or electric, will be the primary implementation partners for the project, acting as a hub to provide a one-stop-shop for the marketing, design, financing and delivery of EE projects. An important objective of the project is to help expand the use of natural gas. Hence, gas utilities such as Xinao Gas will be able to overcome their competitive disadvantage relative to coal by promoting EE measures.

With CHUEE II (2008), the International Financial Corporation (IFC) has committed $170mln of its own capital to expand the partial credit risk guarantee feature of CHUEE I to support EE upgrades in industrial companies (see section 2.2.6 on guarantees).

13. USA - Berkeley FIRST: Small-Scale Solar Initiative (Berkeley, California)						
Launched	Amount	Target end-users	Technical Assistance	Subsidy	Donor/DFI financing	Website
2008	n/a (pilot)	Solar PV systems for households	Yes	Yes, CSI grant from the state - cheap municipal bonds	City, State	www.cityofberkeley.info/ ContentDisplay.aspx?id=26580

This pilot scheme (initially limited to 40 properties) will allow property owners to pay for solar PV system installation as part of their individual municipal property tax. The scheme, developed and administered by the private company Renewable Funding, is the first of a wider initiative in the state of California, called CityFIRST (City Financing Initiative for Renewable and Solar Technology). Under this scheme, the property owner can contract directly with any qualified private solar installer registered with the California Solar Initiative (CSI)[1]. It is understood that the financing works as follows. First, the city issues special bonds (CityFirst bond). Then, Renewable Funding purchases them and transmits the proceeds to individual property owners on demand, who then pay for the cost of the system minus the rebate granted by the state under CSI. The owner services the debt via a surcharge (First Special Tax) on its property. Interest on the loan is attractive because Berkeley can secure long-term (20 years) low-interest debt through these dedicated bonds. The tax stays with the property even if the owner sells, although the owner would have to leave the solar panels. The First Special Tax, like other property taxes, will be secured by a lien on the property, which ranks senior to the first mortgage. Failure to pay property taxes can lead to the foreclosure of a property. This scheme eliminates the two major financial hurdles to wider implementation of solar electric and solar hot water systems—the high upfront cost and the possibility that those costs will not be recovered when the property is sold.

2.2.5. Financing energy access (off-grid communities in rural areas) with micro-finance

14. Bangladesh - Grameen Shakti Solar Home System and Biogas Plant Programmes						
Launched	Amount	Target end-users	Technical Assistance	Subsidy	Donor/DFI financing	Website
1996	n/a	RE, Rural poor	No, apparently	Yes	IFC ($750,000 in 1998)	www.gshakti.org/index.html

The Grameen Bank in Bangladesh has developed an international reputation for its innovative micro-finance approach to assist small rural enterprises. It provides credit to the Bangladeshi rural poor without any collateral. In June 1996 Grameen founded Grameen Shakti (literally "rural energy") with the purpose of supplying RE to unelectrified villages in Bangladesh (70% of the population still has no electricity). Grameen Shakti's two main programmes target solar PV home systems and biogas plants for households and combine soft lending with extended warranties, training and a buy-back scheme. Although the solar home systems are expensive, more than 220,000 have been installed (in addition to 5,000 biogas plants) and the scheme is widely considered a success.

2.2.6. Mitigating perceived risks of local lenders: Loan guarantees

When liquidity is not an issue in domestic financial systems, but financial intermediaries are reluctant to lend to EERE projects because of high perceived risks, risk sharing mechanisms such as loan guarantees (partial credit guarantees (PCGs) or partial risk guarantees (PRGs)) can be the answer. The issue is often the gap between these perceptions and actual risks, which are generally lower. This creates a rationale for an instrument that can narrow the gap at a relatively low cost. While there is a wide variety of risk-sharing mechanisms[13], the examples below from USAID and China mostly illustrate the use of partial risk guarantees.

15. Global - US AID Development Credit Authority						
Launched	Amount	Target end-users	Technical Assistance	Subsidy	Donor/DFI financing	Website
1999	N/A	EE, RE and other areas	Yes	Probably	US Government via US AID	www.usaid.gov/our_work/ economic_growth_and_trade/ development_credit/index.html

Since 1999, the US government (via USAID) can provide PCGs to projects that meet certain criteria, for up to 50% of the loan principal or a loan portfolio. For example, in India USAID is providing Yes Bank with a 10-year $20mln loan portfolio guarantee to increase financing of small-scale RE, EE and water conservation management projects for small and medium enterprises (SMEs). In connection with the guarantee mechanism USAID often provides extensive technical assistance to help borrowers identify projects, develop their business plans, and prepare loan applications.

16. China - ESCO Loan Guarantee Programme (IBRD/GEF)						
Launched	Amount	Target end-users	Technical Assistance	Subsidy	Donor/DFI financing	Website
2003	$22mln	EE	Yes?	Yes, GEF	Yes, IBRD (senior loan)	N/A

In the first China Energy Conservation Project (see item 12 above), the World Bank provided lines of credit to three pilot ESCOs. The second project aims to bring local financing institutions into the industry as sustainable sources of finance for ESCOs. The PCG was selected as the instrument to introduce local banks to the business. In addition, the Second Energy Conservation Project supported the creation of the EMC Association of China (EMCA) as an institution with ESCO mutual support that would also provide technical assistance to newcomers and would act as a representative of this emerging industry for government and other parties.

The guarantee programme is operated by a well-experienced state-owned company, China National Investment and Guaranty Company (I&G), which provides PRGs (with an initial ceiling of 90% set to gradually decrease) for loans involving ESCOs and investments in energy performance contracting. These are counter-guaranteed by $22mln of GEF funds deposited in a special fund held by the government.

The programme was successful (although not all GEF funds were disbursed) but it had two main shortcomings. First, "the longstanding business model of I&G and most other Chinese guarantee companies is to guarantee *all* of the credit risk of loans—in essence to undertake much of the basic loan appraisal and risk mitigation functions usually undertaken by banks, with banks then playing more of an agent, processing and collection role. As a result, the involvement of the banks in appraisal and risk mitigation is less active than in some other models [...]. The uptake of ESCO loan businesses by banks themselves as a result of the program has been slow"[14]. Second, the project structure involving several public and private institutions was "cumbersome and difficult".

2.2.7 Remedying the inability or unwillingness of CFIs to finance EERE projects: Special purpose financing vehicles or windows

Where local banks are weak, risk averse or in the midst of a transition process and as a result unwilling or unable to finance EERE projects, the creation of a special purpose financing vehicle or window, usually by or under the aegis of the government, may be the best strategy. Care should be taken that this vehicle does not compete or undermine private sector financial players. Three examples drawn from Bulgaria (BgEEF), India (IRDEA) and the United Kingdom (Carbon Trust) illustrate this approach below.

17. Bulgaria Energy Efficiency Fund (BgEEF) (IBRD/GEF)						
Launched	Amount	Target end-users	Technical Assistance	Subsidy	Donor/DFI financing	Website
2004	Ca $13mln	EE	Yes	Yes, GEF	Yes	www.bgeef.com/display.aspx

The BgEEF was established in 2004 as a legal entity capitalized entirely with grant funds, including $10mln from the GEF via the World Bank and $1.5mln from the Government of Bulgaria. BgEEF has the combined capacity of a lending institution, a credit guarantee facility and a consulting company. It provides technical assistance to Bulgarian enterprises, municipalities and private individuals in developing EE investment projects. Acting under the strategic guidance of the Donors' Assembly and supervision of a Management Board (where the Government of Bulgaria appoints 2 of the 7 members), the Fund Manager is a consortium of international and domestic consultants. Being a "commercial" entity, but funded with grant monies, it is not clear whether, how and to what extent BgEEF financing is concessional (interest rates are between 7-10% and tenors no more than 5 years). An interesting feature of BgEEF suite of instruments is that it can provide portfolio guarantees to ESCOs and for residential building renovation projects. As of 31 December 2008, BgEEF had financed 62 projects worth BGN25mln (about $18mln), 47 of which consisting of the renovation of (mostly public) buildings.

18. India – IREDA						
Launched	Amount	Target end-users	Technical Assistance	Subsidy	Donor/DFI financing	Website
1987	$1.9 bn (so far)	RE, EE	Yes	?	IBRD, GEF, KfW	http://www.ireda.in/

The Indian Renewable Energy Development Agency Limited (IREDA) was established as a public company by the government in 1987, with the aim of extending financial assistance for RE and EE projects. It is one of the largest dedicated parastatal EERE financiers in the world.

IREDA borrows funds from domestic commercial banks and IFIs (e.g. a $115mln IDA loan in 1992) and its loans appear to be either not concessional or only mildly concessional. IREDA has built up in-house technical expertise, but also relies on some outsourcing. In order to assist in pipeline development, IREDA has built a network of business development centres and strategic allies throughout India, consisting of about 50 organizations. IREDA provides these organizations with training and some financial resources. In addition, they receive incentive payments upon loan disbursement and commissioning. As of March 2007, IREDA had approved 1816 projects worth Rs 8,055 Crores ($1.9bn) in loan commitments.

Its position, once dominant, is now under threat from the fast developing and increasingly competitive Indian banking sector. Increasing liquidity in the banking system and less cumbersome procedures applied by commercial banks in particular to SMEs have led IREDA to lose market share. As the World Bank project performance assessment report noted: "IREDA needs to compete if it is to remain relevant"[15].

19. UK – Carbon Trust, Interest free EE loans for SMEs						
Launched	Amount	Target end-users	Technical Assistance	Subsidy	Donor/DFI financing	Website
2001	£ 123mln (to date)	EE forSMEs	No	Yes, zero interest loan	UK Government (£ 123mln)	http://www.carbontrust.co.uk/energy/Loans/default.htm

The Carbon Trust was set up in 2001 by the Government of the United Kingdom as an independent, not- for-dividend (profits are reinvested) company. Its mission is to accelerate the move to a low carbon economy. The Carbon Trust's core activity consists of helping companies and organisations reduce carbon emissions through providing help, support and advice, including through soft loans and venture capital funding. With funding from the government budget, it recently scaled up its free interest loan scheme targeted at SMEs. The rationale is that commercial banks in the UK do not normally finance energy efficiency investments by SMEs. The Carbon Trust can lend up to £400,000 for up to 4 years to SMEs (possibly each installation if they have multiple sites) provided it can be demonstrated that each pound of loan will save at least 1.5 $kgCO_2$ (which is not overly challenging) and that the energy bill savings associated with the project are estimated to fully cover the cost of the loan amount within 5 years. Interestingly, loans are unsecured, procedures are simple and decisions whether to grant a loan are made quickly (also within a 2-week time). Fast turn-around time and the absence of security and minimum equity contribution are key advantages of the scheme, although it is reserved for fairly small projects. One can, however, wonder why a traditionally pro-market government did not ask commercial banks to run the scheme (as was done in France with a similar zero interest loan scheme ("ECO PTZ") launched this year and which targets households).

2.2.8. Dedicated DFI EE/RE credit lines to local CFIs

Where liquidity of local banks is not sufficient, or the terms of this financing (such as interest rates and tenors) are not attractive, but local CFIs are willing and able, perhaps with some incentives and TA, to serve the EERE market, a wholesale financing mechanism channeling DFI or government funds to local CFIs or ESCOs for on-lending to EERE projects is warranted. This funding can be provided on concessional or market terms, as three examples from Thailand, economies in transition and Tunisia illustrate below.

20. Thailand - Energy Efficiency Revolving Fund (EERF)						
Launched	Amount	Target end-users	Technical Assistance	Subsidy	Donor/DFI financing	Website
2003	$50mln (initially till end-2005)	EE	?	Yes, zero interest rates on loans to banks	Yes: Government tax on oil products	N/A

Thailand's Energy Efficiency Revolving Fund (EERF) was established by the Government of Thailand in 2003 to stimulate investments in EE projects, in conjunction with a grant programme. EERF is funded by the Energy Conservation Promotion Fund (ENCON Fund), which receives revenue from a tax of THB 0.05-0.25 per litre on all petroleum products sold in Thailand. This provides annual inflows of approximately THB 2bn ($50mln) p.a. The EERF in turn provides capital at no cost to 10 participating Thai banks, which then provide low-cost loans for energy efficiency projects of up to a maximum of $1.25mln, at an interest rate of no more than 4% p.a. Frequently, banks set an interest rate lower than this maximum figure, depending on their relationship with the customer. As of mid-2008, the EERF had financed more than 250 EE projects totalling around $500mln in investments, and yielding an estimated $120mln in energy savings p.a. Projects have predominantly been private factories and, to a lesser extent, buildings, such as hospitals and hotels. DEDE, the Ministry of Energy department in charge of the programme, assesses and approves each project and on that basis disburses EERF funds to participating bank. This model contrasts with DFIs' credit lines, as described below.

21. Countries in transition - Sustainable Energy Efficiency Facilities (EBRD)						
Launched	Amount	Target end-users	Technical Assistance	Subsidy	Donor/DFI financing	Website
2004 (first credit line)	€362mln signed out of 653mln approved	EE, RE	Yes, mostly project preparation	Yes: incentive fees paid to banks and end-borrowers	Yes, EBRD (senior loans to CFIs)	www.beerecl.com www.slovseff.eu www.ukeep.org etc.

The EBRD is the leading provider of dedicated EERE credit lines to local banks (Sustainable Energy Financing Facilities) in the countries in transition where it operates. Out of approved credit line frameworks amounting to €653mln, the EBRD has financed 31 credit lines to 25 local banks worth €362mln in Bulgaria, Georgia, Kazakhstan, Romania, Russia, the Slovak Republic and Ukraine, supporting over 24,500 sub-loans. These credit lines have three main features: (i) local banks use the credit line to provide commercial loans, at their own risk; (ii) every credit line is supported by a comprehensive, donor-funded, TA package that helps potential borrowers prepare loan applications and trains local bank loan officers to process sustainable energy investment opportunities (this assistance is provided free-of-charge by a project implementation team consisting of international and local experts); and (iii) often a performance-related incentive fee is paid to the participating banks and to the end-borrowers.

The first credit line was the €155mln Bulgarian Energy Efficiency and Renewable Energy Credit Line (BEERECL), launched in 2004 to jump-start sustainable energy investment in a country that combined high energy intensity and the need to shutdown its largest (nuclear) power plant of Kozloduy for safety reasons. To address the multiple barriers, EBRD partnered with the Kozloduy international decommissioning special fund financed by donors (predominantly the EU), which provided a grant for the substantial technical assistance component and incentive fees to participating banks and end-borrowers. The latter are paid upon project completion and represent between 15% (EE) and 20% (RE) of the sub-loan amount. The project has been very successful in that more than 150 small-scale EE and RE projects have been financed for a total project cost of €131mln, with electricity (equivalent) savings of 875GWh and emissions reductions of 570,000tCO$_2$ p.a.

The €60mln Slovakian Sustainable Energy Financing Facilities (SLOVSEFF), launched in 2007, is worth mentioning for its success in addressing the complex issues of financing the renovation of panel apartment blocks in a region where they constitute a key feature of the urban landscape. By end 2008, some 240 residential projects have been financed to refurbish 11,000 flats.

22. China – EERE credit line to commercial banks (AFD)						
Launched	Amount	Target end-users	Technical Assistance	Subsidy	Donor/DFI financing	Website
2006	€60mln	enterprises in the industrial and service sectors	Yes, €0.6mln (French GEF)	Interest rate subsidy (AFD)	AFD	N/A

Agence Française de Développement (AFD) has rapidly built a portfolio of EERE credit lines to local CFIs in excess of €0.5bn. The Chinese EERE credit line launched in 2006 aims at stimulating small-scale EERE investments in the corporate sector in order to help reach the government's energy efficiency targets. The €60mln AFD concessional loan (Euribor – 100bp) to the Ministry of Finance of China was on-lent to three second-tier commercial banks: Hua Xia, China Merchants Bank and Shanghai Pudong Development Bank. The loan is complemented by a €600.000 TA package aimed at building up participating banks' capacity and funding a Beijing-based advisory team (staffed with Chinese personnel) which advises banks on project eligibility and technical aspects. Banks' margins are capped so that part of the "concessionality" is passed through to end-borrowers. A minimum 20% energy saving is required. The credit line should be fully disbursed by end 2009, financing about 15 projects, which are expected to reduce CO_2 emissions by 1.9 $MtCO_2$ p.a. The cost per tonne of CO_2 avoided would be €7.3, which is quite low (see section 2.3). A shortcoming of the line is that the central advisory team has little room to influence the project design in order to improve the savings potential of EE projects. This is because projects submitted to banks have already been through a feasibility study in accordance with strict Chinese standards and then approved by the local branches of the National Development and Reform Commission of China (NDRC). AFD is working on a follow-on €120mln credit line which will seek to address this issue.

2.3. Monetizing emission reductions: Carbon finance

Carbon finance is not so much a mechanism as an entirely new source of finance for climate change mitigation that has only emerged in the last 10 years. At its simplest, carbon finance can be defined as resources provided to projects generating (or expected to generate) greenhouse gas (or carbon) emission reductions in the form of the purchase of such emission reductions. Carbon finance is inseparable from carbon markets, that is, one or more markets in which various rights to emit GHGs (carbon credits) are traded in order to meet emission reduction targets (including voluntary targets), set at the national, regional or international level.

Table 2.3: The carbon market at a glance (2008 for volumes; as of 21 August for ETS and CDM prices)

Size / value of global carbon markets	4.8Gt - $126bn
Size / value of EU Emission Trading Scheme	3.1Gt – $92bn
Size / value of CDM market (includes secondary)	1.4Gt - $32.8
Size / value of JI market	20Mt - $0.3bn
Size / value of voluntary market	123Mt – $0.7bn
EU ETS price (futures Dec. 2009)	€15.4/t
CDM price (secondary) (futures Dec. 2009)	€13.4/t
Voluntary market price (2008 Over-The-Counter average)	$7.34/t

2.3.1. Carbon markets - Overview

Three carbon markets can be distinguished:

(i)   The "Kyoto market", consisting of three different trading mechanisms created by the 1997 Kyoto Protocol to the UNFCCC which set binding emission reduction targets to be achieved in the period 2008-2012 by 39 industrialised countries (Annex B countries): the Clean Development Mechanism (CDM), Joint Implementation (JI) and International Emission Trading (IET). The first two are project-based (i.e. emission reductions need to be achieved in a project to be sold), while the third is allowance-based (i.e. no actual emission reduction is required to trade[16]). In particular:

(ii)

    a.   JI allows buyers from Annex B countries to buy carbon credits from emission reduction projects implemented in other Annex B countries, e.g. A German utility buying credits from a Ukrainian wind farm.

    b.   CDM allows buyers from Annex B countries to buy carbon credits from emission reduction projects implemented in non-Annex B countries, e.g. A German utility buying credits from a Chinese wind farm.

    c.   IET allows governments from Annex B countries to trade among themselves allowances from their own carbon budget, so-called "assigned amount units" (AAUs).

(iii)   "Cap-and-trade" systems, the largest of which is the EU Emission Trading Scheme (EU ETS), which applies to 30 countries, the 27 members of the EU and Iceland, Liechtenstein and Norway. Cap-and-trade covers a little less then 50% of EU emissions. In a cap-and-trade system, a cap is set on company emissions (such that the overall level of emissions is reduced) and permits (allowances) up to that cap are granted or auctioned to companies. Then, permits can be traded. The first cap-and-trade system was implemented successfully in the US in the early 1990s to curb emissions of sulphur dioxide (SO_2) responsible for acid rain. IET is also a cap-and-trade mechanism, while CDM and JI are "baseline and credit" mechanisms (i.e. emission reductions are calculated relative to a projected level of emissions in the absence of abatement measures – the baseline.)

(iv)   The "voluntary" market, where participants trade Kyoto credits or other credits in the absence of emission targets or regulation, essentially out of ethical, corporate social responsibility or public relations considerations.

2.3.2. Volumes and prices

The carbon market's total value for 2008 was estimated at $126bn (€86bn), twice as much as in 2007 ($63bn), with $4.8GtCO_2$-equ changing hands (3Gt in 2007). However, real emission reductions were barely half that level, as a lot of trades involved the same credits (the "churn").

The EU ETS is the largest market, accounting for two-thirds of the global market, with a total value of $92bn (€63bn) and 3.1Gt traded. The largest trading platform was the over-the-counter (OTC) market, which traded 49% of the volume, with the share of carbon deals traded by exchanges, such as Bluenext and the European Climate Exchange (ECX), up to 37%.

The CDM is the second largest market with some $1.4GtCO_2$-equ changing hands in 2008, worth \$32.8bn (€22.5bn). The secondary market in Certified Emissions Reductions (CER) totalled 1Gt in 2008, corresponding to four-fifths (\$26.3bn) of the total CER market volume. Secondary CERs refer to CERs that have been issued by the UNFCCC and thus are deemed risk-free.

JI remains tiny, with 20Mt exchanged, worth \$300mln. 123Mt valued at \$706mln were exchanged on the voluntary market[17].

The financial and economic crisis has taken its toll on the carbon market. In 2008, the volume and value of *primary* CDM and JI transactions both fell. From their peak of July 2008 (€30 for EU Allowances, and €23 for secondary CERs), prices started falling in the second half of 2008 and have only modestly recovered since February 2009 (€15.2 and €12.5 respectively as of end May 2009). New Carbon Finance, an information provider, expects by the end of 2009 "to see the global carbon market on a level with 2008 at around \$120bn, supported by higher trading activity but lower prices. Growth is then expected to be sluggish to 2012, as the recession has caused prices to remain low in the major schemes, by when it should reach \$408bn (€295bn)."

New Carbon Finance also projects that "assuming a US market does materialise, the world carbon market could grow [...] to \$2.1 trillion (€1.5 trillion) by 2020" and "weighted average global carbon price [could increase] from \$16/t (€12/t) in 2009 to \$61/t (€44/t) in 2020. Prices in Europe would be the highest, potentially rising to \$87/t (€63/t) by 2020, with allowances under a US federal cap and trade likely to be less, at only \$33/t (€24/t) by 2020 due primarily to the large volumes of abatement available at relatively low cost and the potentially greater use of offsets."

2.3.3. A closer look at the "Kyoto market"

From a project financing perspective, the project-based "Kyoto market" (JI/CDM) is more pertinent than IET. The number of projects in the CDM and JI pipeline has reached about 4,700 and 240 respectively, corresponding to cumulative emission reductions of 2.8Gt and 354Mt CO_2-equ respectively by end 2012[18] (7.5Gt by end 2020 for CDM). 1873 CDM projects and 73 JI projects have been registered. 585 CDM projects (340Mt) and 2 JI projects (2.9Mt) are issuing credits[19].

There is a discrepancy between the IEA's BLUE scenario described in section 1.1, which foresees a prominent role for EERE in climate change mitigation, and the picture that emerges from projects in the CDM and JI pipeline. In the JI pipeline, methane reduction (fugitive, landfill gas, coal bed/mine methane) and industrial gases (HFCs, PFCs and N_2O) account for three quarters of forecast ERUs, against 23% only for EERE (15% and 8% respectively, but 46% of the projects). In the CDM pipeline, on the other hand, RE has the biggest share with 36% of forecast CERs (but 64% of the projects), before industrial gases (25%, but 76% of CERS issued so far), and methane (19%), far ahead of EE (12%, with supply-side 11%, and demand-side 1%).

In other words, the number of EERE projects is significant but the bulk of emission reductions will arise from a smaller set of projects deploying other abatement technologies. The main reason is the much higher warming potential of methane and industrial gases relative to CO_2 (which is the main GHG abated by EERE projects) and the much higher profitability of these projects (see below).

2.3.4. Sources of carbon finance

The source of carbon finance is ultimately the primary buyer of carbon credits. Information on buyers is scarce and not reliable, as actual buyers are not always identified in Project Design Documents–the main project preparation document in the Kyoto market. Moreover, primary buyers are not necessarily "compliance" buyers, i.e. Annex B countries and companies subject to a mandatory or voluntary emission reduction scheme.

In the CDM space, the UNEP Centre on Energy, Climate and Sustainable Development (RISOE) has identified about 360 different buying entities. The top 10 buyers account for about 30% of the projects with an identified buyer. In terms of countries of origin, buyers from the UK dominate with a share of 39% in 2008 (for the primary JI and CDM market). This reflects the fact that the most active buyers (developers, carbon funds, financial institutions and traders) operate or are administered from London, which is considered the carbon finance hub of the world.

Buyers belong to the following main categories:

(i)   Governments (Annex B countries), e.g. Austria, Belgium, Denmark, Italy, Japan, the Netherlands, Spain, Sweden.

(ii)   Carbon project developers, e.g. Ecosecurities, Carbon Asset Management Sweden AB, Camco, First Climate, etc.

(iii)   Energy utilities, e.g. EDF Trading, RWE, ENEL, Essent, Endesa.

(iv)   Industrial firms, e.g. ArcelorMittal.

(v)   Public and private carbon funds (it is estimated that close to $16bn have been invested in carbon funds since 1999, close to $10bn of which in pure-play private carbon investment vehicles).

New Carbon Finance has classified them in three categories:

(i)   *Buy side – compliance*. Compliance buyers are either national governments or private companies (e.g. KfW Carbon Fund, or EBRD-EIB's Multilateral Carbon Credit Fund).

(ii)   *Buy side – intermediary*. These entities buy carbon credits from project developers, usually for resale, but do not invest directly in projects and have no direct emissions targets (e.g. European Carbon Fund).

(iii)   *Sell side – project development*. These players invest directly in projects providing capital for equipment as well as bringing know-how in terms of developing the carbon credits through the UN approval procedure (e.g. Climate Change Capital).

The World Bank is the single largest manager of (mostly compliance) carbon funds, with a suite of funds including the Prototype Carbon Fund, the Netherlands JI and Netherlands CDM Facilities, the Community Development Carbon Fund, the BioCarbon Fund, the Italian Carbon Fund, the Spanish Carbon Fund, the Danish Carbon Fund, the Umbrella Carbon Facility, the Carbon Fund for Europe, the Forest Carbon Partnership Facility and the Carbon Partnership Facility. These funds are public or public-private partnerships managed by the World Bank as a trustee. They operate much like a closed-end mutual fund.

Most buyers buy carbon credits till 2012, but some buyers also buy post-2012 credits, and in 2008 five European financial institutions (Caisse des Dépôts et Consignations, Instituto de Crédito Oficial, KfW Bankengruppe and the Nordic Investment Bank) led by the EIB, set up a €125mln carbon fund that buys exclusively post-2012 credits. The Fund is managed by Conning Asset Management (Europe) limited, with First Climate as investment advisor.

2.3.5. Carbon finance and the financing of EERE projects

Despite the growing size of carbon markets, the contribution of carbon finance to the financing of EERE projects is not as significant as usually claimed. Robert Zoellick, the President of the World Bank Group, recently declared that "carbon finance (payment for streams of emission reductions) has a strong multiplier effect on underlying investment in a wide range of sectors", $1 of carbon finance leveraging $3.8 of underlying investment on average and $9 for renewables[20]. The following considerations, however, suggest that carbon finance is not the main cause of this high leverage.

The contribution of carbon finance to project profitability is on the whole rather low for EERE projects, at current low carbon prices. Five main factors determine this contribution:

(i)   Cost of the investment.

(ii) Abatement yield of investment (tCO2 per €1 of investment). This varies across technologies (e.g. the destruction of industrial gases usually necessitates only a small investment).

(iii) Revenue streams. For some projects the carbon revenue is the only revenue and the only reason to undertake the investment (e.g. LFG, N_2O, HFCs). But many projects, comprising all EERE projects, combine carbon revenue and a non-carbon stream (e.g. sale of electricity from a wind farm to the grid, or cost savings from an EE project). The electricity price is key. All things equal, the higher the electricity price, the lower the relative contribution of carbon finance.

(iv) Cost of capital. All things equal, the higher it is (in riskier countries in particular), the lower the *relative* contribution of carbon finance; and not least

(v)   Carbon prices.

Box 2.1: The post-Kyoto mechanisms

Unlike the Kyoto Protocol, which was deliberately a first step in the fight against global warming, the outcome of the negotiations at COP-15 in Copenhagen will most likely represent a permanent regime against climate change. Therefore, whatever the targets agreed upon will be, the role of implementation mechanisms is fundamental. Several proposals have already been put forward and they are being discussed by the Ad Hoc Working Group on Further Commitments for Annex I Parties under the Kyoto Protocol (AWG-KP).

They include:

(i) expansion of CDM to land use, land use-change and forestry activities (such as afforestation and reforestation, reduced deforestation and forest degradation, restoration of wetlands and revegetation);

(ii) expansion of CDM to carbon capture and storage (CCS) activities;

(iii) expansion of CDM and JI to nuclear activities;

(iv) differentiation of Parties' eligibility for CDM and JI through the use of indicators;

(v) sectoral crediting of GHG emission reductions below a previously established ("no-lose") target;

(vi) introduction of GHG emissions trading based on sectoral targets; and

(vii) introduction of modalities and procedures for the recognition of units from voluntary GHG emission trading systems for trading and compliance purposes.

Market-based mechanisms have also been suggested in order to overcome what is widely regarded as the main shortcoming of the Kyoto Protocol, i.e. the lack of a credible enforcement regime. Apart from legally binding provisions, a series of economic incentives are currently under discussion. For instance, countries may commit and pool funds which will be held by an international body until compliance with the targets is reached.

All of these proposals are supported by various coalitions of developed and developing countries. As all of these mechanisms have winners and losers, there is uncertainty about what the new regime will look like and most depends on the concessions each state and coalition will make at the target-setting phase.

The figure below plots mitigation technologies along the first and second of these factors. RE features in the worst quadrant (north-west), combining high investment cost and low abatement yield. EE (south-west quadrant) requires a lower investment but the abatement yield is modest.

Figure 2.1: Cost and Carbon Abatement Yield of Different Mitigation Technologies

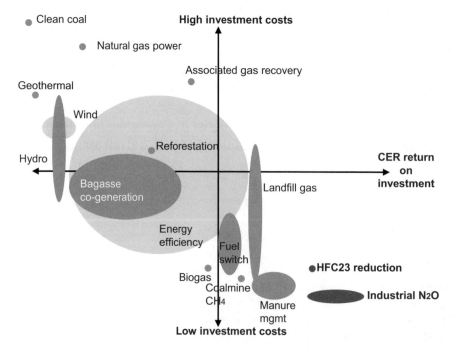

Source: Ellis & Kamel.

Accordingly, the impact of carbon credits on project internal rates of return (median incremental IRR in percentage points) ranges between 2% and 20%, with a median of 2.72%[21]. The table below for China shows a range of between 2% to 26%[22].

For supply-side energy efficiency the boost is a significant 5% and 2% to 3% for wind and hydro projects. Even the "with CDM" IRR is probably over-stated as it assumes (as all PDDs do) an optimistic carbon price (especially since July 2008) and a crediting period that extends beyond 2012 with no certainty that there will be a buyer.

The same source remarks that: "HFC and N_2O projects are excluded from the list because they are funded almost entirely from CDM revenues, giving them a negative IRR [before carbon...]. Landfill gas is the least profitable of the power generation activities, followed by biomass energy, coal mine methane and fossil fuel switch. With different degrees, these all seem to be far from an appealing investment without CDM. Hydro, wind, and to a lesser degree biogas energy have the highest returns [...] without CDM (after EE for own generation), showing that these technologies are relatively more profitable, because of structural (e.g. abundant resources) or market reasons (e.g. high feed-in price)."

Table 2.4: How carbon revenues boost project IRRs in China

	Average IRR w/o CDM (%)	Average IRR with CDM (%)
Biogas Energy	6.17	32.59
Biomass Energy	4.71	10.29
Coal bed/mine methane	5.43	27.86
Landfill gas	3.14	26.36
EE own generation	12.62	17.71
Fossil fuel switch	5.58	9.64
Hydro	6.90	10.45
Wind	6.81	9.00

Source: Ecofys Azure International (Data from registered PDDs to December 2007).

It is hard to escape the conclusion that for the vast majority of EERE projects the impact of carbon finance on returns and the decision to invest is marginal, especially in light of the other issues outlined below.

Financial markets are not yet converting future cash flows into upfront finance. The carbon revenue arises from monetising carbon credits, but emissions reductions materialise over time and capital to finance a carbon mitigation project is needed upfront.

This difficulty can be resolved in mostly two ways:

(i)   *Advance payment*. Some buyers of primary credits agree to make an advance payment, usually of no more than 50% of the value of the Emission Reduction Purchase Agreement (ERPA). However, buyers (in particular private buyers) are increasingly reluctant to do this.

(ii) *Lending against the carbon cash flow*. Theoretically, a bank would lend to the project an amount based on the present value of expected carbon cash flows and it would require as security a pledge of the ERPA, payments into an escrow account, etc. This financial engineering remains however rare, even 10 years after carbon markets came into existence. Given current market prices (primary CDM credits currently fetch less than €10/t) and the lack of buyers beyond 2012, the present value of future carbon cash flows is relatively modest for most EERE projects. Banks are still wary of the mix of regulatory and performance risks that characterises carbon credit projects.

The administrative process to register a project (or obtain final determination for JI projects) with the UNFCCC is slow, laborious, uncertain and costly. This is particularly penalizing for the EERE market as smaller projects and aggregations opportunities, which are crucial for the EE market, are bypassed because of transaction costs and the cumbersome nature of the methodologies and administrative procedures of the "Kyoto markets".

The "Kyoto market" only really benefits a handful of countries. Some other countries and entire regions of the world seem to have missed out on the carbon market. The geographic distribution of sellers is moreover skewed toward a handful of large countries: China, India, and Brazil account for three quarters of forecast CERs (53%, 16% and 6% respectively). Russia and Ukraine dominate the JI market with a 79% share (61% and 18% respectively). These five countries account together for 76% of the Kyoto (CDM+JI) market. At the other end of the spectrum, Africa and the 19 Least Developed Countries have paltry shares of 3% and 1%, respectively.

In conclusion, carbon finance is to an extent a misnomer, at least for most EERE projects: it has not yet been really successful in mobilising the upfront finance that projects need to be built in the first instance. The Kyoto regime, considered as the first concrete step towards the abatement of carbon emission through market mechanisms, need to be upgraded in conjunction with the setting of more stringent emission reductions targets. Likewise, carbon markets need to consolidate if carbon finance is to become more efficient and effective, leveraging much higher levels of investments for climate mitigation. A detailed discussion on proposals to reform the carbon markets is, however, beyond the scope of this section.

3. Complementary technical assistance programmes

The purpose of this chapter is to explain the aims and uses of Technical Assistance (TA), including sources and access to TA programmes and funding sources.

3.1. Purposes of TA

TA is aimed at filling information and skills gaps and is an important "weapon" that architects of financing mechanisms deploy to overcome barriers to investment. TA is a necessary complement to, and component of, the most effective financing mechanisms. In connection with financing EERE investments, TA is useful for the following purposes:

(i)   To understand the environment in which a mechanism is to be established.

Initial diagnosis and market (demand) studies are the first indispensable steps in the process of creating a new financing mechanism. These studies aim to assess the potential for EERE investments, identify the most cost-effective options in light of prevailing energy prices (and feed-in tariffs, if any), identify the main barriers to investment and financing, review the appetite and ability of local CFIs to invest in EERE and identify and assess the capacity of project developers (RE, IPP, etc.), ESCOs and other technical consultants, etc.

(ii)   To raise awareness of the target audience.

Once market targets (technology and client target) have been determined, efforts should be directed at increasing awareness on the benefits of EE, how the new mechanisms work, how they can be accessed, etc. This is less relevant for RE where the client target is, as shown in table 1.2 above, a relatively small number of developers and utilities, where awareness is not an issue. Tools for this include media campaigns (as the one, for instance, just launched by the Turkish commercial bank Sekerbank), conferences targeting certain regions, industries or companies (e.g. SMEs), dedicated websites (see for example for BEERECL), leaflets, etc.

(iii)   To build capacity of participants.

The shortage of relevant skills, possibly more than availability of finance, is the greatest barrier to EERE investment. As discussed in section 1.3, the significant differences between EE and RE require that they be carefully distinguished when designing a capacity building programme. An enumeration of participants in EERE financing programmes and the items they typically need support for is presented below:

a. Local financiers who understand EERE technologies, duly appraise projects, assess the risks and design new financial products;

b. Government agencies and energy regulators who assess the need for EERE projects, select the appropriate type, calibrate and channel subsidies where necessary, create an enabling policy and regulatory environment, issue green and white certificates, design new EERE financing schemes fit to the local context and benchmark programmes;

c. ESCOs, project developers, etc., who make use of model Energy Performance Contracts and monitor and audit projects;.

d. Companies, who train energy or facility managers and

e. Dedicated financing vehicles including lending procedures.

(iv) To facilitate project origination and preparation of:

a. Energy audits or (in UNIDO parlance) systems assessment;

b. Feasibility studies;

c. Environmental assessments; and

d. Contracting, procurement (e.g. of ESCOs).

Energy audits in particular play an important role in highlighting the benefits of EE investments to company managers, who are in most cases positively surprised by the magnitude of the potential savings and IRRs on these investments. Under the BEERECEL in Bulgaria, the project consultant performs full or simplified audits. Note that this cost could be recouped by the participating CFIs by capitalising it in the resulting investment programme. The TA programme could thus provide the seed capital for a revolving energy audit pre-financing facility.

(v)   To evaluate results.

As noted above, the absence of systematic evaluation of existing programmes is a serious impediment to knowledge and experience sharing and as such to the establishment of successful financing mechanisms. On-going (mid-term reviews) and ex-post evaluation are a good use of TA. The standardization of methodologies and terms of reference would be desirable to enable comparisons and the building of a global or regional database of lessons learned.

When using international experts and consultants, the dual objectives of providing immediate support to the host country and sustainability in the long run should be adequately balanced. While international experts may be needed, the aim should be to build domestic capacity. EERE financing mechanisms should therefore provide for a real transfer of skills, in particular by requiring that teams of international consultants always include a strong local component.

3.2. Sources of financing and TA financing flows

While technical cooperation expenditure amounted to about $15bn in 2007[23] there is no specific data on global TA flows in support of EERE financing. A compilation of TA programmes, donor funds and strategies (size, focus, eligibility criteria, etc.) and data on annual flows would be useful. The following is a cursory indication of the main sources of TA funds for EERE.

3.2.1. The Global Environmental Facility (GEF)

The GEF was established in October 1991 as a pilot program in the World Bank to assist in the worldwide protection of the environment and to promote environmental sustainable development. The GEF approach is to fund with grant and concessional funding the "incremental" or additional costs associated with transforming a project with national benefits into one with global environmental benefits. At the Rio Earth Summit in 1994, the GEF was restructured and moved out of the World Bank system to become a permanent independent institution. Since 1994, however, the World Bank has served as the trustee of the GEF trust fund and provided administrative services.

The GEF is also the designated financial mechanism for a number of multilateral environmental agreements or conventions. As such, the GEF assists countries in meeting their obligations under the conventions that they have signed and ratified, including the 1992 UNFCCC.

The GEF implements its projects through multilateral agencies, which are supposed to focus their involvement on GEF project activities "within their respective comparative advantages". These agencies are: the United Nations Development Program (UNDP), the United Nations Environment Programme (UNEP), the World Bank Group, the Food and Agriculture Organization (FAO), the Inter-American Development Bank (IADB), the United Nations Industrial Development Organization (UNIDO), the Asian Development Bank (ADB), the African Development Bank (AfDB), the European Bank for Reconstruction and Development (EBRD) and the International Fund for Agricultural Development (IFAD). Between 1991 and 2007, the GEF has allocated ca $2.4bn to climate change-related activities: 259 full-scale projects amounting to $2.05bn, 86 medium-sized projects amounting to $71mln and 276 so-called "enabling activity" projects amounting to $161mln. In 2006, 32 donors agreed to a 4th replenishment of the GEF resources, in the amount of $3.13bn for the 2006-2010 period.

In 2007, GEF's 15 Operational Programmes were replaced by 6 focal areas, including climate change. The 2007 document introducing the changes ("Focal Area Strategies and Strategic Programming for GEF-4") explains the new thrust of GEF intervention, that is, fewer projects but more activities aimed at building sustained markets[24].

In addition, the GEF further supports capacity building through specific programmes (Global Support Programme to support counties undertaking National Capacity Self-Assessments (NCSA), Country Support Programmes, etc.).

3.2.2. The United Nations system

The UN system, through its various agencies, is a major provider of TA for climate change mitigation[25].

UNEP and the Basel Agency for Sustainable Energy (BASE) jointly manage, with financial support from the UN Foundation, the Sustainable Energy Finance Initiative (SEFI), a platform providing financiers with the tools, the support, and the global network needed to conceive and manage investments in the complex and rapidly changing marketplace for clean energy technologies[26]. SEFI's focus is to develop networks and create partnerships with and within the finance sector to launch innovative financial products tailored to sustainable energy investments. SEFI publishes annually the "Global trends" report[27].

The role of the UN Regional Commissions is also important (see chapters 5-9). However, facilitating EERE financing is not on the whole at the forefront of their TA activities and the geographical distribution of their contribution is uneven[28]. A future potential for TA and capacity-building by the UN Regional Commissions may be realized over the coming years through the Global Energy Efficiency 21 Project, recently launched by the UNECE Committee on Sustainable Energy (see chapter 5).

UNDP focuses its activities on four priority areas: strengthening national policy frameworks, promoting rural energy services, promoting clean energy technology and increasing access to financing for energy[29]. Between 1986 and 2000, UNDP has supported over 200 projects in the area of energy and climate change (using a broader definition than strictly EERE) for an amount of funding of ca $1bn, with a substantial portion from the GEF. One example is a project launched in 2005, with GEF funding on "Increasing energy efficiency and implementing environmental management systems in public schools and health institutions in Jamaica".

UNIDO is also active in the EERE domain with its main focus on policy support, capacity building and technology demonstration[30]. A centerpiece of its work in EE is the promotion of energy management system standards, the purpose of which is "to provide guidance for industrial enterprises to integrate energy efficiency into their management practices using the "plan-do-check-act" approach of the well-known and widely used quality and environmental management systems such as ISO 9001 and ISO 14001".

3.2.3. The Renewable Energy and Energy Efficiency Partnership (REEEP)

Created in 2004, REEEP has the status of an international NGO. It has received donor funding from the Governments of Ireland, Italy, New Zealand, Norway and the United Kingdom. REEEP projects concentrate on the following themes:

(i)   Policy and regulation to attract investors and to guarantee affordable energy services to consumers through the implementation of robust policies and favourable, transparent and stable regulatory frameworks and

(ii)   Innovative finance mechanisms to make small-sized renewable and energy efficient projects bankable and economically attractive by using new forms of financing, risk mitigation and finance models;

REEEP actions are demand-driven and regional. Over 110 projects have been financed to date. For example, REEEP and UNIDO have funded a training package on "Sustainable Energy Regulation and Policymaking for Africa", aimed at reversing the lack of capacity and knowledge on how to foster regulatory and policy environments that support economically and environmentally sustainable methods of energy supply and utilization, both in the industrial, commercial and urban domestic sectors and the rural energy environment in developing countries[31]. REEEP has also initiated a Training and Education Database (TED) as a registry of courses and training in renewable energy and energy efficiency[32].

3.2.4. Regional and bilateral donors

Several countries and organizations are active in funding TA programs that support EERE financing, in particular Germany, Italy, the Netherlands, United Kingdom, the Scandinavian countries and the EU, to name a few. For example, GTZ (Germany's government-owned international technical cooperation agency) is managing a programme called TERNA (Technical Expertise for Renewable Energy Application), which supports partner countries in the assessment and utilisation of their wind energy potential[33].

The EU, for its part, is a significant donor for climate mitigation. However, its funding is scattered across numerous instruments, such that it is not possible to quantify its overall effort in support of EERE financing. A substantial amount is channelled in the form of investment grants and TA through IFIs (EBRD, EIB, KfW), for the most part through its regional policy funds (European Regional Development Fund, Cohesion Fund, IPA, Jessica, etc.)[34]. The EU also supports capacity building. For example, since 2002 its ManagEnergy initiative aims to support the work of actors on energy efficiency and renewable energies markets at the local and regional level. The main tools are training, workshops and online events. Additionally, information is provided on case studies, good practice, European legislation and programmes[35].

3.2.5. International Financial Institutions (IFIs)

IFIs play a key role in designing, financing and supporting EERE financing mechanisms through TA programmes. IFIs have privileged access to international, regional or bilateral donor funding because these donors are either their shareholders, or because IFIs are their institutional partners, such as with the GEF.

IFIs can also finance TA programmes from their own resources, for example AFD typically funds TA programmes from the concessionality embedded in its Overseas Development Assistance (ODA) loans. Since 2008, the EBRD is using some of its retained earnings to fund TA programmes.

3.2.6. Access to TA programmes and funding sources

As this section makes clear, there is a myriad of EERE-related TA programmes implemented across the world under the aegis of international, regional, national agencies or organizations. Yet, it is not always easy to locate and find information about these programmes and ex-post evaluations are either not available or not in the public domain. There is, moreover, significant overlap between programmes and often insufficient coordination between agencies. As a result, the picture is one of a kaleidoscope. This undoubtedly reflects the bottom-up and demand-driven approach of many programmes, but also the tendency of agencies to work in isolation, spend their budgets and achieve their targets with too little regard for the consistency of these schemes and programmes. Finally, there is a lack of global or regional portals that would provide access to this information in a structured way, especially for capacity building.

The creation of UN-Energy was surely a step in the right direction. An interagency mechanism for the coordination of energy-related activities, UN-Energy was established in 2004 to improve the planning and coherence of UN work in the field of energy. It regularly gathers representatives of the above-mentioned (as well as other) agencies and has undoubtedly made a contribution to the field, although it is impossible to quantify the extent to which this has resulted in tangible improvements in the EERE financing area.

4. Creating effective financing mechanisms

This chapter discusses the steps and ingredients to design effective mechanisms fitting different local environments, and with a view to creating sustainable markets (see annex I).

The existence of such a range of mechanisms suggests that one or both of the following things, are happening: (i) the situations and local contexts are so different that only bespoke solutions can work –a conclusion shared by many[36]; (ii) there is not enough exchange of information and experiences to allow lessons to be shared and a body of best practice to emerge. One particular problem is that reliable information on the results and true costs of these mechanisms are scarce, making assessments and comparisons challenging. In particular, very few of these mechanisms have been the object of a proper independent evaluation. IFIs do evaluate some of their projects, but these documents are not always public and not always prepared by independent sector experts. Yet, an evaluation would enable policymakers and practitioners to assess and compare current mechanisms more thoroughly and learn useful lessons for the design of future mechanisms or the adaptation of existing ones.

4.1. Mechanisms must fit the environment in which they will operate

One should guard against the temptation to assume an off-the-shelf model can be simply transplanted to a new setting and work fine. The first requirement to design an effective EERE financing mechanism is to do a diagnosis of the host country environment in which the mechanism is to be created. Delivery systems developed in one institutional environment in one country often do not work effectively in a different institutional context. For success, local institutional environments must be well understood, and general solutions usually need to be at least partly customized for those environments[37].

This is a good use of TA funds (see chapter 3). The initial diagnosis should be thorough and it should consider, among other things, the following aspects:

(i) What are the EERE opportunities?

    a. What is a country's endowment in RE resources?

    b. What is its energy intensity? What are the sectors where EE is significantly below relevant industry and international benchmarks? However, energy intensity is a crude indicator, especially when applied to countries. Climate and economic structure impact energy intensity without implying energy wastage. Some projects, such as the EU funded ODISSEE, aims to remedy these limitations by elaborating new indicators and adjusting energy intensities[38].

(ii)   What are the most cost-effective technology options for climate change mitigation?

A good technical potential does not translate automatically into a good economic potential. Some options for climate change mitigation are, in fact, cheaper than others. A good starting point when designing a financing scheme is to identify the most cost-effective options, which will be prioritized.

   a.   A useful tool is the marginal abatement cost curves that firms such as McKinsey and Vattenfall have popularised[39]. These curves should not be taken at face value. They have, indeed, some flaws. For example, they generally under-estimate the cost of EE by ignoring transaction costs and other market barriers. They can be useful nonetheless to prioritise climate mitigation actions;

   b.   The level of energy prices is a key determinant of the cost-effectiveness of climate mitigation technologies. Where energy prices are low, such as in South Africa, end-users have less incentive to invest in EE, even as the same country has recently adopted attractive feed-in tariffs for RE projects. Fossil fuel subsidization is further discussed below.

   c.   Ideally the diagnosis will also include a market demand study, which will aim at gauging the potential demand for financing in the various segments that yield the best carbon abatement returns by euro or dollar invested. If the budget of the study allows, an initial pipeline of projects is also helpful to kick-start a facility, although experience with such "pipelines" has generally been disappointing as EE projects tend to be relatively small and remain latent until project preparation and financing tools are developed.

The outcome of this analysis is the selection of a set of investment priorities and market targets. For instance, a number of the mechanisms reviewed in section 2.2 have a specialized focus: e.g. SWH (PROSOL), SME projects (BEERECL), Solar PV systems (BerkeleyFirst) and ESCOs (China Energy Conservation Programmes I and II).

(iii) What are the main barriers to EERE investment?

It is important to distinguish real from "self-inflicted" barriers (i.e. a barrier that is the consequence of a government policy). A well-known example is the subsidizing of fossil fuel production and consumption (or over-subsidizing, as the non-internalisation of the climate change externality is tantamount to subsidizing fossil energy.) This is the main barrier to EERE investments as energy subsidies today amount to approximately $250-300 billion globally, of which $180-200 billion are for fossil fuels and only $16 billion or approximately 8% for renewables[40]. Iran and Russia are, according to the IEA, the countries that most subsidize energy consumption (notably gas, electricity and district heating). Unsurprisingly, their energy intensity is among the highest in the world[41].

4.2. Deal flow is no less important than finance

To be effective, a financing mechanism must address, and balance, these two dimensions: supply (the provision of finance) and demand (a steady flow of quality projects). A scheme that is imbalanced in this regard will not yield optimal results. For instance, a good project pipeline may not have access to finance or finance may remain idle for lack of well-developed projects[42].

This means that a scheme must incorporate marketing, project development and technical design functions. It is essential to understand what the host country's capacity is in this regard. Where it is weak, the use of international consultants can fill the gap, but care should be taken that this does not jeopardize or postpone for too long the building of a strong domestic capacity, which is at the core of sustainability (see section 3.1). It is important to consider both sides of the financing equation: the project proponent and the financier. Both may have in-house technical expertise but in many cases both may need to rely on external technical support. This area is another good use of TA. For example, in the BEERECL, a team blending international experts with local consultants provides extensive project preparation support to project proponents, including an energy audit, a priority investment programme, cash flow projections and an IRR calculation. Project proponents are then free to choose which of the 6 participating banks they want to work with.

4.3. The creation of a dedicated financing window should be a last resort

A key objective of policy-makers is to ensure that what they build is sustainable. For that reason, designers of EERE financing mechanisms should look at existing commercial (usually private) providers of finance as their preferred delivery channel. The diagnosis mentioned in section 4.1 should include a review of these providers and their attitude to EERE financing. Local banks, in particular, may be reluctant to finance these projects for various reasons, such as: (i) lack of knowledge of EERE technologies; (ii) insufficient appraisal capacity; (iii) insufficient liquidity; and (iv) perceived risks.

Where the banking system is weak, risk adverse or in the midst of a transition process, it may be unable or unwilling to finance these projects. In this case, the (radical) option of creating a new dedicated EE and/or RE financing vehicle may be considered.

These new vehicles raise issues of their own: often created and controlled by the state, they run the risk of being bureaucratic, slow, inflexible and partisan. They sometimes end up competing with local banks, as in the case of BgEEF and IREDA. When this is the case, they should not be given an unfair advantage that would distort competition. Sustainability is ultimately about creating a real market where multiple commercial institutions compete for customers and use this competition as a leverage to expand volumes and lower costs. Mechanisms which support banks in building their capacity, getting access to funding on better terms (tenor and rates) and becoming less risk adverse are to be preferred. Hence, new dedicated financing vehicles should be considered as a last resort.

4.4. Is funding needed, credit enhancement or both?

Where financing for EERE projects is not forthcoming, one should carefully determine whether the root cause of this situation is scarce liquidity (and/or inadequate terms), high perceived risks, or other factors. If the former is true, then funding will need to be raised from one or several sources; if the latter is true, various forms of credit enhancement may provide the solution. Other factors may include political or economic variables that hinder the availability of funds for EERE.

The lack of funding is generally regarded as a non-issue in most markets, except perhaps since the financial crisis, which has virtually shut down the interbank, syndication and bond markets in many countries. Even when this is an issue, some ways can be found to tap domestic resources. Central banks and bank regulators can prescribe for example that a minimum percentage of new bank loans are made to certain sectors, or for specific purposes. The lowering of bank reserve requirements can be a powerful incentive for lending. Inappropriate financing terms (tenors, rates) in the host market can be a good reason to borrow money from abroad, but this should be managed carefully as excessive foreign borrowings and currency mismatches have been a key compounding factor in the financial crises experienced by some countries.

If liquidity is sufficient and financing terms adequate in the host market, credit enhancement can suffice to address the issue of perceived risks. Credit enhancement is achieved in mainly two forms; guarantee schemes (partial credit or partial risk) or integrating loan payments in a utility bill or municipal tax. The former means that a third party entity will foot some of the cost of a defaulting loan. There are several types of guarantee, which differ in terms of scope (individual project or portfolio), and magnitude of risks shared (first loss, second loss, or else). Many guarantee schemes involve a provider of grants (i.e. a subsidy) as ultimate back-up to the guarantee, for example the GEF in many of the IFC guarantee schemes (Central Europe, China). Guarantees work well in mature banking systems, when such minor support (plus some TA) is enough to nudge banks towards lending to EERE projects. A new study by the EC aims to gauge *inter alia* the extent to which banks in the EU could scale up their EERE lending if guarantees were available on a wide scale and at an attractive cost.

Integrating loan payments in a utility bill or municipal tax is a very attractive idea when the target segment of a scheme is households, e.g. for residential EE, SWHs or solar PV systems. This results in both lower collection costs and reduced credit risk. The lender can be a utility, a supplier, a bank (Prosol) or a municipality (Berkeley First).

4.5. ESCOs are a worthy instrument but success is hard to achieve

ESCOs are a wonderful instrument on paper. They can provide a diagnosis (audit), engineering, procurement, installation, project management, savings guarantee and financing, to name the main functions of ESCOs. The typical ESCO contract is called an Energy Performance Contract (EPC).

There are two main models for energy performance contracting. Under the "shared savings" model, the ESCO is normally the lender and cost savings are shared by the ESCO and the client on a pre-determined basis for a fixed number of years. In the "guaranteed savings" model, a third party finances the project and the ESCO guarantees a certain level of energy savings to the customer: this model has the advantage that interest rates are usually lower (e.g. in the US municipalities can issue tax-free bonds). In contrast, in the shared savings model, the ESCO assumes both the performance and the credit risk[43].

ESCOs, however, remain niche players on the global EE scene. Even in countries where a significant ESCO market has developed such as the US and Canada, they target a niche market, i.e. public sector buildings. China is one of the very few success stories in emerging markets and it is worth referring to[44].

Typical barriers faced by ESCOs include: (i) low energy prices; (ii) complexity of EPCs; (iii) high transaction costs; (iv) difficulties for ESCOs to raise debt and/or equity; (v) complexity of the public procurement process; (vi) issues with calculating and monitoring savings; (vii) reticence of some clients to let ESCOs earn a profit from "their" savings, and (viii) unrealistic pay-back expectations by some managers. Some of the mechanisms reviewed above show that these barriers can be overcome, but these projects are complex and require sustained efforts, as well as a strong commitment and support from governments to decisively tackle barriers.

4.6. Utility Demand-Side Management (DSM) programmes

In the broadest sense, "Demand-Side Management (DSM) program consist in the planning, implementing and monitoring activities of electric utilities which are designed to encourage consumers to modify their level and pattern of electricity usage"[45]. DSM encompasses a wide variety of actions taken by utilities to modify their customers' energy demand, such as programmes that: (i) reduce energy use (e.g., efficient buildings, equipment and processes); (ii) redistribute energy demand to spread it more evenly throughout the day (e.g., load shifting, innovative rates); and (iii) encourage strategic load growth (e.g., electrification programs). Utilities accomplish such goals by using rebates, audits, loans and free installation of energy-efficient equipment, among other options.

These programmes represent an important option for promoting EE investments. Utilities have financial, organizational and technical strength, as well as a unique interface with virtually all energy users. This positions them ideally to offer integrated EE solutions to their customers. Utility DSM schemes are well documented. The major issue is that energy efficiency runs counter to their main business driver (i.e. selling ever more energy) as profit is a function of sales. EE will coincide with the utility's interest if load management is a priority for them in the context of power shortages.

Several countries have tried to alter this business driver and now reward utilities for the EE efforts they make. "White certificates" (also referred to as Energy Savings Certificate) and Energy Efficiency Credits (EEC) are two ways to achieve this[46]. Under these schemes, distributors, suppliers or third parties (ESCOs, installers, retailers, local authorities, etc.) are required to undertake energy efficiency measures for the final user to reach a certain target. If they do not meet the mandated target for energy consumption, they are required to pay a penalty. The white certificates are earned whenever an amount of energy is saved. They can be used for their own compliance needs or sold them to other parties who cannot meet their targets. Several EU countries (such as France, Italy and the UK), some US states (Connecticut, Nevada and Pennsylvania) and the Australian province of New South Wales, among others, are implementing this system. The New York scheme ("EmPower") featured in section 2.2.4 provides an interesting example of a DSM scheme targeted at low-income customers.

4.7. Subsidies run counter to sustainability but are needed to tackle barriers

Subsidies in this discussion are any form of financing that is not subject to normal commercial rules. Subsidies are incompatible with sustainability because subsidies distort the normal operations of markets. That is true if one only considers the end point.

The EERE market is not a well functioning market and, as argued throughout this paper, it is clearly facing a host of barriers. Indeed, referring to climate change, Lord Nicholas Stern, the author of the influential Stern Review, has talked of "the greatest market failure the world has seen"[47]. One should also not forget that governments in many countries are lavishing billions of dollars of subsidies on fossil fuel energy and consumption (see section 4.1).

Subsidies can thus help tackle some of the barriers typically encountered by EERE investments (see table 2.2). They can take various forms, but they all share in common that they buy down costs: cost of financing, cost of reducing risk, cost of investment, cost of transacting, cost of capacity building, etc. Subsidies should not be used to reverse or offset the effects of a negative subsidy, such as low tariffs (policy-makers should remove the latter), but sometimes there is a fine line between tackling genuine barriers and compensating for low tariffs. The levels of subsidies, in particular of investment grants or concessional interest rates, should be set carefully. Most of the mechanisms reviewed in section 2.2 feature some elements of subsidy, either explicitly or implicitly. The debate is then not so much about their legitimacy, as about their effectiveness and cost in doing the job of lifting barriers. Once barriers have been overcome, subsidies should be phased out.

Subsidies in EERE investments normally take one of the following six forms: (i) investment grant (BEERECL, PROSOL); (ii) soft loan terms (Thailand REEF, AFD Tunisia); (iii) guarantees (CHUEE, IBRD 2nd ECP China); (iv) TA (see chapter 3); (v) patient equity (GEEREF, FIDEME); and (vi) feed-in tariffs (i.e. a cross-subsidy among electricity users).

4.8. Grants versus soft loans

Another interesting debate is on the best system to stimulate investments. In particular, DFIs are divided on the strength and weaknesses of concessional lending terms as opposed to investment grants. The IFC and the EBRD, for example, lend funds to banks for EERE projects on a commercial basis, but they mobilise donor grant funds to soften the terms of their guarantees (IFC), fund TA programmes (EBRD, IFC) or pay investment grants to end-borrowers (EBRD). KfW Entwicklung and AFD, which channel almost exclusively ODA funds, still mostly lend at below market interest rate. However, AFD sometimes requires that the concessionality embedded in its funding to local banks will be used for a TA programme or to pay investment grants to end-borrowers (e.g. Mauritius).

Paying investment grants to end-borrowers or beneficiaries as opposed to extending a concessional loan, however, has some advantages. The incentive is more visible, immediate and can be linked to performance as in EBRD BEERECL, where the grant is paid on project completion and is independently verified (see item 21 in section 2.2.8).

4.9. The architecture of financing mechanisms should be simple, flexible, align incentives and allow for evaluation

Designers of financing mechanisms should aim to keep the scheme as simple as possible. Simplicity is an outcome that is difficult to achieve as designers must juggle with, and reconcile, so many considerations;

The design should be flexible to accommodate possible revisions which experience may dictate;

Incentives between participants should be aligned to the extent possible to avoid frictions and conflict;

Last but not least, the scheme should provide for interim and ex-post evaluation, as a way to evolve the scheme if necessary and glean lessons. Performance indicators should be financial and physical (e.g. energy or carbon savings) and could include:

a. Number of projects / systems installed;

b. Energy savings (kWh or MWh) p.a.;

c. RE installed capacity and Plant Load Factors (the amount of "green" energy delivered and GHG emission reductions achieved will depend on both the former and the latter);

d. Mobilization or co-financing ration (total investment cost / loan or equity or guarantee from the scheme);

e. Administrative costs / financing volume or administrative costs / one of the above physical indicators (an indicator of organizational efficiency);

f. GHG emission reductions p.a.; and

g. GHG emission reductions per euro or dollar of investment (or, conversely, the euro or dollar cost by tonne of GHG abated, an indicator increasingly prized by IFIs, or the new Clean Technology Fund). However, reliance on this indicator could restrict the range of climate mitigation technologies financed as financiers would be encouraged to pursue the most cost-effective technologies.

This indicator is particularly important for financing schemes supported by public finance. Public funds are scarce and therefore it is essential that they achieve the highest yield in terms of carbon abatement. The use of indicators such as cost per tonne avoided[48], carbon yield per euro or dollar of investments, loan/guarantee/equity or public funds should thus be made general. Table 4.1 below compares these indicators for three AFD projects developed in 2009 and involving EERE credit lines to local banks, in China, South Africa and Turkey (see also mechanism 22 in section 2.2).

Table 4.1: Cost per tonne of CO_2 avoided and carbon abatement yield for three AFD projects*

	Investment cost per tonne avoided (in €)	Carbon yield of investment (kCO_2 per euro)	Carbon yield of AFD loan (kCO_2 per euro)
China	7,3	137	613
South Africa	10	100	200
Turkey	18,4	54	177

Source: J. Ligot.
*over the economic lifetime of projects (~20 years).

It is illuminating to look at three possible reasons for these different outcomes:

Mobilization ratio (ratio of total investment cost to loan extended by the financing scheme). This varies from 2 (South Africa) to 4.5 (China). The higher the mobilization ratio, the higher the impact of one euro of loan (and in some cases, one euro of embedded public subsidy) on carbon abatement.

Carbon emission factor of electricity, ranging from 0.54 kCO2 per kWh (Turkey) to 0.91 (South Africa). The higher this factor (i.e. the more carbon intensive the electricity generation is) the higher the carbon emissions cut.
Proportion of EE in total investments. EE is cheaper than RE per unit of carbon abated. Hence, the higher that proportion the stronger the carbon abatement impact.

Thanks to its very high mobilization ratio and fairly high carbon emission factor, the Chinese credit line obtains the best score: it achieves the highest return in terms of carbon abatement or the lowest cost per ton of CO_2 avoided. For international donors and DFIs (and assuming they have the choice), a possible conclusion could be to target countries that have the highest carbon intensity (and energy intensity), to give preference to EE and seek higher mobilization ratios.

4.10. Government support is key

Many of the mechanisms reviewed above feature the host governments in some capacity, and strong government support has been crucial to the success of some schemes, such China's First and Second Energy Conservation Programmes (see items 12 and 16 in section 2.2 above, and box 6.2 below).

The government can help through the following: (i) setting policies and targets for EERE (e.g. energy pricing policies, feed-in tariffs, standards, etc); (ii) influencing market players; (iii) streamlining public procurement procedures for ESCOs (e.g. FEMP in the USA); (iv) creating incentives; and (v) if necessary, creating a dedicated financing window.

5. The ECE region

The purpose of this and the following chapters is to present an overview of the regional energy and economic conditions, the local business and investment climates, the national and supranational regulatory frameworks and the major activities by the UN Regional Commissions in the field of energy efficiency.

5.1. Energy overview of the UNECE region

The energy situation of the United Nations Economic Commission for Europe (UNECE)[49] is widely diversified. It reflects both different natural resource endowments and recent political history.

Each country's energy situation has unique features. However, member countries can be roughly divided into two groups. On the one hand, Western European countries and the non-European members Canada, Israel and the United States are characterized by highly developed power markets, use of efficient technologies and universal sustained access to electricity and fuels. On the other hand, Eastern European, Caucasian and Central Asian countries have recently suffered from inefficiencies in production and distribution of energy, lack of investment and occasional shortages. Fast economic development in Eastern Europe and growing intra-regional cooperation promoted by the ECE and other institutions are, however, gradually narrowing this gap.

One thing the two sets of countries have in common is the very high level of energy consumption. The total primary energy supply of the ECE amounted to over 5768 Mtoe in 2008. This means that about half of the global energy production was consumed in the region, which is inhabited by only one fifth of the world's population[50].

The knowledge of the sectors in which energy is consumed, reported below, is fundamental to design effective policies aimed at consumption reduction and rational use. While improvements in the transport sector (33% of total consumption) normally require technological breakthroughs and large-scale investments, efficiency in industry and buildings (54%) can be achieved with financing mechanisms as those surveyed in chapter 2.

Figure 5.1: Total energy consumption per sector in the ECE region (in ktoe)

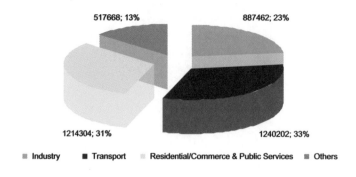

517668; 13%   887462; 23%

1214304; 31%   1240202; 33%

■ Industry   ■ Transport   ■ Residential/Commerce & Public Services   ■ Others

Source: IEA.

The dramatic consumption of energy in the region is somewhat normal given the intense economic activity and the very high levels of GDP per capita. The graph below shows the relation between GDP, energy consumption and CO_2 emission in per capita terms.

Figure 5.2: Carbon Emissions per capita (tCO_2/pop), TPES per capita (Mtoe/2), GDP per capita (US$ PPP) in the ECE region

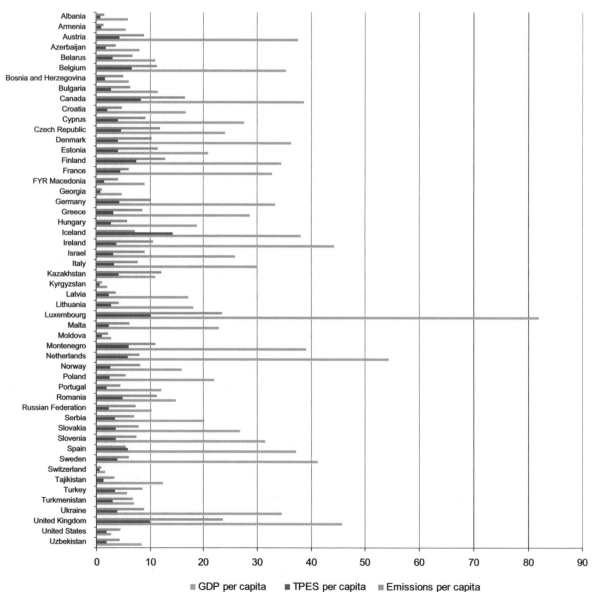

■ GDP per capita   ■ TPES per capita   ■ Emissions per capita

Source: ECE, based on data from ECE, World Bank and IEA.

However, higher levels of wealth do not proportionally reflect increases in energy consumption and GHG emissions. Indeed, a glance at ECE countries proves that some economies are performing much better than others from this point of view. The following tables show the added value produced by the consumption of a toe and those produced by the emission of a kg of CO_2. These statistics are very approximate indicators as they do not account for differences in climate and type of production. Nonetheless, they provide useful guidance in the assessment of the efficiency of the different ECE economies.

Figure 5.3: Carbon intensity (kgCO$_2$/US$ PPP/2), Energy intensity (toe/000US$ PPP) in the ECE region

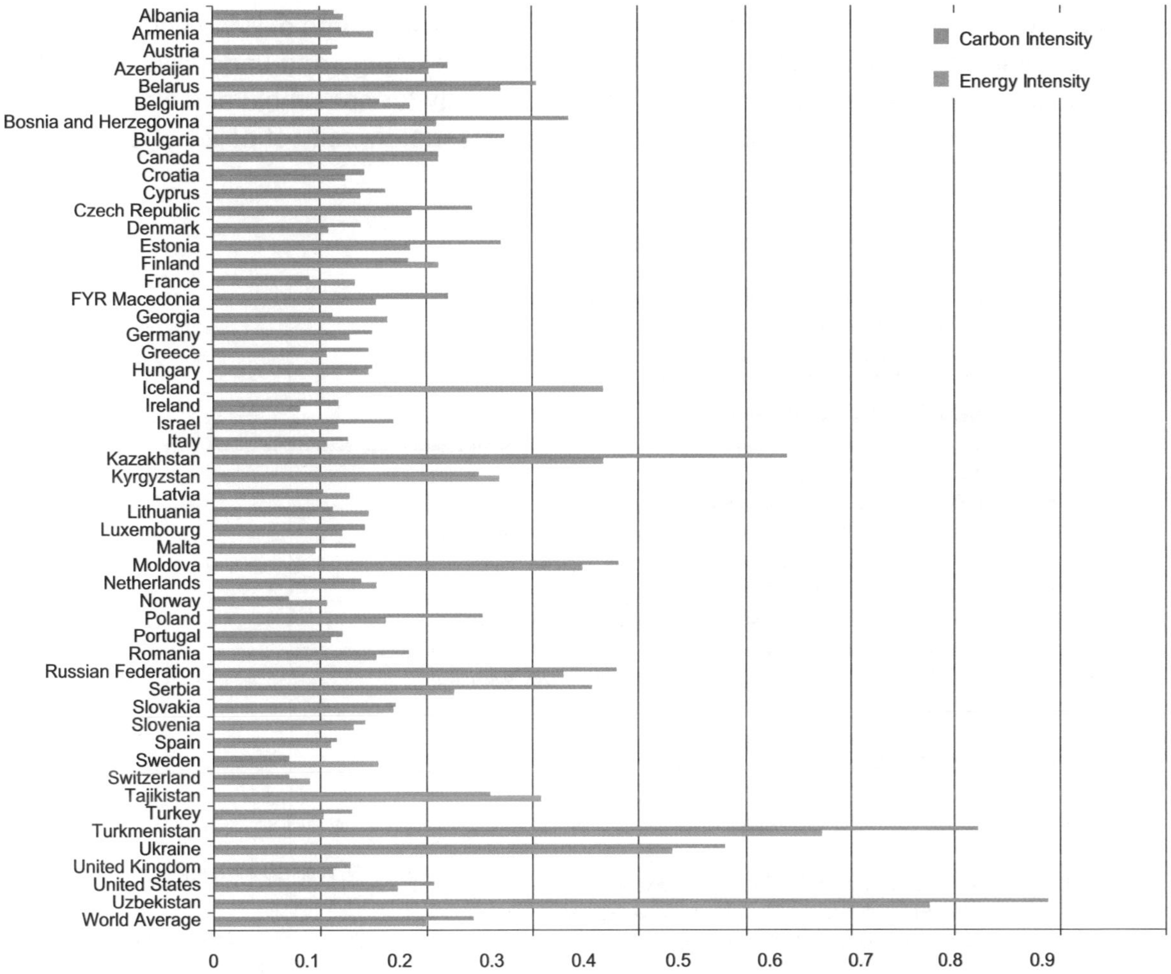

Source: ECE, based on data from UNECE and IEA.

The situation of internal markets is also extremely differentiated. Most ECE countries have been moving from insulated and highly regulated sectors characterized by a single dominant provider to more free and integrated markets. Countries are now situated at different stages of this ongoing process. A major role has been played in this respect by a number of European directives (see box 5.1 and appendix IV)[51] and by their expansions to neighbouring countries through a series of multilateral frameworks and the principle of *acquis communautaire* for EU candidate countries. The current situation of energy sectors in the ECE is outlined below.

Table 5.1: Progress of electricity market liberalization in the ECE region

Energy market structure	Countries
Full liberalization	EU-27, Canada, Croatia, Iceland, Kazakhstan, Norway, Switzerland, USA
Partial or early stage liberalization	Albania, Armenia, Bosnia, Georgia, Israel, Kyrgyzstan, FYR Macedonia, Moldova, Montenegro, Russian Federation, Serbia, Tajikistan, Turkey, Ukraine, Uzbekistan
Liberalization not started	Azerbaijan, Belarus, Turkmenistan

Source: ECE.

Another crucial feature of the power markets is the pricing policy. The issue is delicate as cheap energy and subsidized fuels, while boosting standards of living and sometimes guaranteeing social stability, lead to inefficient use of energy and underinvestment. The following chart shows the average prices of electricity for household and industry users in a selected number of ECE members and reflects the diversity of policy orientations in the region[52].

Figure 5.4: Electricity prices for selected ECE countries (US$/kWh)

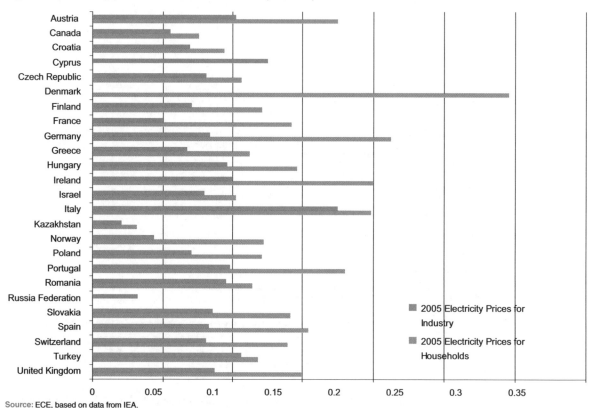

Source: ECE, based on data from IEA.

An additional factor affecting the energy intensity of a country tends to be its own endowment of energy resources. Although all ECE members rely on a mix of domestic and imported sources for their energy needs, most of them have a negative energy balance. The only net exporters in the ECE region are Azerbaijan, Canada, Denmark, Kazakhstan, the Russian Federation, Turkmenistan and Uzbekistan[53]. Countries with a positive energy balance generally tend to be less efficient than net importers. This is partly due to the fact that the activity of producing energy (in particular oil and gas) is highly polluting and energy-intensive and partly to the lower incentives to energy-savings when abundant reserves are available. However, given the global nature of climate change and its indiscriminate effects, such distinction should rapidly lose significance and all countries should be expected to work to reduce CO_2 emissions through efficiency improvements and cleaner energy sources.

5.2. General economic situation in the ECE region

As mentioned in the previous section, ECE countries are among the richest in the world. The degree of differentiation within the region is, however, significant (see figure 5.2 above). The growth rates, as shown in the chart below, are encouraging as poorer economies are generally expanding faster than others.

Figure 5.5: Real GDP growth (2007) in the ECE region

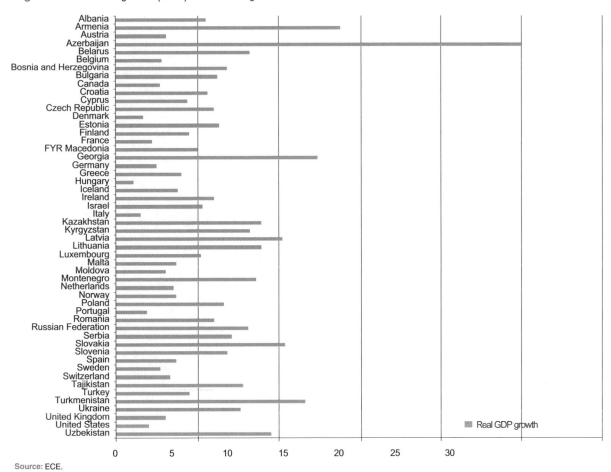

Source: ECE.

Also encouraging are the foreign direct investment (FDI) trends. The main recipients in relative terms are, in fact, those countries where investments in energy efficiency are mostly needed. Likewise, the fact that some of the world largest financers of FDI belong to the region leave plenty of room for intra-regional cooperation, technology transfer and the development of market-based financing mechanisms as those presented in chapter 2. Figure 5.6 shows both inward and outward flows of FDI for ECE countries in 2007.

Figure 5.6: Inward and outward FDI as percentage of gross fixed capital formation (annual average 2005-2007)[54] in the ECE region

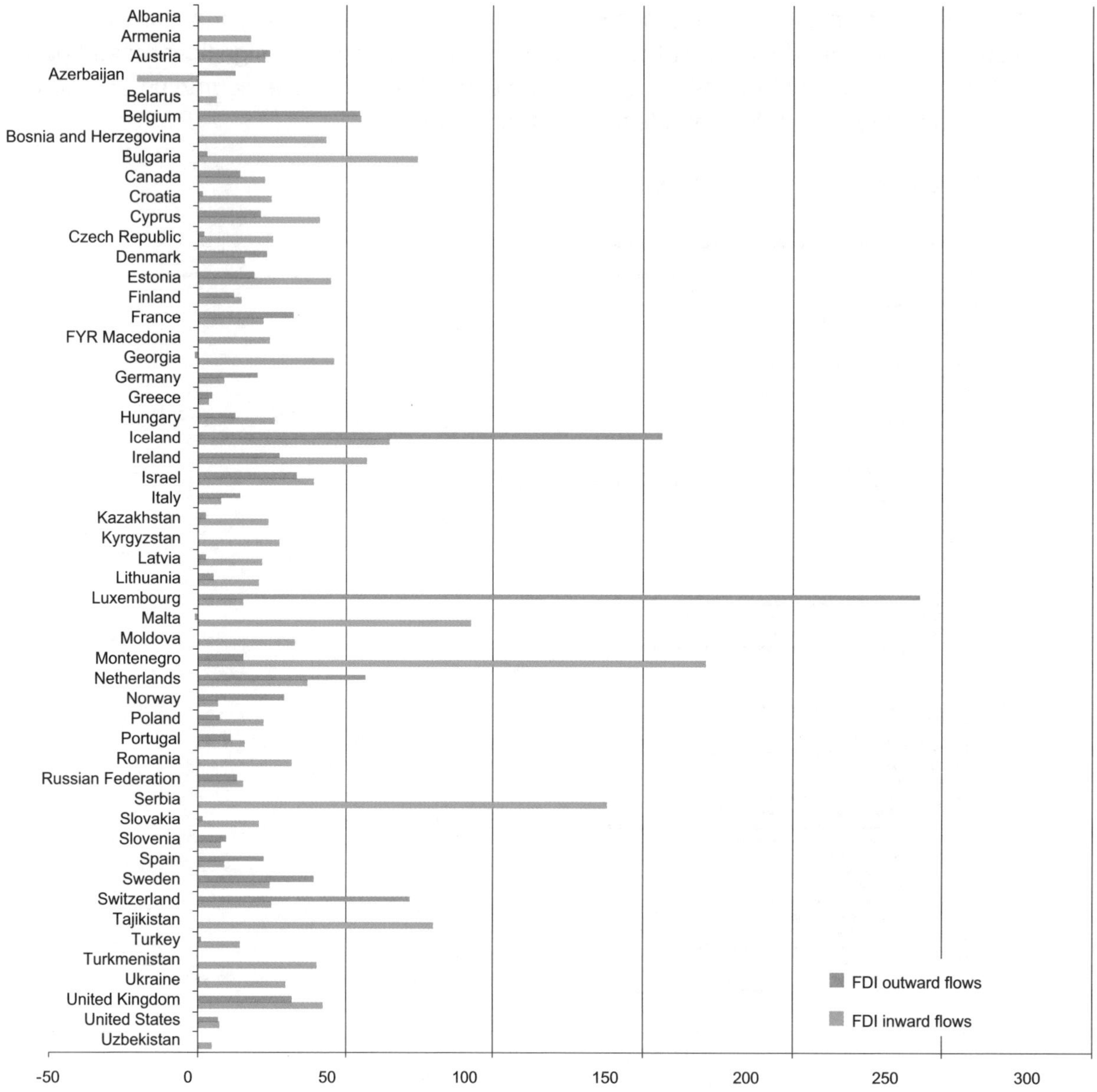

Source: ECE, based on data from UNCTAD.

Indicators assessing the quality of the business environment and the feasibility of investment project (both domestic and foreign) lead instead to less optimistic forecasts. The Corruption Perception Index (CPI) by Transparency International[55] and the Global Competitiveness Index by the World Economic Forum[56], reported in the graph below, show substantial unbalances in good governance practices within the region.

Figure 5.7: Global Competitiveness Index & Corruption Perception Index in the ECE region

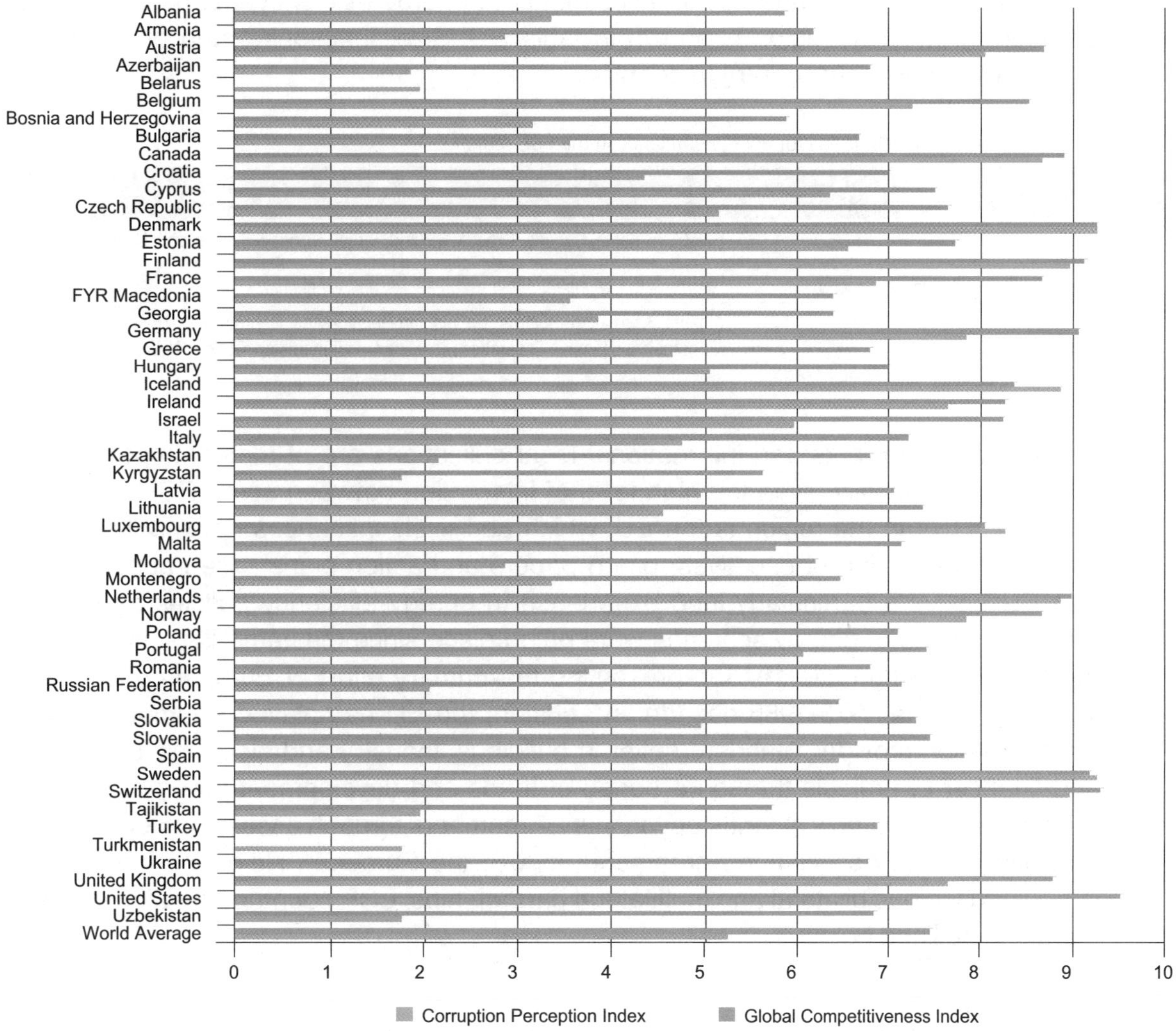

Source: ECE, based on data from Transparency International and World Economic Forum.

5.3. Legislative and regulatory framework

Regulations and legal provisions play a fundamental role in the promotion of energy efficiency investments. As outlined in section 4.10, sound legislation is at least as important as the availability of capital and economic conditions in order to set up effective financing mechanisms. Generally speaking, most ECE member states have in place and have implemented legal frameworks favouring energy efficiency improvements in a variety of sectors, although the progress made has not been uniform across the region. The table below offers preliminary guidance to the variety of legislation in ECE countries.

Table 5.2: National legislation for energy efficiency in the ECE region

Dedicated legislation for EE	Countries
Dedicated legislation (primary and secondary)	EU-27, Canada, Iceland, Israel, Kyrgyzstan, Norway, Switzerland, USA
Dedicated regulation but partial implementation or lack of secondary legislation	Albania, Azerbaijan, Moldova, Russian Federation, Turkey
Regulatory provisions from other frameworks but no dedicated legislation	Armenia, Belarus, Bosnia and Herzegovina, Croatia, FYR Macedonia, Montenegro, Serbia, Uzbekistan
Regulation currently under development	Georgia, Kazakhstan, Tajikistan, Turkmenistan, Ukraine

Source: ECE.

Some countries have gone further and instituted national energy efficiency funds assisting and complementing private sector investments in energy efficiency improvements. The situation in the ECE region is shown in table 5.3. Size, functioning and effectiveness again vary widely from country to country.

Table 5.3: Availability of national funds for energy efficiency in the ECE region

National EE Fund	Countries
Yes	EU-27, Armenia, Canada, Croatia, Iceland, Israel, Norway, Switzerland, USA
Partially established or very limited activity	Kyrgyzstan, FYR Macedonia, Moldova, Serbia, Ukraine
No	Albania, Azerbaijan, Belarus, Bosnia and Herzegovina, Georgia, Kazakhstan, Montenegro, Russian Federation, Tajikistan, Turkmenistan, Turkey, Uzbekistan

Source: ECE.

Multilateral frameworks and international legal obligations are of utmost importance in the region, especially given the high level of integration between some ECE members. A major player in the region is the EU, which decisively influences national legislation through the adoption of directives, green papers and action plans[57] (see appendix IV). The EU enjoys a particularly long experience in energy efficiency policies as savings and rational-use of energy schemes were put in place since the immediate aftermath of the first oil shock in late 1973, representing the primary effort of European institutions in energy for the 1975-1985 decade. In addition, the EU has played an important role as information provider, standard setter in buildings, industry and electronic appliances and financer of projects through a series of funds and development programmes. The outreach of the EU now extends beyond its 27 members through accession negotiations, Stabilization and Association Agreements (SAA), the European Neighbourhood Policy (ENP) and various bilateral and multilateral partnerships. ECE countries' relationship with the EU is outlined below.

Table 5.4: ECE member states and the EU

Relation with European Union	Countries
Members	Austria, Belgium, Bulgaria, Cyprus, Czech Republic, Denmark, Estonia, Finland, France, Greece, Germany, Hungary, Ireland, Italy, Latvia, Lithuania, Luxembourg, Malta, Netherlands, Poland, Portugal, Romania, Slovakia, Slovenia, Spain, Sweden, United Kingdom
Candidates/Applicants	Albania, Croatia, Iceland, FYR Macedonia, Turkey
Interested in membership	Bosnia and Herzegovina, Croatia, Georgia, Moldova, Montenegro, Serbia, Ukraine
Not openly interested in membership	Armenia, Azerbaijan, Belarus, Kazakhstan, Kyrgyzstan, Norway, Switzerland, Tajikistan, Turkmenistan, Uzbekistan

Source: ECE.

An example of effective expansion of EU legislation and policy direction is represented by the Energy Community South East Europe Treaty (ECSEE), entered into force on 1 July 2006. The treaty covers the electricity, natural gas and petroleum sectors and bounds the signatories (enumerated below) to gradually adopt the EU *acquis communautaire* in the relevant fields of energy, environment and competition. Implementation has hitherto proceeded smoothly.

Table 5.5: Membership of the Energy Community

Energy Community Treaty	Countries
Parties	Albania, Bosnia and Herzegovina, Croatia, FYR Macedonia, Montenegro, Serbia
Participants	Austria, Bulgaria, Cyprus, Czech Republic, France, Germany, Greece, Hungary, Italy, Netherlands, Romania, Slovakia, Slovenia, EU Commission, UK
Observers	Georgia, Moldova, Norway, Turkey, Ukraine
Not involved	Armenia, Azerbaijan, Belarus, Belgium, Canada, Denmark, Estonia, Finland, Iceland, Ireland, Israel, Kazakhstan, Kyrgyzstan, Latvia, Lithuania, Luxembourg, Malta, Poland, Portugal, Russian Federation, Spain, Sweden, Switzerland, Tajikistan, Turkmenistan, USA, Uzbekistan

Source: ECE, based on ECSEE Secretariat website.

Box 5.1: The objectives and reach of EU Energy Efficiency Policies

The EU policy-making in the field of EE almost exclusive relies on directives, to which states are abided to adapt their domestic legislation. Directives set policy objective and targets, while member states are free to choose the appropriate means to comply.

The EC Joint Research Centre (EC-JRC), Institute for Energy has collected and categorized the measures implemented by member states in response to EU directives:

(i)   Energy tax
(ii)   Incentives for EE investments
(iii)   Information campaigns
(iv)   Promotion of energy services (ESCOs)
(v)   Equipment Labelling (now standardised at the EU level)
(vi)   Buildings Codes (standards)
(vii)   Energy Audits
(viii) Voluntary programmes (mainly in industry, but also for equipment and cars; progressively run at the EU level)
(ix)   Energy Audits
(x)   DSM programmes
(xi)   Opening up public purchasing (procurement)
(xii)   Measures in the transport sector (road tolls, congestion avoidance, etc.)
(xiii) Guarantee of Origin for the promotion of co-generation.

Despite the fact that EU countries are among the most energy efficient in the world, very large savings can still be achieved (for instance, losses due to inefficiencies and wastes still account for 62.26% of the total primary energy input. In addition, the EC calculated that current policies will result in a 13% reduction in energy consumption by 2020, well below the official target of 20%. The Commission has appealed to member states for a swifter and effective implementation of directives and proposed immediate initiatives for buildings and products (eco-design)[58].

An ambitious yet less successful attempt to regulate the energy sector on a continent-wide scale was made with the Energy Charter Treaty, signed in Lisbon in December 1994. The agreement's main focus is the protection of foreign investment and the promotion of non-discriminatory trade in the field of energy. It also includes a Protocol on Energy Efficiency and Related Environmental Aspects (EEREA), which provides a forum for good-practice exchange but has few legally binding powers. The effectiveness of the Treaty has been thwarted by the refusal of some countries (most remarkably the Russian Federation) to ratify the agreement. The relationship of ECE members with the Energy Charter Treaty and the EEREA is presented in Table 5.6.

Table 5.6: Membership of the Energy Charter Treaty

Energy Charter Treaty	Countries
Parties	Albania, Armenia, Austria, Azerbaijan, Belgium, Bosnia and Herzegovina, Bulgaria, Croatia, Cyprus, Czech Republic, Denmark, Estonia, Finland, France, Georgia, Greece, Germany, Hungary, Ireland, Italy, Kazakhstan, Kyrgyzstan, Latvia, Lithuania, Luxembourg, FYR Macedonia, Malta, Moldova, Montenegro, Netherlands, Poland, Portugal, Romania, Slovakia, Slovenia, Spain, Sweden, Switzerland, Tajikistan, Turkey, Turkmenistan, Ukraine, UK, Uzbekistan
Observers	Canada, Serbia, USA
Parties with pending ratification	Belarus, Iceland, Norway, Russian Federation
Not involved	Israel

Source: ECE, based on Energy Charter Secretariat website.

Box 5.2: Energy Efficiency Policies and the G8

Another institution with significant impact in the region is the Group of 8 (G8). As seven out of eight members belong to the ECE region, the discussions and the outcomes of G8 summits have great relevance to regional policy-making. With regard to EE, the Gleneagles Plan of Action, which calls for "the pursuit of a clean, clever and competitive energy future" mandated the International Energy Agency (IEA) to elaborate a series of recommendations to the most industrialized economies. 25 recommendations were released in 2008:

(i) The IEA recommends action on energy efficiency across sectors. In particular, the IEA calls for action on:

   a. Measures for increasing investment in energy efficiency;

   b. National energy efficiency strategies and goals;

   c. Compliance, monitoring, enforcement and evaluation of energy efficiency measures;

   d. Energy efficiency indicators; and

   e. Monitoring and reporting progress with the IEA energy efficiency recommendations themselves.

(ii) Buildings account for about 40% of energy used in most countries. To save a significant portion of this energy, the IEA recommends action on:

   a. Building codes for new buildings;

   b. Passive Energy Houses and Zero Energy Buildings;

   c. Policy packages to promote energy efficiency in existing buildings;

   d. Building certification schemes; and

   e. Energy efficiency improvements in glazed areas.

(iii) Appliances and equipment represent one of the fastest growing energy loads in most countries. The IEA recommends action on:

   a. Mandatory energy performance requirements or labels;

   b. Low-power modes, including standby power, for electronic and networked equipment;

   c. Televisions and "set-top" boxes; and

   d. Energy performance test standards and measurement protocols.

(iv) Saving energy by adopting efficient lighting technology is very cost-effective. The IEA recommends action on:

   a. Best practice lighting and the phase-out of incandescent bulbs; and

   b. Ensuring least-cost lighting in non-residential buildings and the phase-out of inefficient fuel-based lighting.

(v) About 60% of world oil is consumed in the transport sector. To achieve significant savings in this sector, the IEA recommends action on:

   a. Fuel-efficient tyres;

   b. Mandatory fuel efficiency standards for light-duty vehicles;

   c. Fuel economy of heavy-duty vehicles; and

   d. Eco-driving.

(vi) In order to improve energy efficiency in industry, action is needed on:

    a. Collection of high quality energy efficiency data for industry;

    b. Energy performance of electric motors;

    c. Assistance in developing energy management capability; and

    d. Policy packages to promote energy efficiency in small and medium-sized enterprises.

(vii) Energy utilities can play an important role in promoting energy efficiency. Action is needed to promote:

    a. Utility end-use energy efficiency schemes[59].

The IEA itself has closely followed the implementation of the measures at the national level. A report released in 2009 shows encouraging results. Indeed, 40% of the policies recommended have been "fully" or "substantially" implemented, while for only 12% of them no action has been taken yet. These figures hide, however, sometimes wide sectoral and country differences. According to the IEA report, the United Kingdom was the best performer in the region, while the worst were Italy and the Russian Federation[60].

The commitment of the G8 to EE policies and targets has been confirmed, despite worries about the economic recession, at the Energy Ministers summit of Rome in May 2009. The ongoing gradual expansion of this governance mechanism to the G8+5 Climate Change Dialogue and the G20 is likely to trigger a spread of these measures and compliance policies to a larger group of countries, also outside the ECE region.

At the global level, the main legal instrument which may serve the promotion of energy efficiency investments is the UNFCCC and in particular the Kyoto Protocol adopted at the third Conference of Parties (COP-3) in December 1997. Most of the 39 industrialized countries (mentioned in Annex I of the UNFCCC and in Annex B of the Protocol) with compulsory emission targets are in the region[61]. The mechanisms and markets the agreements set up are described in Section 2.4. Despite these mechanisms, effective implementation has been made very difficult by the refusal to ratify or the late ratification of strategically decisive countries (especially the United States). The status of ECE members in the UNFCCC is outlined below.

Table 5.7: Commitment to the UNFCCC and the Kyoto Protocol in the ECE region

Status under UNFCCC	Countries
Annex I with significant reduction obligations	Austria, Belgium, Bulgaria, Canada, Croatia, Czech Republic, Denmark, Estonia, Finland, France, Germany, Greece, Hungary, Ireland, Italy, Latvia, Lithuania, Luxembourg, Netherlands, Poland, Portugal, Romania, Slovakia, Slovenia, Spain, Sweden, Switzerland, UK, USA*
Annex I without significant reduction obligations	Belarus, Iceland, Norway, Russian Federation, Turkey**, Ukraine
Non-Annex I	Albania, Armenia, Azerbaijan, Bosnia and Herzegovina, Cyprus, Georgia, Israel, Kazakhstan, Kyrgyzstan, FYR Macedonia, Malta, Moldova, Montenegro, Serbia, Tajikistan, Turkmenistan, Uzbekistan

* The United States has not ratified the Kyoto Protocol, adopted by consensus at the COP-3 on 11 December 1997, *de facto* refusing to comply with the agreed reduction target.
** Turkey is included in UNFCCC Annex I but not in the Kyoto Protocol's Annex B, which sets compulsory reduction targets.
Source: ECE, based on UNFCCC website.

5.4. Activities and accomplishments

5.4.1. Implemented and ongoing activities

Energy efficiency has been the concern of several international actors in the ECE region. Numerous projects have been run by several organizations including UNDP, the World Bank, the EBRD and the EIB. Most of them relied on financing provided by the GEF[62]. Bilateral development agencies also play a significant role in the region. The main geographical focus of these projects is Eastern Europe and Central Asia and results have been rather encouraging, even though a full assessment of the projects is difficult to conduct.

The ECE, in particular through its Sustainable Energy Division (SED), has always been a relevant player in the promotion of energy efficiency in the region. Activities started as early as 1990, when member governments agreed in the Bergen Ministerial Declaration on Sustainable Development to initiate the region-wide campaign *Energy Efficiency 2000 (EE2000)*. Its aim was to enhance trade and co-operation in energy efficient, environmentally sound techniques and management practices to close the energy efficiency gap between actual practice and best technologies, as well as between practices in different ECE countries. In addition to national actions and bilateral agreements, the ECE was appointed as major implementing agency of the policy orientations.

The EE2000 Project assisted Central and Eastern Europe and CIS countries in enhancing their energy efficiency and security which eased the energy supply constraints in the crucial stage of the economic transition. In addition, it helped these countries meet international environmental treaty obligations under the UNFCCC. The EE2000 Project ran until 2000 and was notably successful in leveraging modest resources to achieve its stated objectives, although a quantitative assessment is impossible due to the qualitative changes in the ECE economies triggered by the processes of transition and regional integration. EE2000 was also a catalyst for additional bilateral, multilateral and private initiatives. The relevance of its achievements have also to be seen in light of the ongoing process of mainstreaming of sustainable development within the United Nations, to which the ECE contributed both as an implementing agency and as a forum for intergovernmental debate. Such role was clearly recognized by the whole UN System at the Johannesburg Summit (WSSD) in 2002[63].

The work of the ECE in the field of energy efficiency is currently assumed under the *Energy Efficiency 21 (EE21) Programme*. Stemming from EE2000, EE21 is a region-wide umbrella project which aims to assist economies in transition to develop and promote sustainable energy policies, pursue energy efficiency strategies, reduce GHG emissions to meet international treaty obligations and enhance the security of energy supplies. It has produced specific outputs from operational activities in the industry, housing and services, transport and energy sectors through national actions, bilaterally and multilaterally (especially through the ECE). The project is guided and monitored by a Steering Committee composed of delegates from national participating institutions, international organizations and donor agencies. EE21 now focuses on the enhancement of regional cooperation on energy efficiency market formation and investment project developments. Its immediate goal is to accelerate regional networking between national participating institutions and international partners through internet communications, information transfers and training. Moreover, EE21 strengthens participant countries' capacity by disseminating skills and capabilities and promoting economic, institutional and regulatory reforms needed to support energy efficiency investments.

Under the EE21 Programme, the ECE runs five sub-regional projects (Financing Energy and Renewable Energy Investment for Climate Change Mitigation (FEEI), The Regional Network for Efficient Use of Energy and Water Resources in Southeast Europe (RENEUER), Energy Efficiency Market Formation in South-Eastern Europe, Increasing Energy Efficiency for Secure Energy Supply and Development of Renewable Energy Sector in the Russian Federation and CIS Countries; one country-oriented project (Removing Barriers to Energy Efficiency Improvements in the State Sector in Belarus) and one inter-regional project (Global Energy Efficiency 21 (GEE21)). The GEE21 and the two latter sub-regional projects are developed with substantial extra-budgetary support from the Russian Federation. Their features are described below.

The Financing Energy Efficiency and Renewable Energy for Climate Change Mitigation Project (FEEI) assists Eastern European, Caucasian and Central Asian countries[64] to enhance their energy efficiency, diminish fuel poverty arising from the economic transition and meet international environmental obligations under the UNFCCC. The project is developing skills in the private and public sectors at the local level to identify, formulate and implement energy efficiency and renewable energy investment projects. It also provides assistance to municipal authorities and national governments to introduce reforms needed to support these investments and promote opportunities for banks and commercial companies to invest in energy efficiency and renewable energy projects through the development of a new public private partnership investment fund. The main accomplishment has been the institution of a €250 million equity and mezzanine investment fund, which contributed also to a substantial boost in private EERE in the region. The project has also managed to attract significant extrabudgetary support from the United Nations Foundation (UNF), the United Nations Fund for International Partnership (UNFIP), UNEP, GEF and the Fond Français pour l'Environnement Mondiale (FFEM).

The Regional Network for Efficient Use of Energy and Water Resources in Southeast Europe (RENEUER) was founded at the end of 1999 at the initiative of representatives of several countries in the region. It is a typical "bottom up" initiative aimed at facilitating and promoting sustainable development for the municipalities and regions in Southeast Europe through initiatives for the rational use of energy and water resources. All countries participating in the Southeast European Co-operative Initiative (SECI) and the Regional Cooperation Council (RCC) have now joined the Network[65]. RENEUER focuses its activities on regional networking by enhanced Internet communications to provide value added information on project finance. It also promotes energy efficiency investments at the local level, develops skills and capacities and elaborates regional policies to support energy efficiency and the Kyoto Protocol mechanisms.

The Energy Efficiency Market Formation in South-Eastern Europe Project is designed to promote the formation of self-sustained energy efficiency markets in participating countries[66] through the development of skills and capability of the public sector at the local level, the provision of assistance in economic, institutional and regulatory reform to municipal and national administrations and the establishment of a network for information sharing and transfer. Particular emphasis is put on a bottom-up approach.

The Increasing Energy Efficiency for Secure Energy Supplies Project supports the development of energy efficiency investments designed to reduce the domestic consumption of hydrocarbons in the Russian Federation, Kazakhstan and other Central Asia energy exporters in order to release additional energy resources which could be used for either domestic consumption or to increase oil and natural gas exports, thus enhancing continent-wide energy security.

The Development of the Renewable Energy Sector in the Russian Federation and in CIS Countries Project promotes interregional cooperation to overcome political, regulatory, institutional and financial barriers to the development of renewable energy resources in the Russian Federation and the countries of the Commonwealth of Independent States (CIS). The expected accomplishments of the project include an increase in the capacity of national and regional experts to identify and adopt measures to overcome the above-mentioned barriers. An enhanced investment climate for the deployment of renewable energy technologies in the Russian Federation and CIS countries is also part of the objectives of the project.

Removing Barriers to Energy Efficiency Improvements in the State Sector in Belarus is currently the only ECE ongoing country-oriented project in the domain of energy efficiency. It aims at catalyzing investments in energy efficiency in the state sector of Belarus, whose improvement is fundamental for the reduction of the country's energy and carbon intensity as well as for the promotion of energy security and economic development. The project will target municipalities, state and communal enterprises in the district heating, combined heat and power sectors. The project objectives are to strengthen institutional capacity to support energy saving in the state sector, establish a track record for investments in sustainable energy efficiency projects in the state sector, develop straightforward financial "starter" mechanisms in a challenging investment climate to promote investments in the state sector and overcome negative perceptions of incentives for energy saving. Local authorities and state enterprises will also be provided with much-needed market information and training.

Following the positive impact of EE21 (specifically mentioned at the 'Environment for Europe' ministerial conference in Belgrade in 2007 and in the 'Proposed United Nations System-wide Approach to Climate Change' put forward by the United Nations System Chief Executives Board), the ECE Committee on Sustainable Energy mandated in November 2008 the Global Energy Efficiency 21 (GEE21) Project to transfer the experience of the energy efficiency projects in the ECE region to other regions of the world. The goal of the project is to develop a more systematic exchange of experience on capacity building, policy reforms and investment project finance among countries of the other regions of the world through their UN Regional Commissions in order to promote self-financing energy efficiency improvements that raise economic productivity, diminish fuel poverty and reduce environment greenhouse gas emissions. The expected accomplishments of GEE21 are: to increase the capacity of the regional commissions to provide effective energy efficiency services that promote the reduction of GHG emissions to member States, as well as to improve capacity to develop, adjust and implement a global strategy to promote self-financing energy efficiency improvements.

The ECE Sustainable Energy Division (SED) also collaborates with other ECE units on two projects aiming at combining the specific experience and know-how of different divisions to promote energy efficiency in the region. In particular:

The UNECE Action Plan for Energy Efficiency in Housing, a joint project with ECE Committee on Housing and Land Management (CHLM), aims to assist ECE governments to improve energy efficiency in the housing sector and enhance energy performance of buildings. The Action Plan provides a list of gaps and constraints preventing countries from increasing the energy performance of buildings and identifies possible solutions to overcome these constraints, as well as potential partners that could assist in the implementation of solutions. The Action Plan is expected to be a practical tool for decision makers and as such should be developed by policy-makers of member States in cooperation with the Secretariat, possibly through consultations and dedicated workshops. Two such workshops have taken place in 2009 in Sofia and Vienna.

The Wood Energy: Modern and Sustainable Heat and Power from Woody Biomass in South-Eastern Europe Project is a joint project of the ECE Sustainable Energy Division and the ECE/FAO Timber Section. Its goals are to demonstrate the feasibility of converting municipal heat and power systems in the western Balkans to woody biomass from local renewable sources by raising awareness at the policy level and by preparing detailed project proposals for one or two municipalities in each of the participating countries. The project is setting up a network of interested municipalities in the countries of the region and it aims to organize reconnaissance expert missions to the pilot areas to assess the market for woody energy, to collect positive examples for wood energy projects implementation and to prepare regional feasibility reports including business case relevant data. The organization of a sub-regional workshop for policy-makers representing energy and forestry areas from target countries is instrumental to the successful establishment of the network and to raise awareness through the showcase of examples where heat and power providers successfully switched to woody biomass.

In addition to these projects, the ECE provides national governments and institutions with the services of the *Regional Advisor on Sustainable Energy*. The duties of the Regional Advisor are to advise senior officials on energy issues, capacity and institutional building in order to raise the overall effectiveness and efficiency of the energy sector and to promote sound policies. The regional advisor has recently worked with various sub-regional organizations, participated in workshops and provided advisory, consultation and project formulation services in response to ad hoc requests by single countries.

Box 5.3: ECE seminar on policy reform

As many ECE projects involve the implementation of substantial political, economic and institutional reforms, the Ad Hoc Group of Experts on Financing Energy Efficiency Investments for Climate Change Mitigation (AHGE-FEEI) organized a *Seminar on Policy Reforms to Promote Energy Efficiency and Renewable Energy Investments* on 7-8 October 2009 in Geneva. The findings of the Regional Analysis of Policy Reforms to Promote Energy Efficiency and Renewable Energy Investments carried out by Poyry Energy Consulting AG were presented and discussed by the national participating institutions, policymakers from the twelve participating countries and ECE officials. At the end of the sessions, the participants elaborated the following conclusions:

(i) Several barriers for investments in energy efficiency and renewable energy sources are still present in the project region, in particular:

a. The main legal institutional and administrative barriers are: complexity of regulatory frameworks; lack of secondary legislation and operational instructions, tools and procedures; complex and cumbersome authorization procedures; inefficient or limited use of public tendering processes;

b. The main economic and financial barriers are: excessive state intervention in price formation; tariffs levels that limit the profitability of EE projects; limited availability of public funds for financing initiatives and programmes; small size of EERE projects; and

c. The main barriers in the level of awareness, human capacity and professional skills are: overall low level of awareness of the need for EE improvements; lack of experience in financing schemes of commercial banks and lack of training and education possibilities for improving professional skills.

(ii) Energy tariffs not covering costs of production and distribution are an obstacle to increasing EE, as they often make EERE projects non-profitable; energy tariffs that reflect full costs and the elimination of cross-subsidies are mandatory for the energy infrastructure to be properly maintained and upgraded and to attract new EERE investments; and

(iii) The establishment of dedicated loan facilities must be done in combination with technical assistance and training to increase capacity and expertise in the banking sector.

These barriers and shortcomings are not exclusively present in the twelve project countries but a large number of countries both within and outside the ECE region share these problems. These recommended actions are thus not limited to the project participants and deserve attentive analysis. In particular, the Seminar emphasized the following measures:

(i) In the short term:

a. Increased budget flexibility and autonomy to improve the efficiency of government-funded organizations and budgeting principles based on full life-cycle costing in order to capture the benefits of long-term investments; and

b. Transparency in the procedures for project approval, public procurement and tendering, using tools such as Standard Bidding Documents.

(ii) In the short-to-medium term:

a. Establishment or increased use of financial incentives for EERE, such as public funds, with a focus on the sectors and technologies where saving potentials are greater, based on accurate cost-benefit analyses; and

b. Identification and evaluation of needs for upgrade and expansion of transmission capacity, identification of optimal financing mechanisms and the definition of a feasible action plan with specific deadlines for access to the grid by energy producers of RE.

(iii) In the longer run (actions with higher initial costs but also higher returns):

a. Restructuring of tariff levels, tariff designs and customer classifications so that they reflect the true cost of production and internalize environmental externalities;

b. Regular monitoring of policy implementation and communication of policy requirements to all concerned stakeholders;

c. Adjustment of institutional structures to the reformed national policy framework at the national, regional and municipal levels; and

d. Proper training of qualified experts to assess the potential for EERE and to evaluate policy instruments.

5.4.2. Planned activities

The future activities of the ECE in the domain of energy efficiency, as outlined in the *Programme of Work in the Field of Energy for 2010-2011* will continue along similar directions. The development and harmonization of guidelines and strategies to enhance energy efficiency and energy conservation will still be one of the priorities of the Committee on Sustainable Energy. Particular emphasis will be put on the enhancement of regional and global cooperation on energy efficiency market formation and investment project development to reduce GHG emissions. The ECE plans to work to these ends closely with a plurality of actors, such as other international organizations, national institutions, private sector companies, international financial institutions and commercial banks.

6. The ESCAP region

6.1. Energy overview of the ESCAP region

The ESCAP region is characterised by vast social, economic, geographic and development disparities. The region consists of 53 member states and 9 associate member states, including emerging powerhouses such as China and India, large landmasses with considerable fossil fuel resources such as the Russian Federation and the Islamic Republic of Iran, many small island developing states and some of the poorest and least developed countries in the world, including Afghanistan, Bangladesh, Cambodia, Timor-Leste, Tuvalu and Samoa[67].

With a total population of over four billion, the ESCAP region is home to over 60% of the world population. As shown in figure 6.1, approximately 24% of the region's population, or 950million people, live on less than $1.25 a day[68], and the 930 million without access to basic energy services exacerbate this poverty[69]. Approximately 1.8 billion people also depend on traditional fuels to meet their basic energy needs[70]. This is reflected in figures 6.2 and 6.3 which show the total primary energy supply (TPES) per capita by country and the electricity consumption per person by country, respectively.

Figure 6.1: Percentage of the population living on less than $1.25 per day in Asia and the Pacific, 1990 – 2006

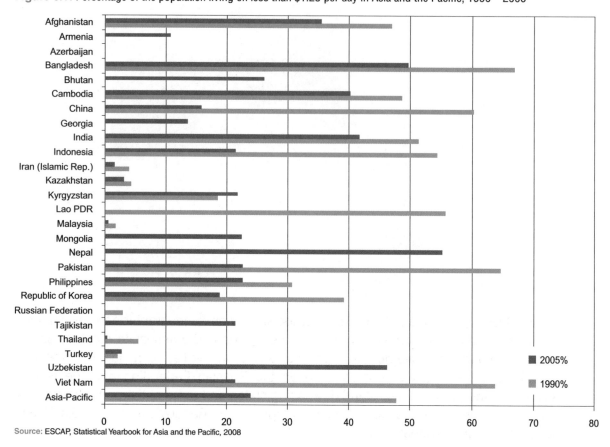

Source: ESCAP, Statistical Yearbook for Asia and the Pacific, 2008

Figure 6.2: Total primary energy supply per person, 2007 (toe per capita) in the ESCAP region

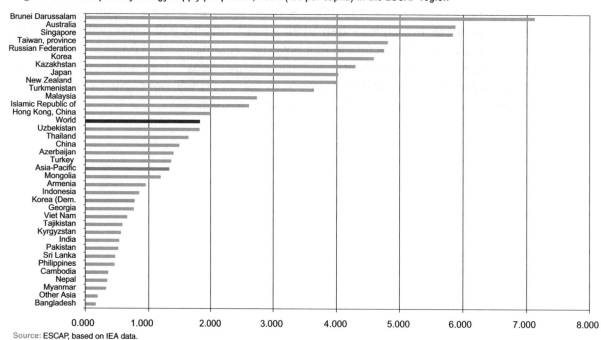

Source: ESCAP, based on IEA data.

Figure 6.3: Total electricity consumption per capita, 2007 (kWh per capita) in the ESCAP region

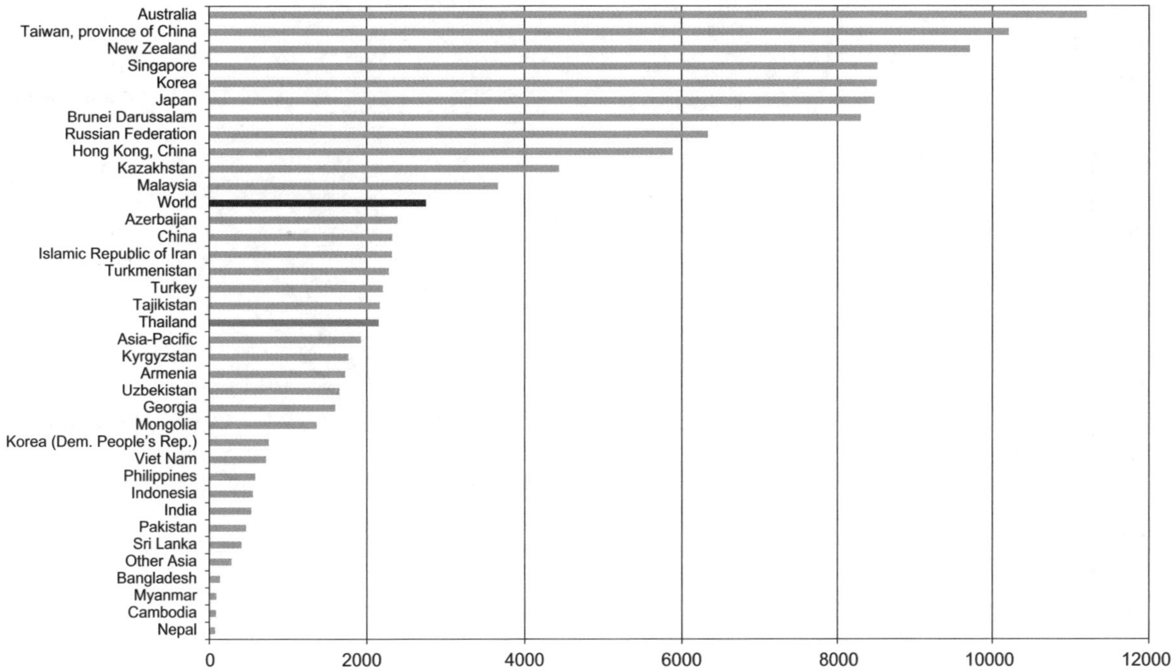

Source: ESCAP, based on IEA data.

Though significant progress has been made toward energy security in Asia and the Pacific, including providing access to clean energy supplies for development, the gap between the energy demand and supply in the region is still vast.

In 2007, the TPES in Asian and Pacific countries was a little over 5.3 billion tonnes of oil equivalent (toe), which was an increase of almost 50% from the 3.6 billion toe TPES of 1995. In 2008, the Asia-Pacific region accounted for 87% of the world's energy consumption growth[71]. Data from the IEA showed that the region's energy consumption as a share of total world energy use increased from 39% in 1990 to 42% in 2007, with China as the fastest growing[72]. This can be attributed to strong economic growth and successful development policies, as over the same period the region's GDP grew 160% from around PPP US$6.7 trillion to $10.6 trillion[73] (a pace which is almost a third higher than the world average in the same period, as figure 6.4 shows). Despite this, it is clear that there is still a considerable unmet demand for energy services in the region.

Figure 6.4: Index of change in GDP for world regions, 1990-2007

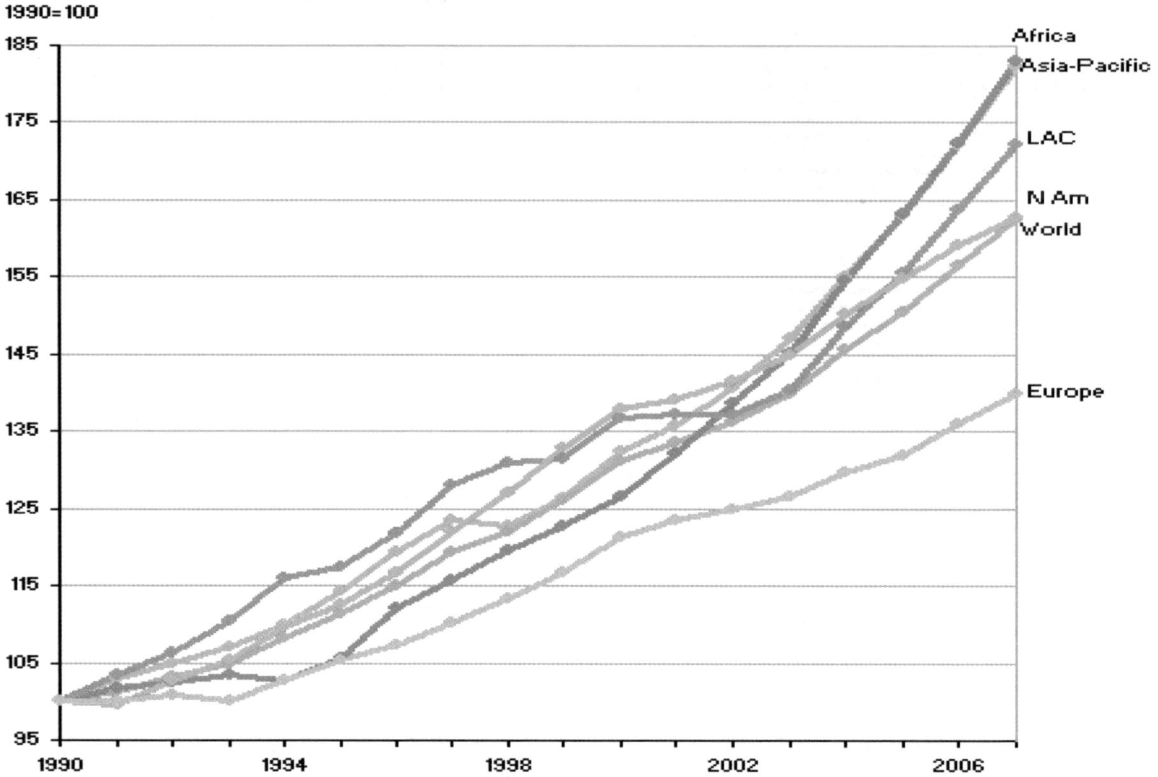

Source: ESCAP.

Although the link between energy consumption and economic development is clear, the use of some energy resources has unfortunately had a high environmental impact which often proves to be an expensive negative externality that can actually undermine the successful development efforts achieved.

This is made worse by Asia and the Pacific's reliance on fossil fuel resources. The actual self-sufficiency rate for the region in 2007 and 1990 was just over one, indicating that the region produces as much energy as it consumes[74]. This highlights the region's considerable reserves of fossil fuels, though unfortunately they aren't dispersed equitably. Table 6.1 shows that, in 2008, the ESCAP region had over half of the world's proven reserves of coal and natural gas and almost a quarter of the world's oil reserves[75]. In addition to this, the region boasts almost 60% of the global uranium reserves and massive potential for clean energy sources such as hydropower, as can be seen from table 6.2.

Table 6.1: Fossil fuel reserves for Asia and the Pacific in 2008

Country	Oil reserves			Natural gas reserves			Coal reserves		
	Billion barrels	% world reserves	Years remaining	Trillion m³	% world reserves	Years remaining	Million tons	% world reserves	Years remaining
Australia	4.2	0.3%	20.4	2.51	1.4%	65.6	76,200	9.2%	190
Azerbaijan	7.0	0.6%	20.9	1.20	0.6%	81.3	-	-	-
Bangladesh	-	-	-	0.37	0.2%	21.4	-	-	-
Brunei Darussalum	1.1	0.1%	16.9	0.35	0.2%	28.8	-	-	-
China	15.5	1.2%	11.1	2.46	1.3%	32.3	114,500	13.9%	41

Country	Oil reserves			Natural gas reserves			Coal reserves		
	Billion barrels	% world reserves	Years remaining	Trillion m³	% world reserves	Years remaining	Million tons	% world reserves	Years remaining
Democratic People's Republic of Korea	-	-	-	-	-	-	600	0.1%	17
India	5.8	0.5%	20.7	1.09	0.6%	35.6	58,600	7.1%	114
Indonesia	3.7	0.3%	10.2	3.18	1.7%	45.7	4,328	0.5%	19
Iran (Islamic Republic of)	137.6	10.9%	86.9	29.61	16.0	>100	-	-	-
Japan	-	-	-	-	-	-	335	> 0.05%	289
Kazakhstan	39.8	3.2%	70.0	1.82	1.0%	60.3	31,300	3.8%	273
Malaysia	5.5	0.4%	19.8	2.39	1.3%	38.2	-	-	-
Myanmar	-	-	-	0.49	0.3%	39.9	-	-	-
New Zealand	-	-	-	-	-	-	571	0.1%	111
Pakistan	-	-	-	0.85	0.5%	22.7	2,070	0.3%	496
Papua New Guinea	-	-	-	0.44	0.2%	> 100	-	-	-
People's Republic of Korea	-	-	-	-	-	-	133	< 0.05%	48
Russian Federation	79.0	6.3%	21.8	43.30	23.4%	72.0	157,010	19.0%	481
Thailand	0.5	< 0.05%	3.9	0.30	0.2%	10.5	1,354	0.2%	75
Turkey	-	-	-	-	-	-	1,814	0.2%	21
Turkmenistan	0.6	< 0.05%	8.0	7.94	4.3%	> 100	-	-	-
Uzbekistan	0.6	< 0.05%	14.6	1.58	0.9%	25.4	-	-	-
Viet Nam	4.7	0.4%	40.8	0.56	0.3%	70.1	150	< 0.05%	4
Other Asia Pacific	1.1	0.1%	12.8	0.39	0.2%	22.1	391	< 0.05%	26

Source: BP, *Statistical Review of World Energy* (2009)

Table 6.2: Hydroelectric potential and uranium reserves in the ESCAP region

	Hydroelectric technical potential, 1997		Uranium reserves, 2003	
	TWh	% world	Metric tons '000s	% world
East and North-East Asia	6,821	14.8%	118	2.8%
North and Central Asia	3,517	7.6%	1,230	28.7%
Pacific	593	1.3%	1,058	24.7%
South and South-West Asia	4,244	9.2%	68	1.6%
South-East Asia	3,461	7.5%	8	0.2%
ESCAP region	18,636	40.5%	2,482	57.9%
Developed ESCAP	1,134	2.5%	1,065	24.8%
Developing ESCAP	17,502	38%	1,417	33.1%

Source: United Nations Energy Database (2007).

Despite volatile oil prices during this period, the region continued to increase its primary energy demand and consumption. Given the initial high cost of alternatives and the limited technical expertise, it is no surprise that development options have been based on the consumption of fossil fuels (figures 6.5 and 6.6), despite the massive potential for renewable energy sources in the region[76]. For example, wind energy in Mongolia could potentially provide 1,100 MW of electricity capacity and approximately 71% of the total land area receives solar irradiation at a rate of 5.5 to 6 kWh/m² per day, with 2900 to

3000 sunshine hours per year[77]. One estimate of geothermal energy in the region, excluding Central Asia and the Russian Federation, indicates a potential of over 4,000 TWh/year for high temperature conventional geothermal plants, and 8,000 TWh/year for high temperature conventional and binary plants, equating to 35% of the global potential[78].

Figure 6.5: Total final consumption by fuel in 2007 in the ESCAP region

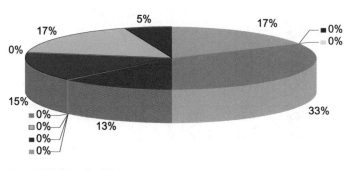

- Coal and coal products
- Peat
- Crude, NGL and feedstocks
- Petroleum products
- Natural gas
- Nuclear
- Hydro
- Geothermal
- Solar/wind/other
- Combustible renewables and waste
- Heat production from non-specified comb.fuels
- Electricity
- Heat

Source: ESCAP, based on IEA data.

Figure 6.6: Total electricity inputs in 2007 in the ESCAP region

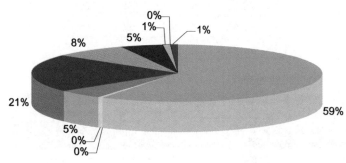

- Coal and coal products
- Peat
- Crude, NGL and feedstocks
- Petroleum products
- Natural gas
- Nuclear
- Hydro
- Geothermal
- Solar/wind/other
- Combustible renewables and waste

Source: ESCAP, based on IEA data

Figure 6.7 shows that the energy intensity in many countries is extremely high, indicating that with some strong policy measures, a large amount of the needed energy resources can be avoided. In addition to this, in some countries, particularly those of central Asia, a large amount of losses occur in the generation and distribution of electricity and heat.

Figure 6.7: Energy intensity (toes/US$1000 year 2000 PPP) in the ESCAP region

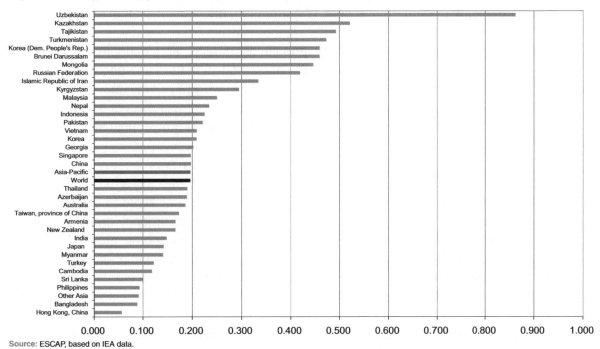

Source: ESCAP, based on IEA data.

The energy intensity, when viewed over time, can also reflect the link between energy consumption, economic development and environmental impacts. On a positive note, however, the energy intensity can also reflect the work towards decoupling the link between energy consumption and economic development. Figure 6.8 shows that the energy intensity of the region has actually improved (decreased) considerably between 1990 and 2006, reflecting efforts to generate wealth while limiting the impacts on natural resources.

Figure 6.8: Index of apparent energy consumption (supply) per unit of GDP in 1990 – 2006

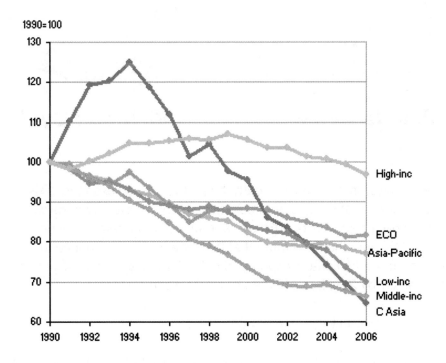

Source: ESCAP.

Many countries are recognising the opportunities and benefits of energy efficiency across the entire energy system - at the point of generation, distribution system and end-user.

However, given the dramatic level of population density and economic growth, EE policies alone do not seem to be enough. According to IEA's "Reference" scenario, by 2030 the region is expected to consume 44% of the world's energy, mostly in the form of fossil fuels[79]. Being the region already responsible for almost 47% of the world's CO_2 emissions, this further increase makes the current model of growth unsustainable[80].

In 2008, the focus of the ESCAP Commission Session was energy security and sustainable development. The key messages from the theme study prepared for this meeting highlighted the fact that the Asia-Pacific region cannot afford to continue along the line of the energy-economy nexus[81]. The region needs to urgently break away from the current vicious cycle of fossil fuels consumption fuelling economic growth by shifting towards a new sustainable energy paradigm. A virtuous cycle of clean energy options that support energy security and economic growth (figure 6.9) has to be created. In practice, however, this new energy paradigm cannot be effectively pursued in isolation from the broader context of a development paradigm. It is required a shift from a conventional development paradigm of "quantity of growth" towards that of "quality of growth".

Figure 6.9: Paradigm shift from a vicious to a virtuous cycle

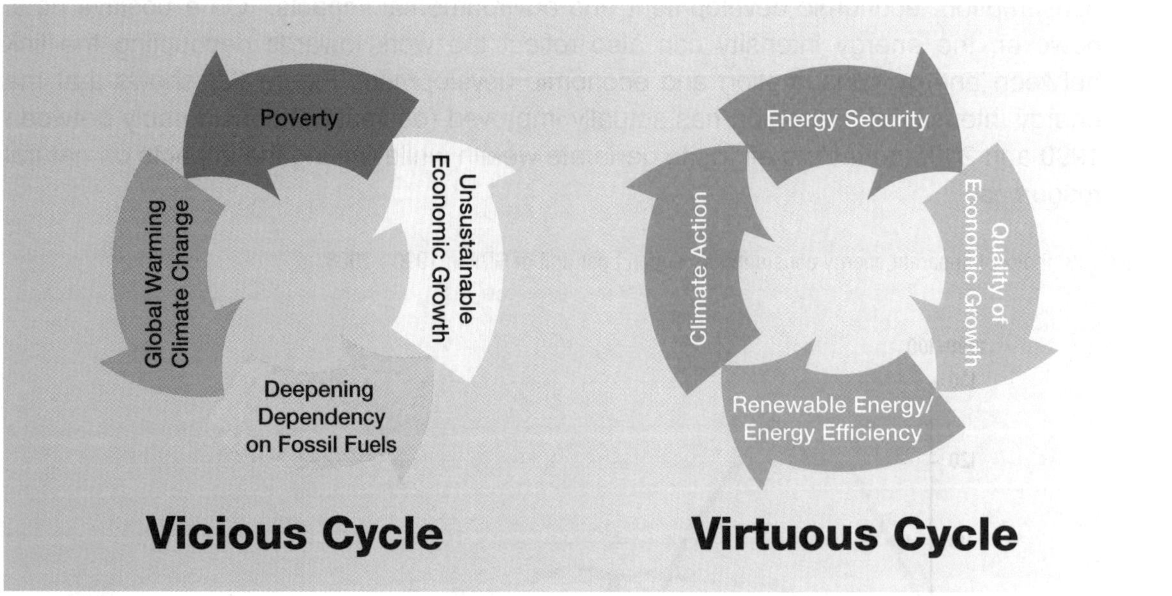

Source: ESCAP.

Initial steps towards this have already been taken. For example, the Government of China recognized that the country could not continue developing the way it was, with an economic growth rate of over 10% p.a. and an annual energy consumption growth rate of around 4%. Thus, the Government at its highest level introduced in its 11th Five Year Guidelines on the National Economy and Social Development a policy to reduce the energy intensity by 20% by 2010 (see box 6.2 below).

6.2. General economic situation in the ESCAP region

The 2008 theme study on Energy Security and Sustainable Development in Asia and the Pacific made a preliminary assessment of the energy sector funding needs to 2030 based on a business as usual scenario and a sustainable energy scenario. This study estimated that between 2006 and 2030, the ESCAP region will need approximately $375 billion annually (or over $9 trillion in total) to expand and modernize the region's energy systems based on a business as usual scenario[82]. Despite this, the needs of those without access to modern energy services will remain unmet. This investment cannot rely solely on ODA, which has generally contributed only $5.4 billion per year to energy projects in developing countries worldwide[83]. Therefore, private sector involvement and more innovative financing and policy options, as those presented in chapters 2 and 3, need to be considered in order to generate domestic financing and attract private sector finance.

The legislative and regulatory framework is one of the most important factors in attracting financing. Especially in the case of developing countries, investors review governance structures to assess whether the laws and contracts are likely to be enforced, whether the regulatory environment is participatory, transparent and accountable, and if their rights are well defined and likely to be respected. Some ESCAP economies have been particularly good at this and, to some degree, this can be reflected by the high level of FDI inflows. In 2008, the ESCAP region remained the largest recipient of FDI of all developing regions, reaching just under $480 billion. However, from figure 6.10 it can be seen that the top 10 countries receiving FDI in Asia accounted for almost 90% of this inflow. Key countries and areas receiving increased inflow of FDI in 2008 were China (third world largest recipient of FDI in 2008[84]), the Russian Federation, Hong Kong (China), India, Singapore and the fully industrialised economies of Japan and Australia.

Figure 6.10: FDI inflow for Asia and the Pacific in 2008 (million US$)

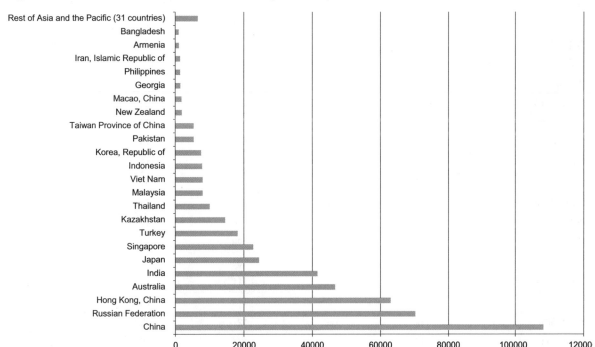

Source: ESCAP, based on UNCTAD data.

According to the World Investment Report 2009, Government policy responses in Asia to the economic crisis have lead to favourable economic conditions for economic recovery, growth and FDI inflows. Specific policy changes have included a removal of FDI ceilings in India, streamlining procedures for approval of FDI projects in China, a rise in foreign equity limits in financial services in Malaysia and an elimination of permits and sub-licenses in Viet Nam[85]. Nonetheless, not all countries have been welcoming with regard to FDI. One example is Kazakhstan which has recently approved a new law on natural resources that allows the Government to change existing contracts in the oil, metals and minerals industries if they have a negative effect on the country's economic interests. In 2008, the Government also announced that it will not negotiate any more production-sharing agreements and that it will impose stricter conditions on foreign investors[86].

Table 6.3 shows the inward FDI performance index, which measures the amount of FDI received compared with the size of its economy. In 2007, the top ranking country according to the index was Hong Kong (China), though Singapore and Georgia were close behind. However, the FDI index does not always reflect the likelihood of investment in various countries, as the most FDI in 2008 went to China and the Russian Federation, followed by Hong Kong (China).

Table 6.3: Inward FDI performance and potential index in the ESCAP region

Country	FDI performance index (ranking)			FDI potential index	
	2005	2006	2007	2005	2006
Hong Kong, China	3	2	1	72	73
Singapore	4	6	7	22	22
Georgia	16	15	9	67	64
Mongolia	17	19	16	117	119
Tajikistan	32	18	17	51	54
Kazakhstan	29	26	23	34	32
Armenia	37	29	39	94	102
Viet Nam	55	62	43	11	10
Kyrgyzstan	48	45	55	86	84
Thailand	49	54	64	103	100
Malaysia	68	67	71	59	61
New Zealand	83	56	76	24	24
Russian Federation	89	82	81	49	46
Pakistan	103	88	83	19	19
Turkey	107	86	84	116	110
China	64	75	88	41	40
Brunei Darussalam	2	64	89	75	71
Philippines	109	99	96	84	86
Myanmar	82	101	99	137	136
India	106	103	104	33	36
Taiwan, Prov. China	132	122	111	119	118
Sri Lanka	108	111	113	77	77
Bangladesh	117	120	121	23	20
Uzbekistan	116	117	124	2	2
Papua New Guinea	112	131	128	123	124
Korea, Republic of	115	126	130	16	17
Australia	130	115	131	97	93
Iran, Islamic Republic	133	133	133	61	63
Japan	135	137	135	69	72
Nepal	137	138	136	95	98
Azerbaijan	1	14	140	79	80

Source: UNCTAD.

Apart from the attitude towards foreign investors, there is a number of other issues to consider in order to boost the availability and the impact of financing mechanisms for EERE, both domestic and foreign. The resilience and reliability of an economy can be synthetically reflected by indicators such as the Global Competitiveness Index and the Corruption Perception Index. Table 6.4 shows the Global Competitiveness Index for 2008 to 2010 for Asian and Pacific countries.

Table 6.4: The Global Competitiveness Index 2009–2010 rankings and 2008–2009 comparisons for the ESCAP region

Country	GCI 2009 Rank	GCI 2008 Rank
United States	2	1
Singapore	3	5
Japan	8	9
Hong Kong, China	11	11
Taiwan, Prov. Of China	12	17
United Kingdom	13	12
Australia	15	18
France	16	16
Korea, Republic of	19	13
New Zealand	20	24
Malaysia	24	21
China	29	30
Brunei Darussalam	32	39
Thailand	36	34
India	49	50
Azerbaijan	51	69
Indonesia	54	55
Turkey	61	63
Russia Federation	63	51
Kazakhstan	67	66
Viet Nam	75	70
Sri Lanka	79	77
Philippines	87	71
Georgia	90	90
Armenia	97	97
Pakistan	101	101
Bangladesh	106	111
Cambodia	110	109
Mongolia	117	100
Tajikistan	122	116
Kyrgyzstan	123	122
Nepal	125	126
Timor-Leste	126	129

Source: ESCAP, based on World Economic Forum data.

Figure 6.11 also ranks countries based on their perceived corruption though it will not necessarily correlate directly with the amount of FDI attracted as can be seen from Kazakhstan, Mongolia and Tajikistan.

Figure 6.11: Corruption Perception Index 2008 in the ESCAP region

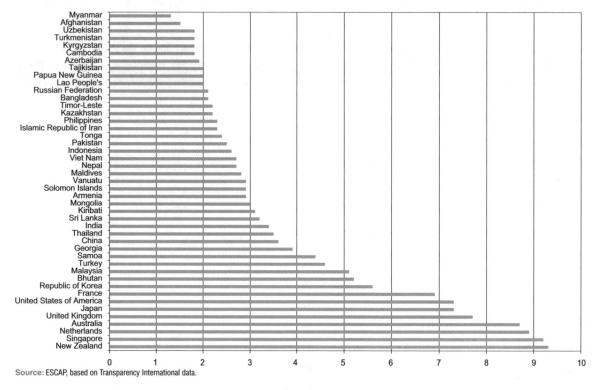

Source: ESCAP, based on Transparency International data.

In general, it can be said that ESCAP countries, despite the above-mentioned intra-regional disparities, are well placed to attract capital and design financing mechanisms for climate change mitigation. Some strong national policies to create the right economic incentives and a good environment for investment can provide a lesson for developing countries in any region of the world. Some examples of good practices are highlighted in box 6.2 at the end of this chapter.

6.3. Legislative and regulatory frameworks

As specified at the beginning of the last section, in order to take full advantage of the generally good economic situation and investment climate in the region and attract capital for sustainable energy investment, sound regulatory frameworks are needed. A large number of countries in Asia and the Pacific have recognized the importance and benefits of energy efficiency and have already implemented legislation or policies to encourage it, as listed in table 6.5 below.

Table 6.5: Energy efficiency legislation in the ESCAP region

Dedicated legislation for EE	Countries
Dedicated legislation and provisions from other legislation	Armenia, Azerbaijan, Australia, China, France, Japan, India, Kazakhstan, Kyrgyzstan, Netherlands, New Zealand, Philippines, Republic of Korea, Russian Federation, Singapore, Sri Lanka, Tajikistan, Thailand, Turkey, United Kingdom, United States, Uzbekistan
Policies and guidelines	Bangladesh, Bhutan, Brunei Darussalam, Fiji, Indonesia, Malaysia, Marshall Islands, Mongolia, Palau, Papua New Guinea, Samoa, Viet Nam
Dedicated legislation to be approved	Georgia, Kazakhstan, Russian Federation

Source: ESCAP.

Given the global nature of the fight against climate change, it is also important to analyse cooperation at the supranational level. As of 2009, most countries in Asia and the Pacific had ratified the *Kyoto* Protocol, including a number of Annex I countries. The status of ratification of countries in Asia and the Pacific are listed in table 6.6.

Table 6.6: Commitment to the UNFCCC and the Kyoto Protocol among ESCAP countries

Status under UNFCCC	Countries
Annex I with significant reduction obligations	Australia, France, Japan, Netherlands, New Zealand, United Kingdom, United States*
Annex I without significant reduction obligations	Russian Federation, Turkey**
Non-Annex I	Armenia, Azerbaijan, Brunei Darussalam, Cambodia, China, Fiji, Georgia, India, Indonesia, Iran, Kazakhstan, Kiribati, Republic of Korea, DPRK, Kyrgyzstan, Laos, Malaysia, Maldives, Marshal Islands, Micronesia, Mongolia, Myanmar, Nauru, Nepal, Pakistan, Palau, Papua New Guinea, Philippines, Samoa, Singapore, Solomon Islands, Sri Lanka, Tajikistan, Thailand, Timor-Leste, Tonga, Turkmenistan, Tuvalu, Uzbekistan, Vanuatu, Viet Nam
Not signed	Afghanistan

* The United States has not ratified the Kyoto Protocol, adopted by consensus at the COP-3 on 11 December 1997, de facto refusing to comply with the agreed reduction target.
** Turkey is included in UNFCCC Annex I but not in the Kyoto Protocol's Annex B, which sets compulsory reduction targets.
Source: ESCAP, based on UNFCCC website.

Box 6.1: ESCAP recommendations on general aspects of energy efficiency promotion

ESCAP came early to the promotion of energy efficiency in the Asia and Pacific region. As early as 1999, it issued a *Compendium of Energy Conservation Legislation in Countries of the Asia and Pacific Region* (New York, United Nations, 1999) where the following principles can be found:

(i) The enactment of a regulatory framework for promotion of energy conservation and energy efficiency can be useful for Asian countries, particularly for countries with rapidly growing domestic energy demand or energy import dependent economies;

(ii) Promotion of energy conservation and efficiency should form an integral part of national energy policy;

(iii) Basic energy conservation laws should codify energy conservation policies and create the principal legal foundation for government intervention aimed at lowering the energy intensity of economic activity;

(iv) Energy conservation legislation should ideally result from a participatory decision making process which adequately involves all stakeholders;

(v) The government should provide the framework legislation from which business opportunities arise. This collaboration between the Government and the business community should lead to energy efficiency and the creation of jobs necessary for development;

(vi) Fiscal and non-monetary incentives should be the preferred tools in achieving the desired conservation and efficiency. Regulatory mechanisms should be in the form of prescriptive or performance-based legislation that can be revised and upgraded; and

Energy conservation legislation should cover both supply of and demand for commercial and traditional forms of energy.

Given the high level of fuel and electricity subsidies in the region, ESCAP focused on the sensitive issue of energy pricing and concluded that:

(i) The feasibility of all energy efficiency promotion activities is largely predetermined by energy pricing and related policies. If possible, energy price subsidies should be reduced. Energy prices should be gradually adjusted to reflect the long-term marginal costs of energy supply;

(ii)   The comparative inelasticity of energy demand makes taxation of all forms of energy an effective tool of fiscal policy which should serve to support energy conservation or energy efficiency objectives;

(iii)   Energy pricing mechanisms should seek to internalize external costs including costs of emission reductions and preservation or rehabilitation of the environment.

The ESCAP region has moreover witnessed a number of measures, taken by groups of individual countries or by existing regional institutions. These have mostly taken the form of policy guidelines or non-binding recommendations and include the following initiatives.

The Asia Pacific Partnership on Clean Development and Climate was launched in 2005 with a Charter, a Communiqué and a Workplan aimed at eight key sectors. Members to the Partnership are Australia, Canada, China, India, Japan, the Republic of Korea and the United States. For each of the eight key areas, a task force was established involving both Government and private sector partners. The eight key sectors that the Partnership focuses on are the aluminium industry, buildings and appliances, the cement sector, cleaner fossil fuels, coal mining, power generation and transmission, renewable energy and distributed generation and the steel sector. Specific actions under a number of these sectors cover initiatives and objectives for improving energy efficiency.

Under the Association of South-East Asian Nations' (ASEAN) Plan of Action for Energy Cooperation 2004 – 2009, member countries of ASEAN have agreed to "strengthen cooperation in energy efficiency and conservation through institutional capacity building and increasing private sector involvement including enhancing public awareness as well as expanding markets for energy efficient products"87. Specific work areas include information sharing, standards and labelling for products, private sector involvement, capacity building, promotion of energy service companies and promotion of energy efficiency in the transport sector. ASEAN member states are Brunei Darussalam, Cambodia, Indonesia, the Lao People's Democratic Republic, Malaysia, Myanmar, Philippines, Singapore, Thailand and Viet Nam.

Within the Asia-Pacific Economic Cooperation (APEC) intergovernmental forum, the APEC Leaders Declaration on Climate Change, Energy Security and Clean Development adopted in 2007, energy efficiency was seen as a cost effective strategy towards achieving energy security. Under this Declaration APEC members agreed to:

a.   work towards achieving an APEC-wide regional aspirational goal of a reduction in energy intensity of at least 25% by 2030 (base year 2005);

b.   encourage all APEC economies to set individual goals and action plans for improving energy efficiency; and

c.   facilitate and review progress through the voluntary APEC Energy Peer Review Mechanism.

APEC Member States within the ESCAP region are: Australia, Brunei Darussalam, China, Hong Kong (China), Indonesia, Japan, Republic of Korea, Malaysia, New Zealand, Papua New Guinea, the Philippines, the Russian Federation, Singapore, Taiwan (Province of China), Thailand, the United States and Viet Nam.

The South Asian Association for Regional Cooperation (SAARC) was formed in 1985 by the Heads of State of Bangladesh, Bhutan, India, Maldives, Nepal, Pakistan and Sri Lanka. Under the SAARC energy cooperation programme, a Technical Committee on Energy was formed to review recommendations related to a number of energy issues relevant to South Asian countries including energy efficiency. A Road Map for implementation by Member States was developed in 2005 and included a number of measures aimed at promoting energy efficiency at the national and subregional level, including standards and labelling harmonization, institutional strengthening and capacity building, knowledge exchange and the promotion of public private partnerships.

In a new initiative, China, Japan and the Republic of Korea have issued a Joint Statement on Sustainable Development on 10 October 2009. In this Joint Statement the countries agreed to work towards developing a "green economy, make joint efforts to facilitate a virtuous cycle between the social and economic system and the natural and ecological system, promote balance between economic growth and social development, and contribute to the realization of sustainable development"88. One of the strategies to achieve this involved strengthening regional cooperation to promote energy efficiency, among other clean energy solutions.

Other international initiatives include the Energy Charter Protocol on Energy Efficiency and Related Environmental Aspects which was adopted in 1994 under the Energy Charter Treaty. Signatories to the Protocol in 2004 were: Armenia, Azerbaijan, Japan, Kazakhstan, Kyrgyzstan, Mongolia, Tajikistan, Turkey, Turkmenistan and Uzbekistan. In principle, the Protocol aims to reinforce energy efficiency policies and programmes based on market mechanisms and pricing that incorporates externalities, transparency, technology transfer, cost-effective policies and the promotion of investments.

Table 6.7: Membership of regional organisations in the ESCAP region

Organization	Members
Asia Pacific Partnership on Clean Development and Climate	Australia, Canada, China, India, Japan, Republic of Korea, United States
ASEAN	Brunei Darussalam, Cambodia, Indonesia, the Lao People's Democratic Republic, Malaysia, Myanmar, Philippines, Singapore, Thailand, Viet Nam
APEC	Australia, Brunei Darussalam, China, Hong Kong (China), Indonesia, Japan, Republic of Korea, Malaysia, New Zealand, Papua New Guinea, the Philippines, the Russian Federation, Singapore, Taiwan (Province of China), Thailand, the United States, Viet Nam
SAARC	Bangladesh, Bhutan, India, Maldives, Nepal, Pakistan, Sri Lanka
Energy Charter Treaty	Armenia, Azerbaijan, Japan, Kazakhstan, Kyrgyzstan, Mongolia, Tajikistan, Turkey, Turkmenistan, Uzbekistan

Source: ESCAP (2009).

6.4. Activities and accomplishments

In 2005, Ministers from across Asia and the Pacific opted to pursue a different development path at ESCAP's *5th Ministerial Conference on Environment and Development in Asia and the Pacific (MCED-5)*. They realized the urgent need to integrate environmental sustainability into development strategies and adopted the concept of an environmentally sustainable economic growth, or Green Growth, as the strategy for the region to attain sustainable development.

Efficient production and consumption of energy was just one component under this concept, which also supports activities in advocating a low carbon development path in the region.

More recent activities relating to energy efficiency have focused on infrastructure development and cities given the economic, social and environmental relevance of urban areas. The way cities are planned, developed and managed will have a major bearing on sustainable development of both regions, including the achievement of the MDGs. As highlighted in the recent United Nations Population Fund's (UNFPA) State of the World Population 2007 report, "although the current concentration of poverty, slum growth, social disruption and environmental degradation paints a threatening picture, urbanization can be positive and has a great potential to play a key role in sustainable development. Cities concentrate poverty, but they also represent the best hope of escaping it. Cities can create environmental problems, but they can also generate the solutions. The challenge is in learning how to exploit these possibilities."[89]

This was emphasized in a recent Policy Dialogue in Beijing on Energy *Efficiency for Low Carbon Development in Cities*, held back to back with the Asia Pacific Forum on Low Carbon Economy organized by ESCAP in partnership with the Energy Research Institute of China and the National Development and Reform Commission of China. These meetings emphasized the link between urbanization and environmental impacts, including climate change. Delegates from various cities across Asia discussed possible measures and policy options at the city level to promote energy efficiency broadly and within specific sectors such as transport, buildings and urban planning.

In addition to the Beijing meetings, ESCAP has partnered with ECLAC to implement the project *Eco-efficient and Sustainable Urban Infrastructure Development in Asia and Latin America*. Though this project focuses broadly on urban development including water, waste, transport and energy infrastructure, a small component specifically considers energy efficiency in the context of applying eco-efficiency as a key criterion for sustainable infrastructure development and as a basis for expanding infrastructure financing opportunities. The project contributes to this by equipping policy-makers and planners with a set of methodologies, indicators and tools to assess the eco-efficiency and social inclusiveness of urban infrastructure in an integrated manner and to develop strategies and policies to improve this. In doing so, the project builds the capacities of target groups through a learning by doing approach (by conducting city and sector level assessments, case studies, national roundtables), increases awareness and understanding of the issues through analysis and capacity building workshops (at national, regional and inter-regional levels), and facilitates the participation in clean energy and energy efficiency investment, and in carbon markets, by identifying opportunities.

Also supporting this project is the *Kitakyushu Initiative for a Clean Environment*, which was adopted in 2000 at the 4th Ministerial Conference on Environment and Development in Asia and the Pacific. This initiative focuses on building the capacity of local governments to enhance environmental management through the exchange of information, their participation in seminars and demonstration projects on successful policy measures. Under this initiative, a number of activities have focused on promoting energy efficiency, particularly in municipal buildings in Mongolia and Tajikistan. ESCAP also plans to continue its work on this issue and is preparing further activities, specifically in urban areas.

The Special Programme of Economies of Central Asia (SPECA) is jointly administered by ESCAP and ECE with the aim of building subregional collaboration among Central Asian countries on various issues, including energy. In 2006, the SPECA Coordinating Committee endorsed the *Baku Initiative on Energy Efficiency and Conservation*. The Baku Initiative focuses on promoting energy efficiency improvement through partnerships among the central governments, industries and commercial entities.

The Baku Initiative includes seven broad components:

(i)	strengthening legislative support;
(ii)	strengthening stakeholder involvement;
(iii)	setting effective minimum performance standards;
(iv)	strengthening institutional support;
(v)	providing research development and dissemination support;
(vi)	disseminating best practices; and
(vii)	enhancing public awareness.

Since then, various meetings have aimed to define the activities under the Baku Initiative and to raise funding for its implementation. One activity planned in 2010 will focus on establishing the baseline of the current situation in various countries, identifying specific activities needed in order to move countries towards developing energy efficiency policies, and building partnership through cooperation at the subregional level. This would include developing a subregional concept to guide national policy development and identify possible barriers and opportunities to subregional collaboration that supports national energy efficiency activities. For example, a long term goal on developing a set of subregional standards and labels for electrical appliances could be a mutually beneficial subregional activity. The national studies should also identify specific further potential projects and activities at the national level.

Another ongoing activity which includes Central Asia, but also South-East Asian and South Asian countries, is the project *Strengthening Institutional Capacity to Support Energy Efficiency in Selected Asian Countries*. The project aims to review existing institutional arrangements in promoting energy efficiency in the region to identify good practices and enhance the capacity of Governments in furthering their efforts to ensure effective implementation of energy efficiency. In undertaking this project and most other activities, ESCAP often works in partnership with various international, subregional and national partners such as the Association of Southeast Asian Nations (ASEAN), the Asia Pacific Centre for the Transfer of Technology (APCTT), the South Asian Association for Regional Cooperation (SAARC), the Asian Development Bank (ADB) and the Eurasian Economic Community (EurAsEC).

All of these will feed into the *Global Energy Efficiency 21 (GEE21) Project* which is planned for Asia and the Pacific. A proposal is currently under development and it will aim to replicate the successful ECE *Energy Efficiency 21 Programme*, which works with countries to support the formation of an energy efficiency market through building the capacity of local experts to develop projects, working with local authorities on government policy reforms and facilitating opportunities for project finance through externally managed public-private partnership investment funds.

The Asian Development Bank (ADB), Asia's sole multilateral development bank, has initiated a number of programmes to aid its developing member states in the Asia-Pacific region with a growing portfolio of technical and financial support designed to move the region from inefficient, carbon-intensive technologies to an energy-secure, low-carbon pathway that promotes growth and mitigates climate change (see annex III). ADB has recognized the effectiveness of energy efficiency as paramount in energy policy, such that improving energy efficiency by examining both demand- and supply-side alternatives has become a priority of the Bank. The *Energy Efficiency Initiative (EEI)* represents the Bank's flagship clean energy programme. Launched in July 2005, EEI seeks to catalyse investments in renewable energy and energy efficiency in Asian cities. The EEI program will invest at least $1 billion a year between 2008 and 2010 in clean energy projects. In 2008, the plan achieved investments of $1.7 billion[90]. In 2008, EEI was initially focused on projects in the People's Republic of China, India, Indonesia, Pakistan, Philippines and Vietnam and has been expanded in 2009 to include projects in Afghanistan, Bangladesh, Cambodia, Lao People's Democratic Republic, Mongolia and Uzbekistan.

Box 6.2: Country best practices in the ESCAP region

(i) China

China has initiated a number of programmes and policies to support energy efficiency in various sectors. In 2006, China published its 11th Five-Year Guidelines on the National Economy and Social development (2006-2010) setting the factors that will be the most influential in shaping China's social and economic trajectories during that period. In these Guidelines, the Government set an aggressive energy efficiency target for reducing energy consumption relative to economic growth by 20% between 2006 and 2010. By 2010, China seeks to improve energy efficiency by 20% and reduce emissions of greenhouse gases by 10%[91]. Following the establishment of the Five-Year Guidelines, the Energy Conservation Law, originally enacted in 1997, was amended in 2007 to highlight the importance of energy conservation as a national policy in addition to making achievements of energy efficiency goals a component of the performance evaluation of local cadres[92].

The China *End Use Energy Efficiency Program (EUEEP)* was initiated in 2005 as part of a 12-year government plan to dramatically improve the efficiency of China's buildings and industry, which tend to be major energy users. The program is designed to remove barriers to the widespread application and practice of energy conservation and efficiency to support the development and implementation of a comprehensive system of policies and regulations for energy conservation. These range from technological innovations to the creation and revision of design codes, the development of training materials and energy conservation guidelines for architects, engineers and industrial managers to improve the efficiency of industrial equipment, household and office appliances. UNDP and the GEF, in partnership with government agencies, research institutes, bilateral donor countries, non-governmental organizations and enterprises will also help introduce and test new technologies, methodologies and market-based mechanisms and tools. According to UNDP, the estimated carbon dioxide emissions avoided over the 12 year programme will be approximately 279 million tonnes.

(ii) Japan

To support the 2006 New National Energy Strategy, the Front *Runner Plan* has been established to specify measures for improving end-use energy efficiency by 2030. This plan looks at establishing medium and long term measures to reduce energy consumption in addition to the short-term energy conservation measures adopted. A number of tax and subsidy schemes are in place to promote energy efficiency across all sectors. In particular, taxation measures such as a green automobile tax and an acquisition tax for fuel-efficient and low emission vehicles are in place to deter the purchase of inefficient vehicles. For industries and commerce, Japan has implemented a tax system which would provide a credit or special depreciation for organizations introducing efficient equipment.

(iii) Republic of Korea

The Republic of Korea is pushing to transform their society into one that promotes Green Growth. Some activities being undertaken include encouraging industry to conserve energy, subsidizing the installation of high-efficiency equipment and appliances, along with raising the design criteria for energy saving in buildings. In 2004, the Government established the *General Energy Conservation and Efficiency Improvement Plan* to improve the national energy intensity through various energy efficiency initiatives. In 2006, long term goals were also established for the transport and building sectors. Some of the most recent strategies to promote a low carbon economy include:

a. Providing financial support for companies to invest in energy efficiency and undertake energy audits;
b. Promoting compact and hybrid vehicles and raising fuel efficiency standards;
c. Implementing an energy efficiency standards and labelling programme for buildings and appliances; and
d. Supporting additional initiatives undertaken by state or local governments.

As the Republic of Korea is fully dependent on oil imports to run its fast-paced economy, the Government has instigated a fuel tax which has been ranked as the 3rd most expensive in Asia[93]. From the 1990s the Government of the Republic of Korea has been consistently pursuing a high-handed policy to maintain high fuel surcharge for non-commercial vehicle users in order to deter the waste of valuable energy. As part of its own energy security, the Government has kept pace with raising fuel taxes in accordance with increasing international oil prices. In terms of the road fuel tax (commonly called transportation tax) to internalize the costs of the environmental impact of transport, the Government has introduced a series of energy tax reforms to increase diesel and LPG prices in line with OECD standards for environmental and economic reasons. In addition, environmental improvement charges had already been levied since 1992 for diesel-engine vehicles with differential rate increases depending on the age and size of the vehicles[94].

(iv) Thailand

Thailand's *Programme on Electrical Energy Efficiency* was initiated in 1993 with the objective of building the institutional capacity of the electric power sector to deliver cost-effective energy services to the country and to pursue policies and actions that would lead to a more energy efficiency society. A number of activities were initiated under the Programme, including a labelling scheme and the piloting of energy service companies, energy efficient building practices, testing and labelling of appliances and audits for various sectors. Key to the implementation of this Programme was the Energy Conservation Promotion Act. An energy conservation fund was established under the Energy Conservation Promotion Act to support energy efficiency efforts. This fund was based on revenues from petroleum products and provided an average annual income of 2 billion baht. Agencies eligible to apply for funding of energy efficiency activities include Government agencies, state enterprises, educational institutions and non-profit organizations. Initially it was used as a source of revenue for programmes and to fund subsidies, though more recently it has been utilized for tax incentives to end users[95].

(v) Philippines

The Philippine *Efficient Lighting Market Transformation Project* was initiated in 2004 and aimed to address the barriers on the widespread utilization of energy efficient lighting systems in the Philippines, and to reduce GHG emissions. The project consists of various preparatory activities which will culminate in the design of a multi-component programme that addresses the removal of the remaining technical, financial and market barriers to the accelerated introduction or large-scale promotion and commercialization of energy-efficient fluorescent lighting systems in the Philippines. Many of the electric distribution utilities are already committed to sponsor lighting-focused DSM programmes, but are not prepared to field them. The project thus focuses heavily on overcoming such technical and market capability barriers.

The Philippine *National Energy Efficiency and Conservation Program*[96] was declared a national policy to promote the judicious conservation and efficient utilization of energy resources through the adoption of cost-effective options for the efficient use of energy to minimize environmental impacts. The aim of the

Programme is to achieve a savings of 229 million barrels of oil equivalent between 2005 and 2014. It is projected that about 50.9 million tonnes of CO_2 equivalent greenhouse gas emissions will also be avoided during this period. As part of this Programme, 4.45 million compact fluorescent light bulbs (CFLs) will be distributed within Manila, Calabarzon and Bulacan. The replacement to CFLs aims to provide direct economic benefits to the country by reducing energy demand and displacing imported fuel. The expected benefits of this initiative are likely to be a reduced peak demand by 450 megawatts, reduced oil imports by $120 million each year, clean development mechanism revenues of about $10 million for 2010-2012 and an energy efficient market. In addition to the CFL replacement initiative, the Programme includes a number of other initiatives such as retrofitting of government buildings and public lighting, expanding energy efficiency labels and standards, establishing a lamp waste facility and energy service companies, collaborating with the private sector, initiating green building projects, and communication on energy efficiency and social mobilization.

7. The ECLAC region

7.1. Energy overview of the ECLAC region

As a result of the policies pursued by the different countries of the region and the local availability of natural resources, primary energy production in Latin America and the Caribbean[97] has been mainly based on petroleum. Its share as an energy source has, however, fallen steadily since the 1970s and it accounted for 43% of total energy production in 2006 (down from 62% in 1970). On the other hand, in the early 1970s, natural gas accounted for 11% of primary energy production and its share has steadily increased since than, accounting for a quarter of total primary energy supply (TPES) in 2006. It is possible, then, that its share of total production will increase in the near future owing to greater availability and the stronger push by the countries of the Southern Common Market (MERCOSUR) to integrate their gas markets. Hydroelectric power peaked at 11.5% of the total in 2000. Since then, its share of total production has declined to stabilize at about 9%. This decline is due to reforms and the pattern of investments in the electricity industry, which has emphasized building fossil-fuel power plants (thermal, for example). Finally, geothermal and nuclear energy production is still minimal in the region (0.2% and 1% of total energy production, respectively)[98].

Table 7.1: Primary energy production by source in the ECLAC region, 1970-2006

Source	1970	1980	1990	2000	2005	2006
Petroleum	61.48%	56.94%	49.99%	47.39%	42.28%	43.31%
Natural gas	10.53%	15.24%	18.89%	21.95%	26.81%	25.44%
Coal	2.55%	2.95%	3.78%	4.51%	5.59%	5.40%
Hydroelectric power	3.76%	6.23%	9.14%	11.51%	8.51%	8.72%
Nuclear	0.00%	0.19%	0.58%	0.65%	0.70%	0.85%
Geothermal	0.00%	0.12%	0.32%	0.40%	0.26%	0.28%
Biomass (of which Firewood)	21.22% 17.43%	17.81% 13.47%	16.54% 10.79%	12.92% 8.16%	14.64% 8.92%	14.96% 8.80%
Millions of barrels of oil equivalent	2,285	3,103	3,783	4,599	5,138	5,226

Source: ECLAC, based on OLADE data.

Figure 7.1: Primary energy production by source in the ECLAC region

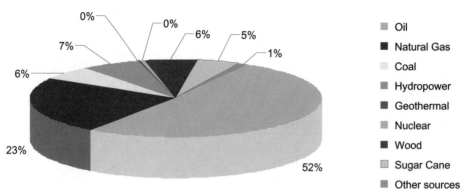

Source: ECLAC, based on OLADE data.

Per capita energy consumption in Latin America and the Caribbean reached 6.2 barrels of oil equivalent (BOE) in 2006, compared with the world average of 9.9 BOE per capita. Nevertheless, although still below world average, average consumption has risen steadily in the last 25 years, bucking the global trend. The region today consumes 12% more energy per capita than it did a quarter of a century ago. At the sectoral level, final energy consumption changed significantly in the 1970s, owing to the stronger economic growth seen in that decade. In the 1980s and 1990s, the breakdown did not change greatly, with the exception of the rapid growth of the transport sector's share of total consumption[99].

Table 7.2: Energy consumption by sector in the ECLAC region, 1970-2006

Sector	1970	1980	1990	2000	2006
Transport	26.8%	32.3%	32.4%	35.8%	35.5%
Industry	32.7%	34.9%	36.5%	34.7%	33.3%
Residential + tertiary	34.1%	26.7%	25.9%	25.1%	25.8%
Other	6.3%	6.2%	5.2%	4.4%	5.4%
Final consumption (million boe)	1,240	1,943	2,311	2,929	3,507

Source: ECLAC, based on OLADE data.

Figure 7.2: Energy consumption by sector in the ECLAC region, 1970-2006

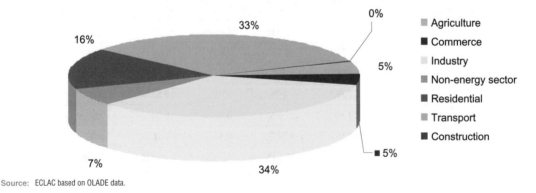

Source: ECLAC based on OLADE data.

Table 7.3: Energy consumption by source in the ECLAC region, 1970-2006

Energy Source	1970	1980	1990	2000	2006
Natural gas	6.90%	10.57%	11.96%	11.77%	13.93%
Coal	1.17%	0.82%	1.05%	1.40%	1.61%
Firewood	29.32%	16.88%	13.03%	9.43%	9.16%
Other primary sources	0.79%	0.69%	0.98%	1.18%	1.24%
Total from primary sources	38.18%	28.97%	27.02%	23.78%	25.94%
Electricity	6.19%	9.38%	12.71%	15.80%	15.92%
Liquefied petroleum gas	3.17%	3.91%	5.52%	6.69%	5.73%
Gasoline	17.81%	18.90%	19.70%	19.69%	18.19%
Fuel oil	12.47%	11.57%	7.07%	4.76%	3.06%
Other	22.17%	27.27%	27.98%	29.29%	31.17%
Total from secondary sources	61.82%	71.03%	72.98%	76.22%	74.06%
Total (Million boe)	1,210	1,966	2,382	3,043	3,676

Source: ECLAC, based on OLADE data.

Energy intensity in Latin America and the Caribbean remained stagnant from 1980 to 2005, in contrast with the progress made in other regions (see figures 7.3 and 7.4). This is at odds with the ideal trend of industrial development, which implies a gradual decline in energy intensity and carbon intensity over time.

Figure 7.3: Energy intensity by region, 1971-2005

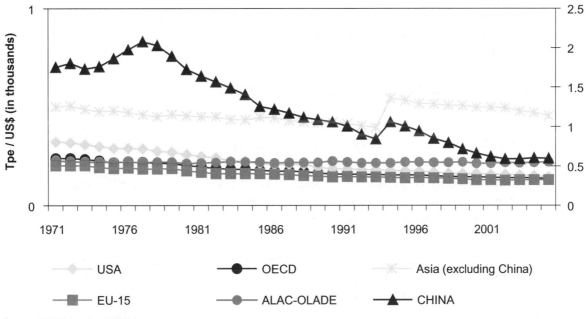

Source: ECLAC, based on OLADE data.

Figure 7.4: **Change in energy intensity by region, 1971-2005**

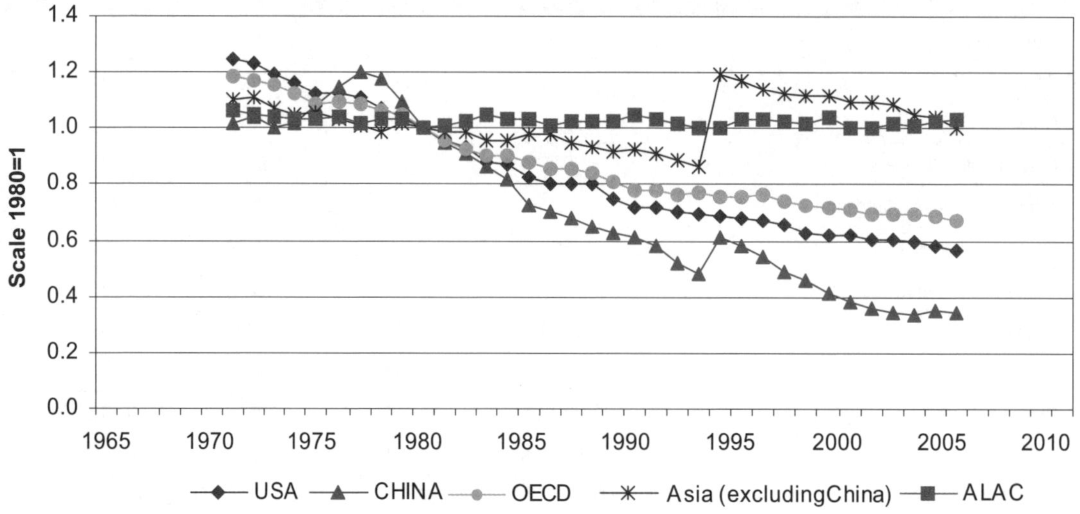

Source: ECLAC, based on OLADE data.

The failure to reduce energy intensity in the region stems from the following factors:

(i) The *economic structure* of the region and the fact that the primary sector (in particular, energy-intensive natural resource development) still accounts for a share of GDP that is well above the world average. The countries of the Organisation for Economic Co-operation and Development (OECD) have the opposite economic structure, with the services sector accounting for the　largest share of GDP, and the primary sector for a lower share of GDP than in the countries of Latin America and the Caribbean.

(ii) The region's sluggish economic growth from 1980 to 2005 has been comparable to the (also modest) increase in the energy supply (an average of 3% and 2%, respectively). Energy intensity has then remained static rather then declining as it often happens when sustained growth leads to changes in the economic structure.

(iii) The *low priority* accorded by the countries of the region until now to energy-efficiency policies. Rising per capita electricity and transport consumption, in keeping with also-rising income levels in developing countries.

As for the trends in carbon intensity in the region, they are also the result of the above-mentioned conditions, as well as of the primary energy supply mix. When comparing Latin America and the Caribbean with the most developed countries, it can be noted that improvements have been meagre on a relative basis. With respect to the levels of emissions per unit of energy consumed, the gap between OECD countries and the ECLAC region has in fact been widening. Whereas in 1971 the OECD countries outstripped the region by a factor of two to one, the spread had narrowed to four to one by 2005. Similar dynamics can be observed in the comparative levels of CO_2 emissions per capita, as outlined in table 7.4[100].

Table 7.4: **Indicators of emissions in OECD and Latin America**

OECD/ Latin America (%)	1971	1980	1990	1991	2000	2001	2004	2005
CO2/TPES	52.71%	39.79%	38.33%	36.12%	24.12%	23.62%	24.86%	24.20%
CO2 per capita	548.5%	488.8%	525.3%	520.6%	436.9%	436.8%	437.8%	427.3%

Source: ECLAC, based on OLADE data.

According to International Energy Agency (IEA) statistics, the situation in the world in 2006 in terms of energy intensity and carbon intensity in various countries was as shown in figure 7.5.

Figure 7.5: Energy Intensity and carbon intensity in the ECLAC region (toe/US$2000; kg/US$2000)

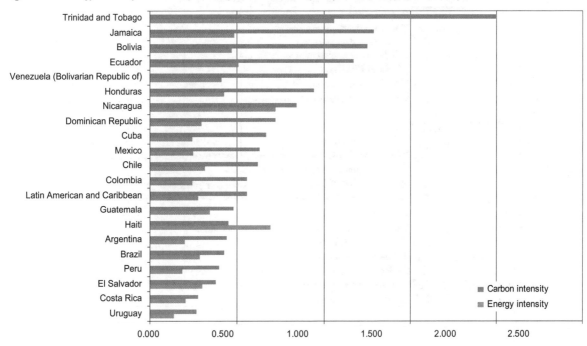

Source: ECLAC, based on OLADE data.

7.2. General economic conditions of the ECLAC region

In 2005, Latin America and the Caribbean had 556.4 million inhabitants, or 8.6% of the global population. According to ECLAC figures, per capita GDP in the region in 2006 was US$ 3,856 (in constant 2000 dollars). Figure 7.6 below shows real GDP growth for the countries of the region in 2007, 2008 and 2009[101].

Figure 7.6: Change in real GDP in the ECLAC region in 2007, 2008 and 2009

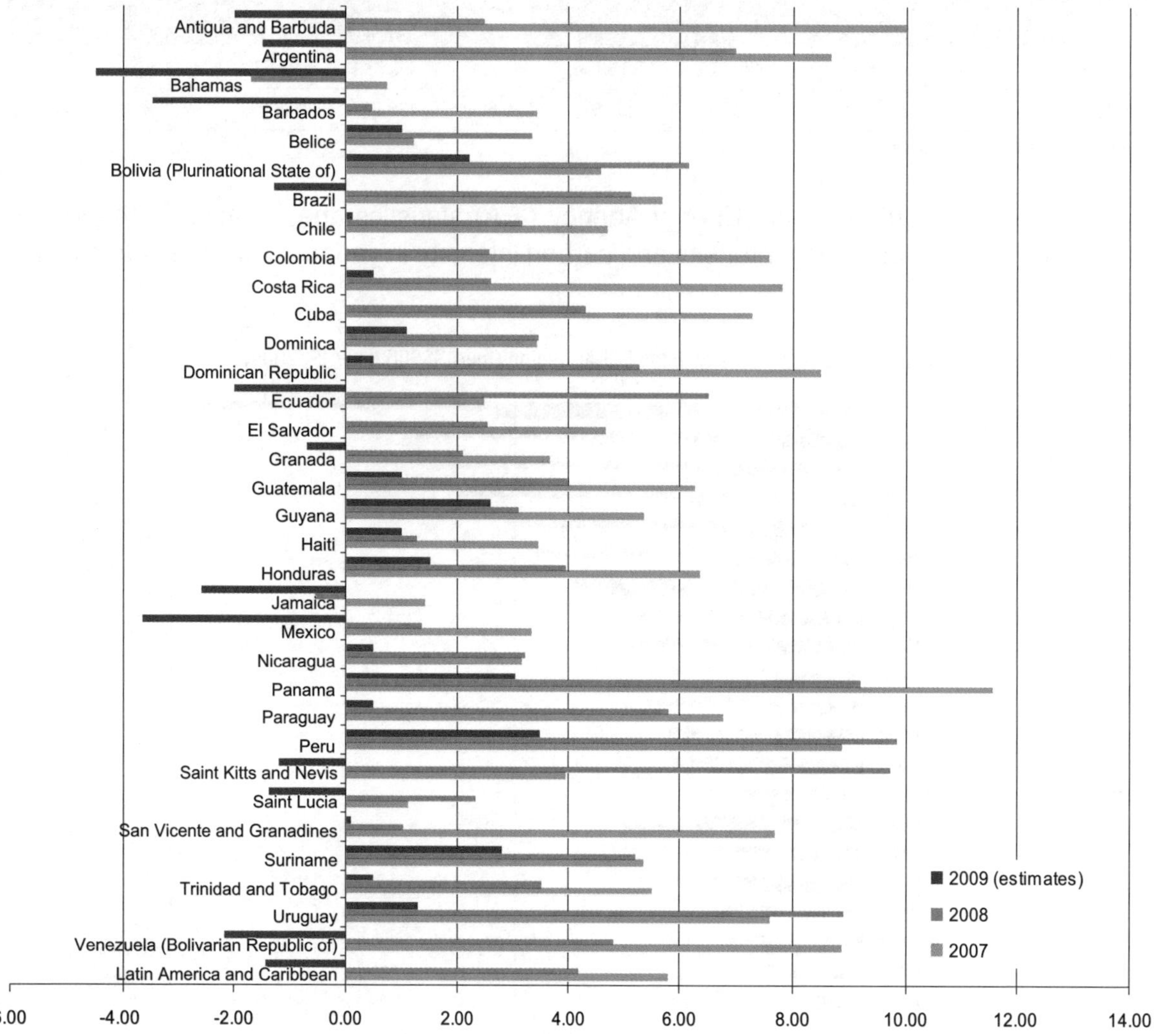

Source: ECLAC.

As shown in figure 7.7, Brazil received about one-third of all foreign direct investment in the region in 2008; other large recipients are Chile, Colombia and Mexico.

Figure 7.7: FDI inflows in the ECLAC region

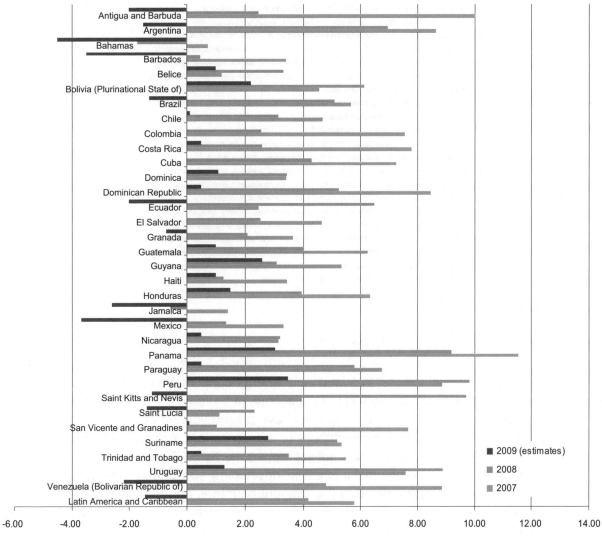

Source: ECLAC, based on UNCTAD data.

As shown by the Index of Economic Freedom, the level of freedom and competitiveness of the economic environment varies significantly in the region. In 2009, Chile was by far the best performer, while Cuba and Venezuela where the only countries to score below 50.

Figure 7.8: Index of Economic Freedom in the ECLAC region

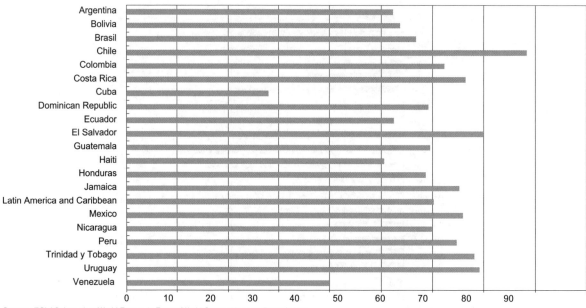

Source: ECLAC, based on World Economic Forum (World Competitiveness Report) data.

7.3. Legislative and regulatory frameworks

Strong international interest in sustainable energy consumption patterns has prompted numerous countries of the region to take actions to promote a more efficient use of their energy resources. The different countries have placed varying degrees of emphasis on this issue and allocated varying amount of resources to it and only one country in the region (Saint Kitts and Nevis) has not yet signed the Kyoto Protocol (see table 7.7). This underscores the Governments' interest in developing sustainable energy. The energy efficiency policies implemented in the different countries and the availability of national EE funds are listed in tables 7.5 and 7.6 below. A more detailed overview of national legislation is provided in Annex IV.

Table 7.5: National legislation for energy efficiency in the ECLAC region

Dedicated energy efficiency legislation	Countries
Dedicated legislation (primary and secondary)	Brazil, Colombia, Costa Rica, Mexico, Peru, Uruguay
Dedicated regulation but partial implementation or lack of secondary legislation	Argentina, Dominican Republic, Ecuador, Nicaragua
Regulatory provisions from other frameworks but no dedicated legislation	Barbados, Bolivia (Plur. State of), Cuba, El Salvador, Grenada, Guyana, Haiti, Honduras, Jamaica, Panama, Paraguay, Suriname, Trinidad and Tobago, Venezuela (Bol. Rep. of)
Regulations currently being developed	Chile, Guatemala

Source: ECLAC, 2009.

Table 7.6: Availability of national funds to promote energy efficiency in the ECLAC region

National energy efficiency funding	Countries
Yes	Brazil, Chile, Cuba, Mexico
Some funding available has been made available or only limited promotion efforts have been carried out	Argentina, Barbados, Bolivia (Plur. State of), Colombia, Costa Rica, Dominican Republic, Ecuador, El Salvador, Guatemala, Guyana, Honduras, Jamaica, Nicaragua, Panama, Peru, Suriname, Uruguay, Venezuela (Bol. Rep. of)
No	Grenada, Haiti, Paraguay, Trinidad and Tobago

Source: ECLAC, 2009.

Table 7.7: Kyoto Protocol status in Latin American and the Caribbean

Kyoto Protocol	Countries
Ratified	Antigua and Barbuda, Argentina, Bahamas, Barbados, Belize, Bolivia (Plur. State of), Brazil, Chile, Colombia, Costa Rica, Cuba, Dominica, Dominican Republic, Ecuador, El Salvador, Grenada, Guatemala, Guyana, Haiti, Honduras, Jamaica, Mexico, Nicaragua, Panama, Paraguay, Peru, Saint Lucia, Saint Vincent and the Grenadines, Suriname, Trinidad and Tobago, Uruguay, Venezuela (Bol. Rep. of)
Not ratified	Saint Kitts and Nevis

Source: UNFCCC 2009.

Although the degree of emphasis on this goal varies from one country to another, since adopting objectives to encourage sustainable energy consumption, Governments in Latin America and the Caribbean have tended to harmonize their regulations relating to the development of projects, programmes and activities for the promotion of rational and efficient energy use. Currently, three international organizations address energy issues in the ECLAC region. One of them, the Latin American Energy Organization (OLADE), which focuses specifically on this field, was founded immediately after the 1973 oil shock. The other two, the Bolivarian Alternative for the Americas (ALBA) and the Union of South American Nations (UNASUR), were created more recently and focus on energy as part of a broader agenda of economic, social and political cooperation.

OLADE was designed to undertake common efforts to achieve integration and development in the region's energy market. It provides information used for statistics and national legislation, promotes agreements among its member countries and carries out actions to ensure that their energy needs are met through various sustainable energy sources. In energy efficiency, OLADE promotes periodic ministerial meetings and aims to strengthen the impact of jointly implemented measures through coordination, capacity-building and technical assistance.

Table 7.8: Membership of OLADE

OLADE	Countries
Member countries	Argentina, Barbados, Bolivia (Plur. State of), Brazil, Chile, Colombia, Costa Rica, Cuba, Dominican Republic, Ecuador, El Salvador, Grenada, Guatemala, Guyana, Haiti, Honduras, Jamaica, Mexico, Nicaragua, Panama, Paraguay, Peru, Suriname, Uruguay, Trinidad and Tobago, Venezuela (Bol. Rep. of)
Observer	Algeria

Source: OLADE website.

ALBA was created in December 2004 as an agreement between the Bolivarian Republic of Venezuela and Cuba. It subsequently expanded to several other countries in the region. It is an organization for international cooperation based on the idea of social, political and economic integration among the countries of Latin America and the Caribbean. Its scope includes nearly all facets of inter-government cooperation, including democracy, human rights, finance, defence and tourism. Given that the organization was created only a few years ago, its agenda has only just begun to take hold at an institutional level and it is difficult to predict its future path. In view of the preponderant role played by the oil-rich Bolivarian Republic of Venezuela, any developments within ALBA in the field of energy should be closely monitored.

Table 7.9: Membership of ALBA

ALBA	Countries
Member countries	Bolivia (Plur. State of), Cuba, Dominica, Ecuador, Honduras, Nicaragua and Venezuela (Bol. Rep. of)

Source: ALBA website.

For its part, UNASUR is an intergovernmental union established in May 2008 to integrate two customs unions (MERCOSUR and the Andean Community of Nations) as part of the ongoing process of South American integration. Clearly patterned on the European Union model, UNASUR may be expected to follow in the footsteps of its European counterpart in the field of energy. The various ambitious projects carried out under its aegis include those relating to trade liberalization, the free movement of people, defence, infrastructure and cooperation on energy. Of particular interest is the South American "energy ring", a pipeline that will provide Argentina, Brazil, Chile, Paraguay and Uruguay with natural gas from several sources, such as the Camisea gas project in Peru and the Tarija gas deposits in Bolivia. This will constitute a reasonably clean source of energy in the region. The project will also allow for the development of the natural resources of some of the poorest ECLAC members.

Table 7.10: Membership of UNASUR

UNASUR	Countries
Parties	Argentina, Bolivia (Plur. State of), Brazil, Chile, Colombia, Ecuador, Guyana, Paraguay, Peru, Suriname, Uruguay and Venezuela (Bol. Rep. of)

Source: UNASUR website.

7.4. Activities and accomplishments

In the last few years, ECLAC has undertaken a series of activities to boost the capacity of its member States to manage and ensure the sustainable use of their natural resources in general and to make efficient use of energy in particular.

The following are the most notable technical assistance and cooperation activities carried out in the area of energy efficiency:

(i)   The project *Energy Efficiency in Latin America and the Caribbean* (1999-2001), jointly financed by the EC's Directorate-General for Energy and Transport. Outcomes include the preparation of the text and technical support for the discussion of the draft Law on Energy Efficiency of the Bolivarian Republic of Venezuela, Colombia and Peru;

(ii)   The *Europe-Latin America Dialogues on the Promotion of Energy Efficiency* (2000-2002). Three dialogues were held between members of the European Parliament and members of national parliaments of the countries of the region;

(iii)   The *Regional Inter-Governmental Meeting on Energy Efficiency* (2009). This was the first regional initiative on the topic organized by ECLAC with the cooperation of the German Government. High-level representatives from 15 countries in the region participated; and

Sectoral documents published by ECLAC. Between 1998 and 2009, numerous documents on energy efficiency policies were published[102].

ECLAC has an ambitious programme for cooperation in energy efficiency planned for 2010-2011 that is supported by cooperation from the Governments of Germany and Italy. One priority is the creation of a regional energy efficiency fund for Latin America and the Caribbean that will help establish an intra-regional and international dialogue on the best practices to be applied in the region.

This action couples the significant initiatives undertaken at the national level by ECLAC member countries and the adoption of ambitious policy targets encouraging sustainable energy consumption. The most significant of these programmes are presented in box 7.1 below, where also an assessment of their results is attempted.

Box 7.1: Achievements of selected national programmes in the ECLAC region

(i) Brazil

The results in terms of investments and savings of the three major energy efficiency programmes are presented in the tables below.

National Electricity Conservation Programme (PROCEL) of Electrobras:

Expenditures (R$ millions)	1986 – 2003	2004	2005	2006
From Electrobrase budget	252.01	27.18	37.17	29.24
From Global Reversion Reserve	412.00	54.00	44.60	77.80
Energy Efficiency Programme (with GEF)	2.09	12.97	16.23	6.20
Total Investment	666.08	94.15	98.02	113.24
Benefits				
Saved energy (billion kWh/year)	17.22	2.37	2.16	2.84
Saved capacity (MW)	4.633	622	585	772
Equivalent postponed power generation (MW)	4.033	569	518	682
Postoponed investment (R$ billions)	10.65	2.50	1.77	2.23
Estimate cost saving per unit (R$/kWh)	38.7	39.7	45.4	39.8

Source: Electricity Conservation Programme (PROCEL), Brazil, 2008.

Energy Efficiency Programme of the National Electricity Regulatory Agency (ANEEL):

Sector or type of project	Investment (R$ million)	Saved energy (GWh/year)	Saved capacity (MW)
Residential	304.9	511.5	183.5
Government	55.1	178.7	25.9
Industrial	26.4	38.9	7.7
Public services	22.4	27.1	6.1
Services	58.1	64.8	16.5
Rural	4.6	1.3	1.3
Solar heating	6.4	7.6	3.6
Total	477.9	830.0	244.7

Source: Brazilian Electricity Regulatory Agency (ANEEL).

National Programme for the Rational Use of Oil Derivatives (CONPET) of Petrobras (indicators of activity):

Indicator	2007	2008
Monitored vehicles (thousands)	130	138
Diesel oil saved (million litres)	320	381
CO2 emissions avoided (thousands of tons)	436	499

Source: National Programme for the Rational Use of Oil Derivatives (CONPET).

(ii) Costa Rica

The project *Efficient Lighting Programmes: Three-for-Two Promotion for Compact Fluorescent Lightbulbs* was carried out in February 2008 targeting the residential sector which is the single largest electricity consumer in the country (40.2% of total consumption according to 2007 data). Through an alliance with importers and distributors, people were offered three compact fluorescent lamps (CFLs) for the price of two. The goal was to reduce consumption in the national electrical system by 30 MW and save an investment of around US$ 30 million in fuel during the lifetime of the CFL. The results up to February 2009 are as follows:

a. CFLs sold: 1,475,224 units

b. Energy savings: 11,902 MWh

c. CO2 not emitted: 1,547 tons

The project *Training in the Inter-Institutional and Communal Network for Social Projects (RICEPS) in the Ipis Region* was concluded in December 2008. The following results had been obtained:

Participation	
Total number of participants in Network	207
Number of participants in Ipis	159
Total participants in the education sector	174
Total participants in the trade sector	18
Total	558
Average savings achieved through the programme	9.47%

(iii) Honduras

Project to implement compact fluorescent lamps in the residential sector delivered six million compact fluorescent lamps (CFLs) to residences, resulting in the quick switch to their use in the homes served by the National Electric Power Company. Out of these CFLs, 4 million were purchased or acquired through cooperation with Cuba and other 2 million were procured from a private company in Honduras. Students at public schools were the programme's pioneers, providing their time and skills free of charge. Figures on the results are presented below:

Lamps replaced	6,000,000
Energy saved	480 MWh/day - 175.20 GWh/year
Power savings	119 MW during peak night-time power usage
Amount	US$ 8,700.00
Emissions avoided	113,880 tCO2e

Source: National Electric Power Company (ENEE).

(iv) Mexico

Programmes of the National Commission for Energy Efficiency (CONUEE) accomplished the following results:

Programme	Thousands of barrels of oil equivalent		Equivalent (MXN millions)	Emissions avoided ('000 tons of CO2
	2001-2006	2007	2007	2007
Standardization	66,039	16,314	9,870	6,591
Federal government building	544	136	82	55
Public-sector industry	23,654	3,131	1,894	1,265
Private-sector industry	3,200	1,007	609	407
Transport	747	298	180	120
Total	98,184	20,886	12,635	8,437

Source: National Commission for Energy Efficiency (CONUEE).

(v) Uruguay

Electricity savings programmes have been implemented in the public sector since 2005[103].

"A Todas Luces" (Full Beam) Programme delivered fluorescent lamps acquired by the electrical utilities and transmissions body UTE. It was started under the coordination of the National Energy and Nuclear Technology Directoratee. To date, 1,589,830 light bulbs have been delivered. This represents a saving of 75% of the energy consumed by each bulb replaced. This is the first landmark achievement in the equipment labelling programme. A high percentage of residential lighting now uses CFLs rated class A by the Uruguayan Technical Standards Institute. The savings generated by the initiative are over 12 thousand tons of oil equivalent, and 2,716 tons of CO_2 emissions have been avoided.

(vi) Grenada

In 2007, Grenada, within the framework of the activities carried out by Cuba in the member countries of PETROCARIBE, replaced 133,253 incandescent light bulbs with energy-saving ones.

The results of the programme were as follows:

1. 133,253 incandescent light bulbs replaced;

2. 38.3-watt power saving per replaced light bulb;

3. 23,205 homes visited;

4. Reduction in energy consumption of 33kWH per month per household;

5. Reduction in peak demand of 1,891 kW (energy savings of 10,152 MWh/year);

6. The estimated savings are US$ 2,269,669 in generation capacity plus US$ 1,182,691 per year in reduced fuel imports (equivalent to 23,440 tonnes); and

7. 6,690 tons of CO_2 emissions avoided, worth US$ 28,100.

(vii) Dominican Republic

Under the programme to replace incandescent light bulbs with CFLs in cooperation with Cuba, 13 million CFLs were acquired. The energy savings have not been measured, but the National Energy Commission estimates that 20MW were saved for every million 100W-bulbs replaced by 18W-CFLs. If the 13 million bulbs were effectively used to replace incandescent ones, the drop in demand (during peak usage times) would be approximately 200 MW. US$ 25 million was invested in the programme, equivalent to US$ 125 for each kilowatt reduction in power.

8. The ECA region

8.1. Energy overview of the eca region

The ECA Region is comprised of the following 53 countries of different sizes, demographic characteristics, socio-economic development levels[104]. Patterns of energy production and consumption are very diverse on the African continent. Africa is known to be lagging behind other major world's regions in terms of level of industrialization, modern energy consumption, electrification rates and hence to contribute marginally to global trade and wealth creation, Africa has the lowest electrification rate in the world and it is anticipated that half of the population living in Sub-Saharan Africa (SSA) will still be without access to electricity by 2030 if strong policy measures are not taken to reverse the current situation[105], as illustrated in figure 8.1 below.

Figure 8.1: Electrification rates in world's region in 2005

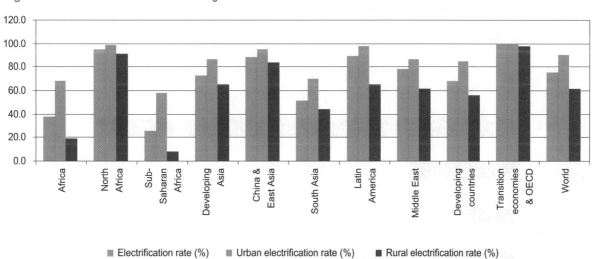

■ Electrification rate (%) ■ Urban electrification rate (%) ■ Rural electrification rate (%)

Source: ECA based on IEA data.

Yet, the region is endowed with fairly significant energy and other natural resources, accounting for 10.6% of world's proven oil reserves, 8.0% of world's proven natural gas reserves, 3.9% of world's recoverable proved reserves, 22.75% of world's recoverable reserves of uranium at up to US$130/kgU (16.7% recoverable at up to US$80/kgU), 10.8% of world's net hydropower generation, 7000 MW of geothermal energy potential and a high potential for wind power, biofuels production and solar power generation[106]. However, these resources are unevenly distributed among countries of the region and are often found far from the main energy demand centres. Oil and gas reserves are found in North and West Africa (Algeria, Libya, Egypt, Nigeria and Angola), coal reserves are located in Southern Africa with South Africa accounting for 95% of the total, with the bulk of hydropower potential is found in Central Africa (DR Congo) and East Africa (Ethiopia)[107].

In spite of the low level of development of its energy resources, the ECA region is a net energy exporter, as it produces more energy than it consumes, particularly in the case of oil and natural gas. Africa accounted for more than 12.5% of the world's total oil production in 2008 with 10.3 million barrels per day (mb/d), but its consumption was only 3.4% of the world's total with 2.9 mb/d. On the other hand, Africa accounted for 7.0% of world's natural gas production with 214.8 billion cubic meters (bcm), but its consumption was only 3.1% of the world's total with 94.9bcm[108]. More specifically for conventional oil production in SSA, a survey conducted by the IEA in the ten largest hydrocarbon-producing countries revealed that they produced 5.6 mb/d in 2007, about 91% was exported (501mb/d)[109]. Most of these exports were crude oil as the sub-region is suffering from inadequate refinery capacities.

Given the difficulty of dealing with the 53 member countries of the ECA Region, it is useful for analytical reasons to divide the African continent into two main sub-regions: North Africa comprised of countries bordering the Mediterranean Sea (Algeria, Egypt, Libya, Morocco and Tunisia) and SSA comprised of the 48 countries south of the Sahara Desert. Within the latter group, it is sometimes useful to treat the Republic of South Africa (RSA), in light of its particular history and economic conditions, as a separate entity.

Figure 8.2 below gives an indication of the per capita electricity consumption for 2006 with the 47 SSA countries, excluding RSA, averaging less than 150 kWh/cap and representing just over 5% of the world average. The most industrialized North African countries and RSA registered a higher per capita electricity consumption representing 46% and 180% of the world's average respectively[110].

Figure 8.2: Per capita electricity consumption in the ECLAC region, 2007 (kWh/pop)

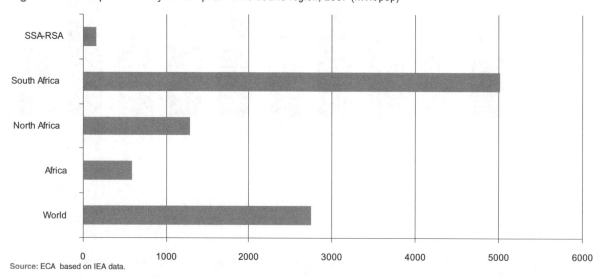

Source: ECA based on IEA data.

Likewise, figures 8.3 to 8.6 break down the total primary energy supply per energy source for different groups of countries. This demonstrates the importance of biomass fuels in SSA (direct consequence of the lack of electricity), which almost accounts for two thirds of the total primary energy supply and even reaches 79% if RSA is excluded from the group. On the other hand, North African countries are heavily reliant on oil and gas[111].

Figure 8.3: Total primary energy supply in the ECA region, 2006

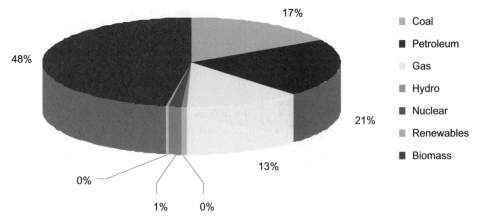

Coal
Petroleum
Gas
Hydro
Nuclear
Renewables
Biomass

Source: ECA based on IEA data.

Figure 8.4: North Africa primary energy supply in 2006

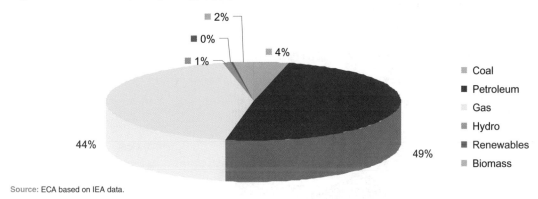

Coal
Petroleum
Gas
Hydro
Renewables
Biomass

Source: ECA based on IEA data.

Figure 8.5: SSA total primary energy supply in 2006

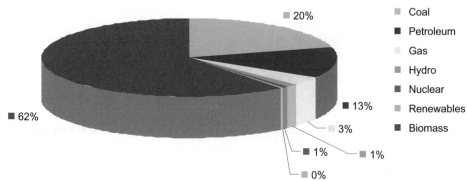

Coal
Petroleum
Gas
Hydro
Nuclear
Renewables
Biomass

Source: ECA based on IEA data.

Figure 8.6: SSA-RSA total primary energy supply in 2006

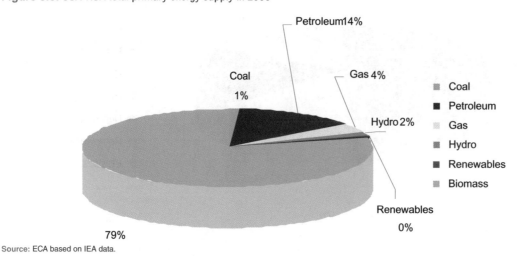

Source: ECA based on IEA data.

If only the grid-connected power sector is taken into consideration, the overwhelming dominance of fossil fuels in Africa's energy mix can be better appreciated, as they contributed to more than 80% of the region's total electricity generation in 2006. This is mainly due to coal-fired power plants that contribute to more than 90% of RSA power generation (amounting alone to 43% of Africa's total) and gas- and oil-fired power plants in North Africa and Nigeria, as illustrated in figure 8.7 and figure 8.8[112].

Figure 8.7: Electricity generation by energy source in the ECA region

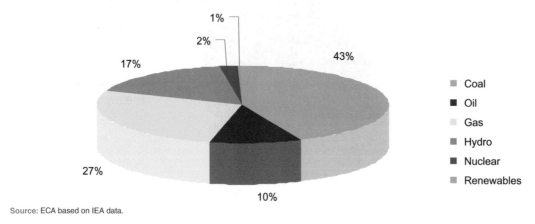

Source: ECA based on IEA data.

Figure 8.8: RSA electricity generation by energy source

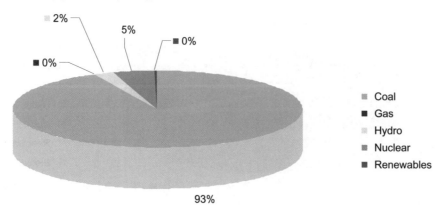

Source: ECA based on IEA data.

The low level of industrialization of the continent is translated into an energy consumption pattern overwhelmingly dominated by the residential sector, normally in the form of biomass fuels for cooking and heating. It can be noted from figures 8.9 to 8.13 that resource-rich North Africa and industrialized RSA have a more balanced demand[113].

Figure 8.9: Final energy consumption by sector in the ECA region

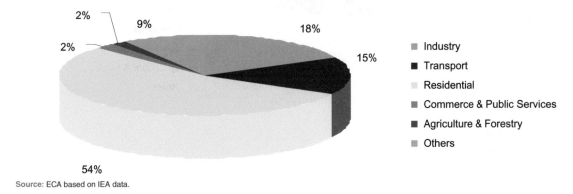

Source: ECA based on IEA data.

Figure 8.10: North Africa energy consumption by sector

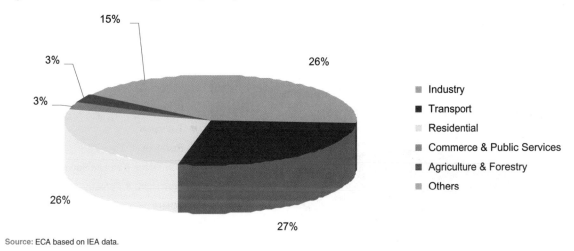

Source: ECA based on IEA data.

Figure 8.11: SAA final energy consumption by sector

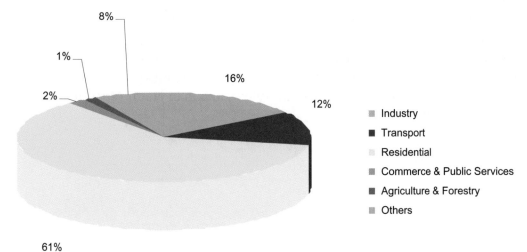

Source: ECA based on IEA data.

Figure 8.12: SSA-RSA final energy consumption by sector

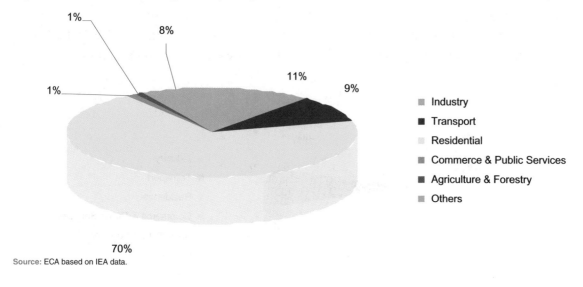

Source: ECA based on IEA data.

Figure 8.13: RSA final energy consumption by sector

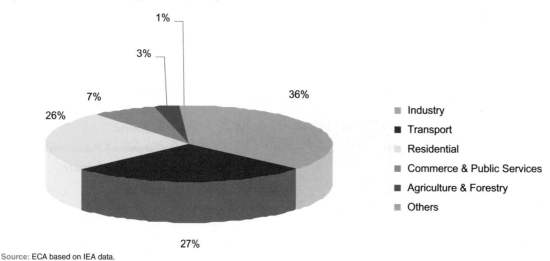

Source: ECA based on IEA data.

The ECA region make a very inefficient energy use, as its energy intensity is over two and a half times higher than the world's average, although timid signs of improvements can be observed in the two following figures. Figure 8.14 gives an indication of energy intensity for the world, Africa, North Africa, sub-Saharan Africa (SSA), South Africa (RSA) and sub-Saharan Africa excluding South Africa (SSA-RSA). Similarly, the region has higher carbon intensity than the world's average as illustrated in figure 8.15 below. This mainly due to fossil fuels based electricity generation in North Africa (oil and gas) and South Africa (coal).

Figure 8.14: Energy intensity in the ECA region 2005-2007

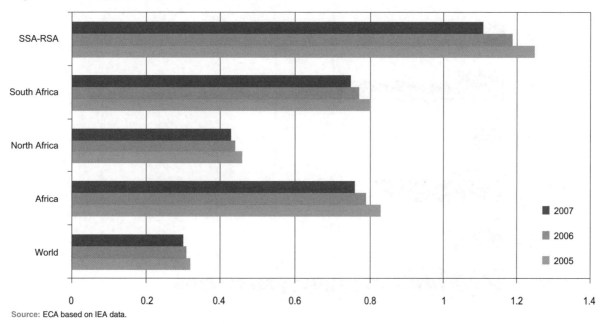

Source: ECA based on IEA data.

Figure 8.15: Carbon intensity in the ECA region, 2005-2007

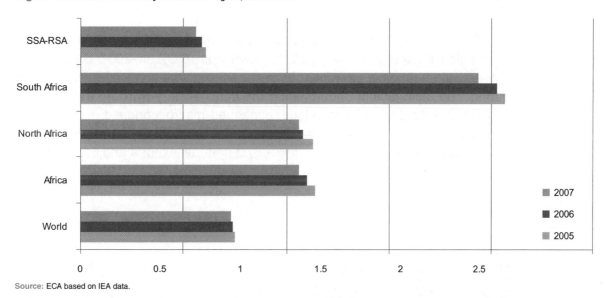

Source: ECA based on IEA data.

Figure 8.16 provides a summary of the relation between GDP, total energy consumption and carbon emissions on a per capita basis for all the groupings taken into consideration and the world average. Both the consumption of energy and the level of emissions are heavily correlated with the levels of economic activity and standards of living, although the figures clearly show the highly inefficient use of energy in SSA and, to a lesser extent, North African countries, as well as the enormous carbon intensity of RSA.

Figure 8.16: Per capita CO_2 emissions, GDP and TPES

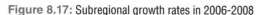

Source: ECA based on IEA data.

8.2. General Economic Situation in the ECA Region

According to the Economic Report on Africa 2009 prepared by ECA, economic growth in the ECA Region slowed to 5.1% in 2008, down from 6.0% in 2007. Despite this deceleration and the economic slowdown ignited by the global financial crisis, growth remains strong. The main factors underpinning the continent's growth are multiple and include high commodity demand and prices, continued macroeconomic management and commitment to economic reforms, increased domestic investment and productivity, recent debt write-offs, private capital flows, increased non-fuel exports and consolidation of peace in various parts of the continent[114].

Figure 8.17: Subregional growth rates in 2006-2008

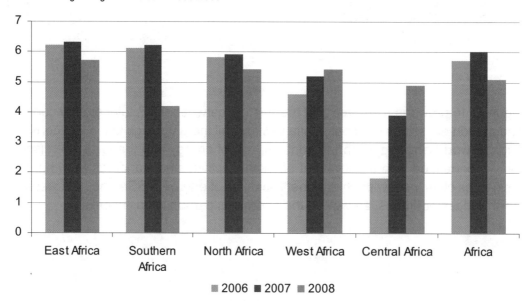

Source: ECA.

The continent's prospects for 2009 are subject to strong uncertainties stemming mainly from the global economic crisis. Based on its weak integration into the global financial system, it was first assumed that the crisis would have relatively small direct effects on the continent. However, a general fall in primary commodity demand and prices, as well as reduced export revenue due to a decrease in imports in developed and emerging markets led to more pessimistic forecasts. The real GDP growth rate in Africa is now expected to fall to 2.0% in 2009 from 5.1% in 2008. Subregional growth rates in 2009 are projected to range from -1.2% in Southern Africa, to 1.9% in Central Africa, 3.1% in North Africa, 3.1% in West Africa and 3.8% in East Africa[115].

According to the World Investment Report (WIR) 2009 published by UNCTAD, FDI inflows in Africa rose to another record level of US$88 billion in 2008 ($69 billion in 2007) despite the financial crisis, as illustrated in figure 8.18 below. FDI inflows to Africa were US$53 billion in 2007, according to figures provided in the WIR 2008.

Figure 8.18: FDI inflows in the ECA region, 2006-2008

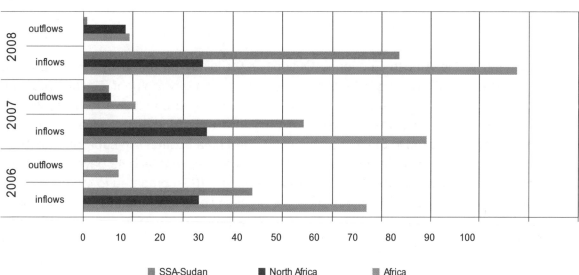

Source: ECA based on UNCTAD data.

FDI inflows increased in all subregions of Africa in 2008, except North Africa (including Sudan). While Southern Africa attracted almost one third of the inflows, West African countries recorded the largest percentage increase (63%). In 2009, a decline in the FDI inflows to Africa is likely to be witnessed, after six years of interrupted growth. The main reasons for this are the slowdown in the global economy, lower global commodity prices and a worsening of the financial crisis in many developed and fast-growing developing economies. Figure 8.19 below illustrates the evolution FDI inflows to the African subregions for the period 2005-2007.

Figure 8.19: FDI inflows to African subregions in 2006-2008

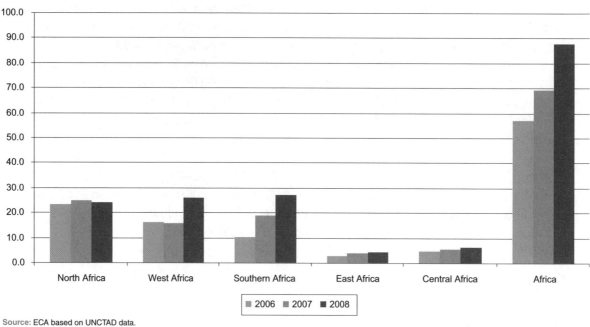

Source: ECA based on UNCTAD data.

According to the African Economic Outlook 2009 jointly prepared by OECD and the AfDB, Africa is still lagging behind in terms of business environment. Despite profound improvements in the pace of reforms to make them more conducive to domestic and foreign investment, business environments in Africa are still less attractive to firm entry and growth, compared to the rest of the world. Starting a business in sub-Saharan Africa is the most difficult in the world. It entails 10.2 procedures that take 49 days to complete. Only Latin America outranks SSA in the length of days (65, compared to 49) to complete a business start up, but in Latin America, the process costs less and the minimum capital requirements is lower. In addition, registering a property in SSA also involves more procedures and costs than in other regions. However, SSA is close to the world's average in terms of contract enforcement, duration of bankruptcy procedure and the subsequent recovery rate[116].

Figure 8.20: African Index of Economic Freedom 2005-2009

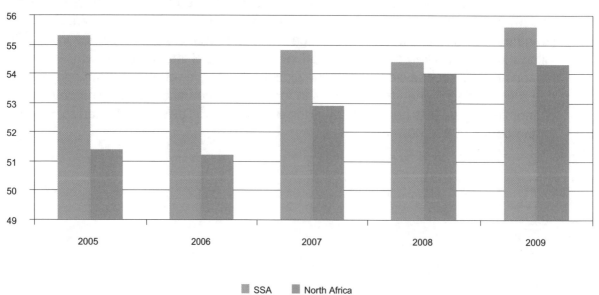

Source: ECA based on African Economic Outlook 2009.

8.3. Legislative and regulatory framework

As table 9.1 below shows, most African countries, particularly in SSA, do not have specific legislation for energy efficiency, but include at least directives or policy guidelines for promoting energy efficiency and conservation in their national energy policies.

Table 9.1: National legislation for energy efficiency in the ECA region

Energy efficiency legislation	Countries
Dedicated frameworks or programmes	South Africa
Provisions from other regulatory frameworks	Ghana, Kenya, Morocco, Namibia, Tunisia, Zimbabwe
No legislation	Algeria, Angola, Benin, Botswana, Burkina Faso, Burundi, Cameroon, Cape Verde, Central African Republic, Chad, Comoros, Congo, Democratic Republic of the Congo, Cote d'Ivoire, Djibouti, Egypt, Equatorial Guinea, Eritrea, Ethiopia, Gabon, Gambia (The), Guinea, Guinea-Bissau, Lesotho, Liberia, Libya, Madagascar, Malawi, Mali, Mauritania, Mozambique, Niger, Nigeria, Rwanda, Sao Tome and Principe, Senegal, Seychelles, Sierra Leone, Somalia, Sudan, Swaziland, Tanzania, Togo, Uganda, Zambia

Source: ECA.

The top priority in climate change mitigation policies has been the ratification of the Kyoto Protocol by ECA member States. 51 out of 53 African countries have so far ratified the Kyoto Protocol. Seven countries ratified the Protocol following the call by the Heads of State and Government of the African Union (AU) in their Declaration on Climate Change and Development in Africa adopted at their Summit held in Addis Ababa on 29-30 January 2007. Zimbabwe has been the last African country and 184th in the world to ratify the Protocol on 30 June 2009. Only Chad and Somalia have not yet ratified the Protocol, with the former being a party to the UNFCCC, while the latter having only observer status. The above-mentioned declaration also called, among other things, for developing and strengthening research and development (R&D) in climate change in Africa, particularly in renewable energy, forestry and agriculture, to increase the continent's resilience and adaptation to climate change.

Table 9.2: Commitments to UNFCCC and the Kyoto Protocol in the ECA region

Kyoto Protocol	Countries
Ratified	Algeria, Angola, Benin, Botswana, Burkina Faso, Burundi, Cameroon, Cape Verde, Central African Republic, Comoros, Congo, Democratic Republic of the Congo, Cote d'Ivoire, Djibouti, Egypt, Equatorial Guinea, Eritrea, Ethiopia, Gabon, Gambia (The), Ghana, Guinea, Guinea-Bissau, Kenya, Lesotho, Liberia, Libya, Madagascar, Malawi, Mali, Mauritania, Morocco, Mozambique, Namibia, Niger, Nigeria, Rwanda, Sao Tome and Principe, Senegal, Seychelles, Sierra Leone, South Africa, Sudan, Swaziland, Tanzania, Togo, Tunisia, Uganda, Zambia, Zimbabwe.
Not ratified	Chad, Somalia

Source: UNFCCC website.

Because of the large number of countries that make up the ECA Region, the best approach adopted by African leaders to address the issue of small and fragmented national economies and the uneven distribution of energy resources within the continent has been regional cooperation and integration so as to benefit from economies of scale. This had led ECA to assist member States in the establishment of some of the five subregional economic groupings (known as regional economic communities or RECs).

These include:

(i)   the 15-member Economic Community of West African States (ECOWAS), dominated
       by Nigeria in economic terms;
       the 15-member Southern African Development Community (SADC), dominated by
       RSA in economic terms;

(ii)   the 19-member Common Market for Eastern and Southern Africa (COMESA),
       dominated by Egypt in economic terms;

(iii) the 10-member Economic Community of Central African States (ECCAS); and

(iv)   the Maghreb Arab Union (UMA), comprised of North African countries, excluding
       Egypt, but including Mauritania.

The RECs were established to form the building blocks of the African Economic Community. Most of these RECs have developed their regional energy programmes and sometimes their regional power development master plans. These RECs have also established power pools to operate as specialized institutions for operation and management of regional energy markets within their regions. These are: (i) the Southern African Power Pool (SAPP), established in 1995; (ii) the West African Power Pool (WAPP), established in 2000; (iii) the Central African Power Pool (CAPP/PEAC), established in 2003; (iv) the East African Power Pool (EAPP), established in 2005; and (v) the Comité Maghrebin de l'Electricité (COMELEC). With regard to EE and RE, provisions are generally included in the energy protocols of the RECs (e.g., the ECOWAS Energy Protocol is an integral part of the Revised ECOWAS Treaty).

The ECOWAS has recently established the ECOWAS Centre for renewable energy and energy efficiency. According to the statement of ECOWAS Energy Ministers meeting in Guinea Bissau on 31 August 2008, it is expected to conduct integrated training programmes for target groups such as high-level decision-makers and staff of national and regional institutions in energy and related sectors in order to increase awareness of EE and RE opportunities and to support the implementation of EE and RE policies, programmes and projects.

The COMESA has recently adopted the COMESA Model Energy Policy Framework in which EE and conservation issues are given due importance, particularly within the energy policy objectives seeking to improve effectiveness and efficiency of the commercial energy supply industries and manage environmental, health and safety impacts of energy production and utilization.

The SADC Council of Ministers has approved a regional power conservation programme to facilitate DSM at a one-day meeting held in Botswana in February 2008. The SADC road map includes the development of minimum EE standards for all new electrical connections, implementation of renewable energy technologies and the phasing out of incandescent light bulbs replaced by a preference for Compact Fluorescent Lights (CFLs). The Southern African Power Pool (SAPP) Coordination Centre, which is managing the regional electricity market and is operating a short term energy market (STEM) that allows power utilities to purchase or sell on a day-ahead basis, helps in monitoring results achieved by its member utilities in implementing the DSM and power conservation programmes. In addition, Lesotho, Malawi, Mozambique, Namibia, RSA, Zambia and Zimbabwe are involved in a Biomass Energy Conservation (BEC) programme financed by GTZ.

Table 9.3: Regional integration in the ECA region

Organization	Membership	Legislative Framework	Institutional Framework
ECOWAS	Benin, Burkina Faso, Cape Verde, Cote d'Ivoire, Gambia, Ghana, Guinea, Guinea Bissau, Liberia, Mali, Niger, Nigeria, Senegal, Sierra Leone, Togo	ECOWAS Energy Protocol Article 43 on Energy Efficiency calling member States to establish energy efficiency policies and appropriate legal and regulatory frameworks	ECOWAS Centre for Renewable Energy and Energy Efficiency
COMESA	Burundi, Comoros, DR Congo, Djibouti, Egypt, Eritrea, Ethiopia, Kenya, Libya, Madagascar, Malawi, Mauritius, Rwanda, Seychelles, Sudan, Swaziland, Uganda, Zambia, and Zimbabwe	COMESA Model Energy Policy Framework, particularly within the policy objectives of improving effectiveness and efficiency of commercial energy supply industries and managing environmental, health and safety impacts of energy	
SADC	Angola, Botswana, DR Congo, Lesotho, Malawi, Madagascar, Mauritius, Mozambique, Namibia, Seychelles, South Africa, Swaziland, Tanzania, Zambia and Zimbabwe	SADC Protocol on Energy SADC Council of Ministers' approval of SADC Energy Ministerial Task Force on Power Conservation programme (PCP) and DSM programme	ADC Directorate of Infrastructure and Services Southern African Power Pool (SAPP)

Source: ECA.

8.4. Activities and accomplishments

The ECA's Energy Agenda derives from its general mandate and the African priorities in the sector of energy. As the regional arm of the United Nations in Africa, ECA is mandated to support the economic and social development of its 53 member States, foster regional integration, and promote international cooperation for Africa's development. ECA, like other UN Regional Commissions, is not a funding agency, but helps to promote and disseminate its work through the three broad means of (i) policy analysis and advocacy; (ii) consensus building; and (iii) technical assistance.

The focus of ECA's interventions on energy is based on priorities and commitments made in the framework of the World Summit on Sustainable Development (WSSD), the New Partnership for Africa's Development (NEPAD) energy initiatives and other energy priorities related to the achievement of globally agreed objectives such as the Millennium Development Goals (MDGs). Under this agenda, ECA is assisting member states to formulate policies and strategies aimed at lifting institutional barriers, promoting good practices and accelerating the development of the African energy sector. Areas of intervention include:

(i)   improving energy accessibility, especially to the disadvantaged population;
(ii)   improvement of energy policies and management; and
(iii) development of RE sources.

In implementing its mandate, ECA has made collaboration and partnership-building its preferred strategic approach in order to optimize its resources and enlarge the scope and beneficiaries of its actions. In addition to NEPAD, privileged relationships and partnerships are developed with the African Union (AU), the RECs, the African Energy Commission (AFREC), the African power sector organizations such the Power Pools, the African Development Bank (AfDB), and UN organizations active in energy in Africa through UN Energy/Africa. ECA's subregional offices play an important role in these partnerships, particularly with the RECs.

In order to ensure more effectiveness of the UN system's actions in Africa, and in particular to provide a more coherent support to NEPAD, ECA is convening the *Africa Regional Coordination Meeting (RCM)* on an annual basis. The RCMs are organized around nine clusters of issues, including infrastructure, which comprises a sub-cluster on energy. With regard to the sub-cluster on energy, ECA coordinates efforts of UN organizations with a view to creating an inter-agency coordination mechanism called UN-Energy/Africa, which provides a framework for all stakeholders, including UN and selected non-UN agencies, such as the AU, the AfDB, the NEPAD Secretariat and the African Energy Commission, to discuss, identify and implement joint activities aimed at achieving the objectives of the NEPAD energy agenda. UN Energy/Africa serves as the sub-cluster on energy in support of NEPAD.

ECA has worked to improve Africa's energy sector management and to promote its regional integration through the following actions:

(i)   Improving reliability of energy supply through power pooling arrangements

ECA conducted a study and organized an ad hoc expert group meeting on "assessment of power pooling in Africa". The meeting took place in Addis Ababa on 24-26 June 2003. It was attended by energy experts from the power pools and utilities operating in Africa such as the Southern African Power Pool (SAPP), the West African Power Pool (WAPP), the Communauté Electrique du Benin (CEB), the Volta River Authority (VRA), the Compagnie Ivoirienne d'Electricité (CIE), the Uganda Electricity Transmission Company Limited (UETCL) and the Ethiopian Energy Power Corporation (EEPCO), as well as the African Energy Commission (AFREC), the African Development Bank (AfDB) and the World Energy Council (WEC). The objective of the meeting is to consider and validate the main findings of the above-mentioned study and elaborate action-oriented recommendations aimed at assisting member States in making decisions on their possible involvement into cross-border electricity trading and the operation of regional power pools. The meeting highlighted the importance of hydropower development in ensuring cheap and sustainable energy supply within inter-country and regional power pooling arrangements in Africa.

(ii)   Providing technical assistance in the formulation of energy policy

ECA provided, in 2004, TA to the Government of Sierra Leone for the formulation of a national energy policy. The proposed energy policy gives due consideration to improving access to reliable and affordable modern energy services and to mitigating negative environmental impacts of energy production and consumption.

(iii) Strengthening human resources and capacity building in energy planning

To address the issue of poor planning considered as one of the main causes of the energy crisis experienced by many African countries, ECA has embarked on implementing capacity building activities in the area on integrated resource planning for energy and electricity in Africa. ECA has organized, in partnership with the International Atomic Energy Agency (IAEA), a training workshop for experts from power pools, river basin organizations and regional economic groupings on the use of planning and modelling tools developed by the IAEA in order for them to make informed investment decisions for energy and power development in the future. In addition, ECA is working closely with the UN Department of Economic and Social Affairs (UNDESA) to implement the Development Account Project on *Capacity building for inter-regional electricity access and supply in Africa*. The project aims at assisting the less-developed power pools in Central and Eastern Africa to build their capacity in terms of planning power systems interconnection, preparing bilateral power sales agreements and creating and maintaining energy databases.

(iv) Improving power sector reform for the provision of sustainable energy

ECA, in partnership with UNEP and within the framework of UN Energy/Africa, carried out an in-depth analysis of the economic, social and environmental impacts of power sector reforms in Africa. The study entitled *Making Africa's Power Sector Sustainable* maps the way forward for making Africa's power sector more sustainable with regard to social and environmental objectives. It covered 14 countries in varying degrees and was completed in December 2005. A high-level policy dialogue forum was organized on 15-16 December 2005 in partnership with UNEP and UNDESA to validate the assumptions made and the conclusions and recommendations of the study. The main findings of the study were presented at the First Conference of African Ministers responsible for Electrical Energy organized by the African Union in Addis Ababa in March 2006.

(v) Promoting regional integration in energy

To address the challenges of uneven distribution of energy resources in Africa and the small size of energy systems and markets on the continent, ECA is assisting member states and the RECs in promoting regional energy cooperation and integration leading to economies of scale through inter-country energy trade and the establishment of sub-regional power pools. In this regard, ECA commissioned a study on hydropower development and interconnection of electricity grids in West Africa, which came up with an indicative regional power master plan within ECOWAS. This master plan served as the basis for the establishment of the West African Power Pool. ECA also organized an ad hoc expert group meeting to consider the main recommendations of a study on *Prospects for energy and power development and connectivity in Central Africa*, which resulted in the adoption of a roadmap for the establishment of the Central African Power Pool (Pool Energétique d'Afrique Centrale). Finally, ECA hosted the meeting of East African Energy Ministers for the launching of the East African Power Pool.

(vi) Cooperation with the African Union

ECA contributed to the preparation of background documents, including thematic maps on energy infrastructure development to be considered at the AU Summit held on 1-3 February 2009 in Addis Ababa on the theme of Transport and Energy Infrastructure Development in Africa.

ECA also commissioned a number of studies on renewable development in Africa. These include:

(i) Renewable Energy Technologies (RETs) for Poverty Alleviation

ECA prepared a paper on renewable energy sources for presentation and discussion at the third meeting of the Committee on Sustainable Development (CSD-3) held in Addis Ababa in October 2003. Given that both the NEPAD and the WSSD emphasized the importance of increasing access to modern energy services for achieving the MDGs and eradicating poverty in Africa, the paper focused on the potential contribution of renewable sources of energy to reducing poverty. CSD-3 recommended, among other things, (i) to promote RETs in order to improve delivery of energy services for the poor and expand opportunities for income-generating activities; and (ii) to facilitate access to RET-based energy services for the poor through setting up innovative financing mechanisms, such as micro-credit, that can provide low-income households and small businesses with access to capital, via loans that typically include flexible repayment schemes, fee schedules matching customer income streams and longer repayment terms.

(ii) Promotion of a *Rural Energy Development Facility for Africa*

As a follow-up to recommendations of CSD-3, ECA proposed at the International Conference for Renewable Energies, held in Bonn (Germany) in June 2004, a project proposal for the creation of a *Rural Energy Development Facility for Africa*. The main features of the facility include: (i) capacity strengthening for energy policymakers, energy entrepreneurs and micro-finance institutions; (ii) development of entrepreneurship for decentralized renewables-based energy production; and (iii) provision of rural finance facilities for financing access to energy services as well as productive uses of energy in rural areas. This project proposal has also been submitted to other UN Agencies working in Africa within UN Energy Africa for possible joint implementation.

(iii) Sustainable Energy: A framework for new and renewable energy in Southern Africa

ECA Sub Regional Office for Southern Africa released in March 2006 a publication entitled *Sustainable Energy: A Framework for New and Renewable Energy in Southern Africa*. Before its finalization, experts in RE policy development and regional integration reviewed the publication during a meeting held in Lusaka, Zambia, in November 2005. The study reviews the constraints to RE in the Southern Africa sub-region. These include inadequate policies, legal, regulatory and institutional frameworks and limited financial flow for the development and provision of sustainable energy. The framework calls for member States from SADC to improve the environment for private sector participation in the development of appropriate renewable energy technologies and the supply of these technologies to communities at affordable prices. The framework emphasizes the importance of energy as a factor of production for economic empowerment and diversification of economic activities in rural areas. The policy framework establishes a clear relation between access to affordable, reliable and sustainable energy and social and economic uplifting.

(iv) Improving energy accessibility

ECA completed a study in 2007, entitled *Unleashing Energy Access in Africa: Rural Energy Access Scale-Up Mechanism*. It sought to identify best practices in rural energy development in Africa, and mainstream its key findings into policy formulation in Africa. In addition, it helped establish the contours of a *Rural Energy Access Scale-Up Mechanism* (REASUMA) and draw lessons and best practices in scaling up rural energy access, including use of renewable energy technologies (RETs) based on the main findings of a regional survey conducted in a dozen of countries.

(v) Innovative financing mechanisms for new and renewable energy projects

ECA through its sub-regional office for North Africa is implementing this development account project in collaboration with UNDESA. The project seeks to explore mechanisms for disseminating, in North Africa, the lessons learnt from successful experiences based on a comparative study of the feasibility of existing and new technical and financial mechanisms for each country and each type of renewable energy. In the project, particular emphasis will be placed on capacity building as well as the development of information and knowledge networks so as to effectively share lessons learned and enhance peer learning. The choice of North Africa as a starting point is mainly justified by the fact that most countries in the subregion are ready to consider the utilization of new and renewable energies in order to promote the use of environmental friendly energy in the sub-region.

Finally, ECA has just launched the African Climate Policy Centre (ACPC) to serve as the Climate Information for Development in Africa (ClimDev-Africa) knowledge-management and policy-facilitation arm. The ClimDev programme is being developed and implemented by the three continental institutions (ECA, AU and AfDB) as a follow up to the Declaration on Climate Change and Development adopted by AU Summit in January 2007.

9. The ESCWA region

9.1. Energy overview of the ESCWA region

The energy sector of the ESCWA region[117] has played and will continue to play an important role globally as well as within the region. It serves as a main source of revenue through oil and (to a lesser extent) gas export and it could potentially satisfy energy needs for economic and social development. However, more than 20% of the population in rural and urban poor areas do not have access to energy services and as many are highly underserviced[118]. Moreover, in many cases, the efficiency of energy production and consumption in the region requires improvement[119].

On the production side, the energy sector in the ESCWA Member Countries is characterized by a vast oil and gas sector and a large electric power sector which is dominated by thermal power generation (more than 90%)[120].

Figure 9.1 shows the primary energy production in the region and clearly underscores the dominant role of oil and gas in the energy mix of the region.

Figure 9.1: Primary energy production by source ('000 toe) in the ESCWA region

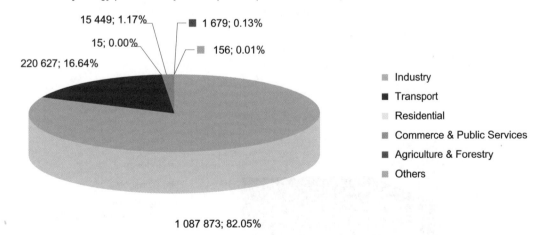

Source: ESCWA, based on IEA data.

The oil and gas sector in the ESCWA region represents the largest economic sector. In 2007-2008, the total proven reserves of crude oil represented about 53% of the world's total, while those of natural gas represented about 27% of the world's proven reserves[121].

The total crude oil production of ESCWA Member Countries is estimated to have been 20.2 million barrels per day on average in 2008, with an increase of 3.6% from the previous year[122]. The ESCWA region gross revenues from oil exports are estimated to be $637.1 billion in 2008, with an increase of 41.8% from previous year[123]. The projections for 2009 estimate an average daily production equivalent to 17.5 million barrels. Such significant reduction is mainly due to compliance of OPEC member countries in the ESCWA region with new OPEC quotas. This, along with the fall in oil prices of late 2008, led to a reduction of more than 50% in oil revenues, projected to amount to only $307.7 billion[124].

The region also enjoys good RE resources with 7,491 megawatts (MW) of installed hydroelectric capacity. Solar resources vary between 1,460 and 3,000 kilowatt-hours per square meter (KWh/m^2) per year. Wind resources are also available in several ESCWA countries at utilizable average speeds[125].

The total primary energy supply, visually represented in figure 9.2, confirms the strong role of hydrocarbons even with regard to consumption. It is, however, interesting to note the larger share of gas as opposed to the primary production as oil is more massively exported. Other sources still have a marginal impact on both production and consumption.

Figure 9.2: Primary energy supply by source ('000 toe) in the ESCWA region

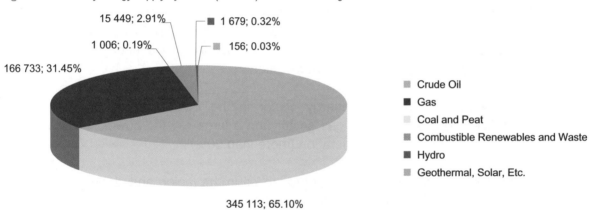

15 449; 2.91%   ■ 1 679; 0.32%

1 006; 0.19%   ■ 156; 0.03%

166 733; 31.45%

345 113; 65.10%

- ■ Crude Oil
- ■ Gas
- ▨ Coal and Peat
- ■ Combustible Renewables and Waste
- ■ Hydro
- ▨ Geothermal, Solar, Etc.

Source: ESCWA, based on IEA data.

Over a third of this energy is destined to transport. The industry and residential sectors also represent significant shares.

Figure 9.3: Energy consumption by sector in the ESCWA region

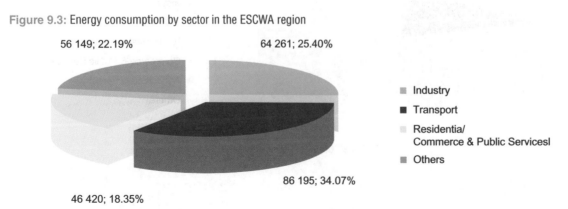

56 149; 22.19%   64 261; 25.40%

86 195; 34.07%

46 420; 18.35%

- ▨ Industry
- ■ Transport
- ▨ Residentia/ Commerce & Public Servicesl
- ■ Others

Source: ESCWA, based on IEA data.

An important development in the energy sector of the region is the increased regional cooperation in the electric power and gas sub-sectors. In the former, regional interconnections have been approved and in some cases main portions of the works have been commissioned. These interconnections include:

(i)   The Egypt, Jordan, Syria, Lebanon, Iraq, Palestine, Turkey and Libya interconnection (partially implemented till now). Out of the eight countries involved in the interconnection, the first six are ESCWA Member Countries. This interconnection opens the possibility for the ESCWA region to be connected to the ECE through Turkey and ECA through Libya.

(ii)   The GCC (Gulf Cooperation Countries) interconnection (under implementation).

(iii) Planned interconnections Saudi Arabia - Egypt and Saudi Arabia - Yemen.

(iv)   Planned interconnection linking Egypt, Sudan and the rest of East Africa countries. This interconnection, would allow the ESCWA and ECA regions to be connected.

(v)   As for the gas sub-sectors, several pipelines connect the ESCWA members and some others are planned:

(vi)   The Euro-Arab Mashreq gas pipeline connecting Egypt, Jordan, Syria and Lebanon (project in the final stages of execution). This pipeline is planned to be extended to Turkey, opening the doors to the ECE region.

(vii) The Dolphin Gas Project linking Qatar to the UAE with plans of extension to Oman. The pipeline came on stream in 2006.

(viii) Planned rehabilitation of the existing pipeline between Iraq and Kuwait.

(ix)   Other pipelines under consideration include pipelines to connect the GCC countries, Qatar - Kuwait and Qatar - Bahrain pipelines and Egypt - Libya pipeline.

Figure 9.4 depicts the energy intensity and the carbon intensity indicators for the ESCWA countries, where GDP is taken on a nominal dollar basis. As it is usually the case in countries with GHG-emitting extractive industries, harsh climates and availability of large domestic energy resources, these figures tend to be well above world average. Likewise, as figure 9.5 shows, total primary energy supply (TPES) and carbon emissions per capita are related to the level of per capita GDP as the use of energy increases with the improvement of economic conditions of the population. No country seems to be an exception to this rule, signalling that alternative paths based on less energy-intensive development and low-carbon energy supplies have not been taken or have not yet achieved significant results.

Figure 9.4: Energy intensity and carbon intensity (toe/US$; kg/US$) in the ESCWA region

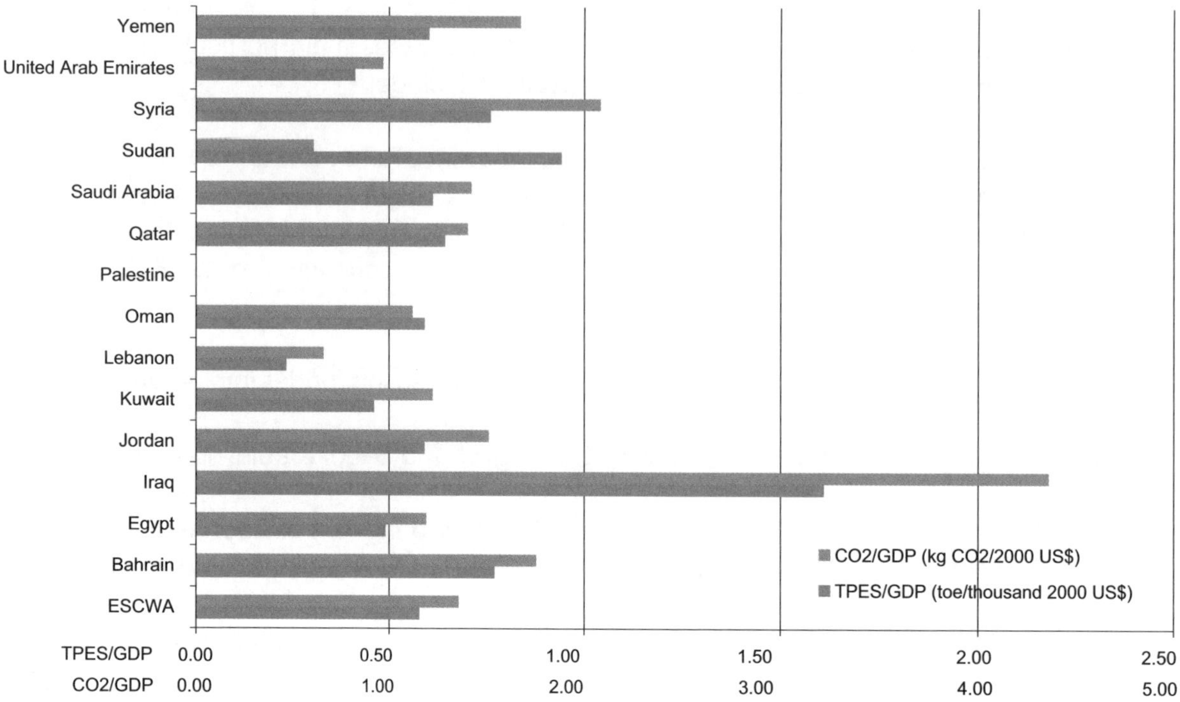

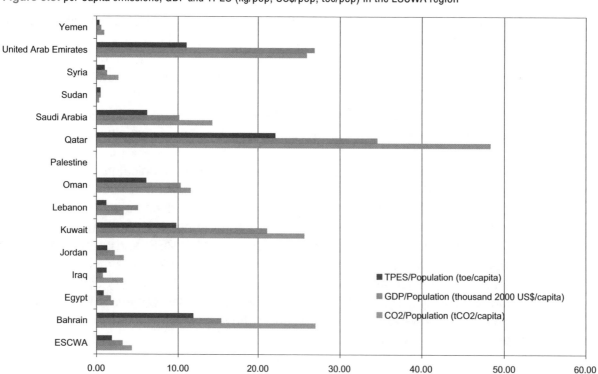

Source: ESCWA, based on IEA data.

Figure 9.5: per Capita emissions, GDP and TPES (kg/pop; US$/pop; toe/pop) in the ESCWA region

Source: ESCWA, based on IEA data

Nonetheless, climate change is a variable which has to be seriously taken into consideration in the region. It affects all countries, but ESCWA members are expected to bear some specific adverse consequences, hindering the achievement of the MDGs and other regional economic and social development targets. In addition, energy production will be one the economic sectors mostly affected, as the potential effects of climate change are likely to boost demand and dwarf supply at the same time, especially in the ESCWA region. For instance, more frequent droughts will reduce the capacity of hydropower stations and lead to electricity shortages, while risen sea levels may partially submerge some energy-generating installations, particularly offshore oil-extraction platforms and coastal power plants. Changes in sea levels may also damage national and regional electricity grids, electricity linkage lines and natural gas pipelines lines in affected areas. At the same time, however, the need for energy-intensive air-conditioning and cooling systems and water desalination will grow due to higher temperatures and desertification.

9.2. General economic situation in the ESCWA region

The ESCWA region has a diversified economic situation. GDP growth rates in 2008 vary between negative values in the Occupied Palestinian Territory and a peak of 16% in Qatar. Figure 9.6 shows the real GDP growth estimates per country for the years 2007, 2008 and forecasts of the year 2009 as of March 2009.

Figure 9.6: Real GDP growth rate in the ESCWA region 2007, 2008 and 2009 (estimates)

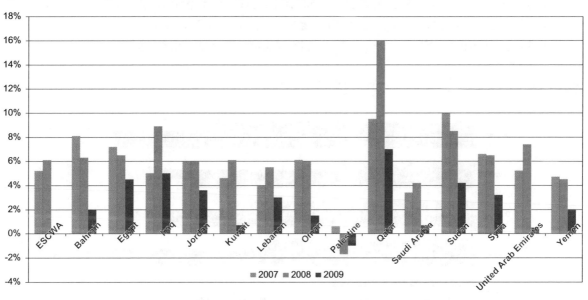

Source: ESCWA.

The inflow of FDI in the ESCWA region is also widely differentiated. Figure 9.7 shows the FDI inward flow for the years 2005, 2006 and 2007 as per the World Investment Report 2008 issued by UNCTAD. The variance is both explained by the economic conditions (which make some countries more attractive to investors than others) and the very different political and legal frameworks. In the ESCWA region, some of the world most FDI-friendly countries coexist with some of the most restrictive.

Figure 9.7: FDI inward flow in the ESCWA region, 2005-2007

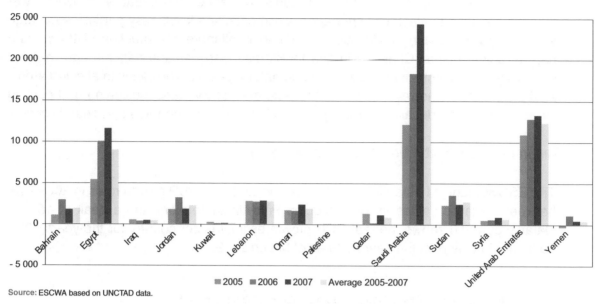

Source: ESCWA based on UNCTAD data.

More information on the economies of the region and their business environment can be found in the following graphs. Figure 9.8 shows the Economic Freedom Index[126], the Corruption Perception Index (CPI) and the Global Competitiveness Index.

Figure 9.8: State of the economy indicators in the ESCWA region

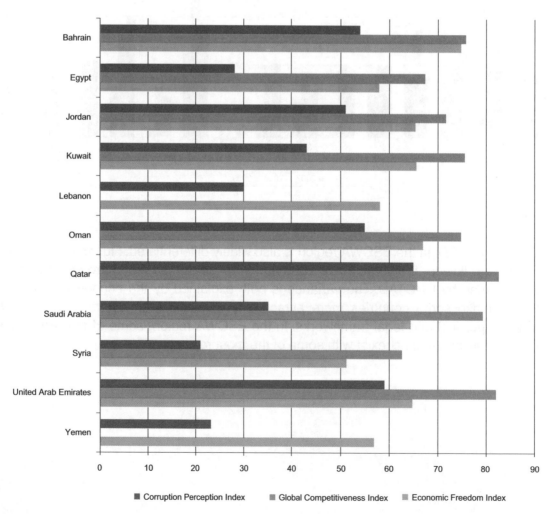

Source: ESCWA, based on data from Heritage Foundation, World Economic Forum and Transparency International.

9.3. Legislative and regulatory framework

As the adoption and reinforcement of sustainable patterns of energy consumption and production are gaining attention worldwide, the ESCWA member countries have taken several steps towards developing policies and regulations in the energy sector that would contribute to achieve sustainable development. Emphasis on the EE and RE differs from country to country, but as 12 countries in the ESCWA region have ratified the Kyoto protocol, concrete steps have been followed.

Below are two summary tables of the overall national and international frameworks in the ESCWA region. Annex IV presents the detailed legislative and regulatory framework by country in each of the ESCWA Member Countries.

Table 9.1: National legislation for energy efficiency in the ESCWA region

Energy efficiency legislation	Countries
Dedicated frameworks or programmes	Syria
Provisions from other regulatory frameworks	Egypt, Jordan, Qatar, Sudan, Yemen
Policy directives or guidelines but no legislative framework	Iraq, Palestine, Saudi Arabia, United Arab Emirates
Dedicated legislation to be approved	Lebanon
No legislation	Bahrain, Kuwait, Oman

Source: ESCWA.

Table 9.2: Commitments to UNFCCC and the Kyoto Protocol in the ESCWA region

Kyoto Protocol	Countries
Ratified	Bahrain, Egypt, Jordan, Kuwait, Lebanon, Oman, Qatar, Saudi Arabia, Sudan, Syria, United Arab Emirates, Yemen
Not ratified	Iraq, Palestine

Source: ESCWA.

9.4. Activities and accomplishments

9.4.1. Implemented activities

In light of the situation described above and the mounting challenges ahead, ESCWA has been closely working with national government and industries in the region to promote sound policies and regional cooperation. In particular, in the last two years, ESCWA has implemented a set of activities to enhance the capacity of Member Countries to sustainably manage their natural resources[127]. These activities can be divided into four categories:

(i) Enhance capacity of member countries to formulate and adopt integrated environmentally-sound policies and to introduce mechanisms for improving the sustainable management of natural resources, with a particular emphasis on water, energy, environmental protection and production sectors:

    a. A study on rationalizing energy consumption and improving energy efficiency in major energy production sectors in selected ESCWA Member Countries (2007);

    b. A cooperation agreement between ESCWA and Qatar on improving energy efficiency in the Qatari electricity sector (2006-2009); and

    c.   The Fourth Middle East and North Africa Renewable Energy Conference (Syria, 21-24 June 2007).

(i)   Enhance capacity of member countries to formulate, adopt and implement policies to improve the sustainable management of natural resources, with particular emphasis on the fulfilment of the MDGs:

    a.   Expert Group Meeting on *Sustainable Consumption and Production* (Abu Dhabi, 17-19 March 2008);

    b.   Technical support activities undertaken for Yemen (included a workshop, a seminar and a training programme conducted in 2008);

    c.   Expert Group Meeting on *Best Practices and Measures for Promoting RE Applications in the ESCWA region* (Lebanon, 3-4 February 2009);

    d.   Several non-recurrent publications on energy for sustainable development; and

    e.   Follow up of electricity and natural gas sector regional integration projects.

(ii)   Strengthening cooperation between member countries on energy issues:

    a.   Participation in the programmes of the Council of Arab Ministers for electricity of the League of Arab States;

    b.   Participation in the programmes of the Council of Arab Ministers for environment of the League of Arab States; and

    c.   Cooperation with UN organizations on climate change issues.

(iii)   Enhancing the capacity of member countries to implement best practice in improving rural sustainable development and small and medium enterprises" (SMEs) competitiveness by using environmentally sound technologies.

Moreover, the following activities have been accomplished in the year 2009:

(i)   A report on *Progress Achieved Towards Sustainable Transport in the Arab Region*;

(ii)   An Expert Group Meeting on *Progress Achieved Towards Sustainable Transport in the Arab Region in support of the Arab Ministerial Declaration on Climate Change*;

(iii)   A report on *Promoting Large Scale Renewable Energy Applications in the Arab Region, an Approach for Climate Change Mitigation*; and

(iv)   A study on *Enhancing regional cooperation on energy issues towards achieving sustainable development and the Millennium Development Goals in ESCWA Member Countries*.

In addition to the above activities, the ESCWA Energy Programme is supporting member countries in building their capacity in the field through training workshops, advisory services and field projects on both energy efficiency and renewable energy. In this respect, since 2000 ESCWA has initiated a regional mechanism for *Energy Uses for Sustainable Development* to promote intra-regional cooperation among its member countries in the field.

Moreover ESCWA, UNEP and the League of Arab States (LAS) have effectively cooperated in many areas related to environment and energy concerns, along with sustainable consumption and production issues. ESCWA is also participating in the ECE Global Energy Efficiency 21 (GEE21) Project with the other UN Regional Commissions.

Box 9.1: Selected national activities of member countries

The initiatives, programmes and activities related to the EERE undertaken by different ESCWA countries are numerous. An outline of the policy and legislative measures implemented by each national government can be found in annex IV. This box provides an overview of some success stories and remarkable achievements in the ESCWA region.

(i) Egypt

Egypt is committed to moving forward in RE and EE. In this regard, it has initiated the New & Renewable Energy Authority (NREA). It has invested in RE to reach a total wind based electric generation installed capacity of 365 MW in 2008 (projected to rise to 430 MW in 2009). During 2008, 847GWh of electricity has been generated from wind farms[128]. New projects funded by the World Bank for Clean Technology include three wind farms for a capacity of 200 MW and a 140 MW solar thermal power plant. A 250 MW new wind project in Jabal AlZeit is also anticipated[129].

(ii) Jordan

Jordan has been able to gather funds from different donors to promote RE and EE projects. These donors included GEF, AFD and FFEM. The total funds raised are in the range of US$60 million in grants or soft credit lines extended directly to major Jordanian banks for EERE investments[130]. Moreover, the EU Commission's Jordan Country Strategy for 2007-2013 includes financing two pilot projects: a wind power testing station and a concentrated solar power plant[131].

(iii) Saudi Arabia

Saudi Arabia has initiated the National Energy Efficiency Program (NEEP). NEEP has concentrated on conducting energy audits for selected building and facilities, initiating energy efficiency training and awareness programmes, issuing energy efficiency standards and labelling for selected household appliances, developing EE codes for new buildings design and establishing benchmarks for buildings and building services. NEEP energy audits concluded that an estimated annual EE market of SR1.2 billion is available in educational buildings, shopping malls and industrial sectors alone[132].

(iv) United Arab Emirates

The UAE's largest Emirate, Abu Dhabi, has launched the MASDAR Initiative and committed more than $15 billion in renewable energy programs. The MASDAR Initiative underscores twin commitments to the global environment and diversification of the UAE economy. The MASDAR Initiative focuses on the development and commercialization of technologies in renewable energy, energy efficiency, carbon management and monetization, water usage and desalination. The Initiative's partners include some of the world largest energy companies and most prestigious institutions, such as BP, Shell, Occidental Petroleum, Total, General Electric, Mitsubishi, Mitsui, Rolls Royce, the Imperial College London, the Massachusetts Institute of Technology (MIT) and the World Wildlife Fund (WWF).

MASDAR is characterized by key elements:

a. An innovation centre to support the demonstration, commercialization and adoption of sustainable energy technologies;

b. The MASDAR Institute of Science and Technology with graduate programmes in RE and sustainability, located in MASDAR City, the world's first carbon-neutral, waste free, car-free city;

c. A development company focused on the commercialization of emissions reduction and CDM solutions as provided by the Kyoto Protocol; and

d. A Special Economic Zone to host institutions investing in RE technologies and products[133.]

9.4.2. ESCWA planned activities

(i) ESCWA activities planned for 2009-2011 addressing climate change mitigation in the energy and transport include the following:

(ii) An Expert Group Meeting on The Role of Energy Networks in Regional Integration (December 2009);

(iii) A field project on Capacity Building on Renewable Energy Technology Applications for Poverty Alleviation in Rural Areas in the ESCWA Member Countries (2010-2011);

(iv) Parliamentary documentation on Energy Policies and Measures for Promoting Climate Change Mitigation in ESCWA Countries (2010);

(v) Promotional material on Improving the Efficiency in the Electric Power Sector in the ESCWA Region (2010);

(vi) Study on Policies and Measures Promoting Sustainable Energy Use in the Transport Sector in the ESCWA Region (2011);

(vii) Expert Group Meeting on Approaches for Promoting Emission Reductions from the Transport Sector in the ESCWA Region (2011); and

(viii) Advisory services on Promoting the application of energy efficiency measures in the ESCWA region (2010-2011).

Conclusions

This publication shows that models for designing financing instruments and sources of financing are readily available and the potential for EE improvements is vast in every region of the world, allowing the elaboration of win-win solutions for the mitigation of climate change, the fight against poverty and the quest for sustainability and energy security.

Nonetheless, several significant steps have yet to be taken to overcome the numerous obstacles that still hinder their diffusion and dwarf their positive effects. The nature of these measures, as repeatedly underlined throughout the report, has to be adjusted to the local contexts and their needs, even though some lessons can be drawn on their general validity.

Firstly, it is decisive for the mainstreaming of the benefits of EE to raise awareness and skills by enhanced communication, information transfer and dissemination using multilingual platforms, interactive tools and exploiting the full potential of web-based technology. Likewise, the organisation of meetings and seminars to diffuse knowledge and relevant expertise among policymakers, practitioners in the energy and banking sectors and local communities is a key for success and instrumental in the usefulness of bottom-up initiatives.

In the mid to long-run, however, the self-sustainability and the cost-effectiveness of EE investments can be ensured only through sound reforms at the local, national and international level. Measures such as the promotion of Action Plans for EE and RE, the drafting or revision of dedicated legislation, the promulgation of secondary regulation and implementation decrees are necessary to establish a regulatory framework suitable for investments.

A politically more costly yet fundamental step to take is the restructuring of subsidies for traditional sources of energy and fossil fuels. A consensus for their gradual phase-out seems to be emerging but further action is required in order to ensure the smooth and timely application of the agreement and the assistance to the most hardly hit groups, especially in developing countries. Policies against the consumption of traditional sources have also to be accompanied with positive incentives for EE and RE, under the form of public funds, public sector investment and demonstrative projects.

Ultimately, the successful spread of EE practices rely on the ability of the international community to create a regime providing strong incentives for lower consumption levels and ensuring the availability of appropriate knowledge, technology and financing at the global scale. In this respect, a transition from the Kyoto Protocol to a regime of larger reach and greater impact after 2012 is fundamental to fully deploy the potential of such financial mechanisms and the next Conference of Parties to the UNFCCC will decisively determine their future usefulness and applicability.

Annexes

1. EERE Financing mechanisms – Building blocks

Instruments
(i)   Financing
   - a.   Debt: most mechanisms
   - b.   Equity: EnErcap
   - c.   Quasi-equity: FIDEME

(ii)   Credit enhancement
   - a.   Partial risk guarantees: CHUEE
   - b.   Loan payments integrated in utility bills or taxes: PROSOL, EnergyCity

Financing Vehicles
(i)   Mainstream
   - a.   Commercial banks: BEERECL
   - b.   ESCOs: Enemona
   - c.   Utilities: Brazil Wire-Charge Programme
   - d.   Suppliers: SunEdison

(ii)   Quasi-mainstream
   - a.   Specialised subsidiary of commercial bank: Grameen Shakti
   - b.   Dedicated financing vehicle
   - c.   Debt and guarantees: BgEEF
   - d.   Debt: IREDA
   - e.   Equity or quasi-equity funds: CAREC, EnerCap

Wholesale Funding (to the above Financing vehicles)
(i)   Types and sources
   - a.   Debt: DFIs, Governments
   - b.   Equity: GEEREF, Governments, DFIs
   - c.   Grants: CTF, GEF, Governments

(ii)   Terms
   - a.   At market interest rates: EBRD
   - b.   At zero or subsidised interest rates: Thailand EERF, GEF
   - c.   Contingent grants or grants: GEF, EC

Subsidy
   a. Investment Grant: BEERECL, PROSOL
   b. Concessional loans (below market interest rates): Thailand REEF
   c. Guarantees: CHUEE, IBRD 2nd ECP China,
   d. Technical Assistance
   e. Patient equity: GEEREF, FIDEME
   f. Feed-in tariffs

Technical Assistance
   a. Project preparation
   b. Capacity building
   c. Information/outreach campaigns

Energy utility involvement
   a. As a hub: IFC/GEF CHUEE
   b. To enhance credit and/or facilitate collection and lower its cost: integrated loan payment and utility bill: PROSOL
   c. As a one stop shop: CHUEE

Carbon finance

2. Main public finance mechanisms

Pfms	Description	Financial barriers addressed	Financial market characteristics	Applicable market segment	LP	Example
credit line for senior debt	Debt facilities provided to commercial FIs for on-lending, and usually on a full-recourse basis. Typically meets 50-80% of project cost. Can also be offered on limited or non-recourse basis depending on FIs willingness to take project risk.	(i) lack of funds among FIs; (ii) shortage of long-term funds; (iii) high interest rates.	Underdeveloped financial markets where there is lack of liquidity and borrowing costs are high.	(i) large scale and medium scale RE and EE; (ii) wholesale loans for energy access market.	L to M	Thailand Energy Efficiency Revolving Fund; CORFO credit line programme.
Credit line for subordinated debt	Debt provided to CFIs for on-lending, in combination with senior debt to improve security for senior lender. Typically meets 10-25% of project cost. Can take other legal structures such as convertible debt or preferred shares.	(i) lack of available equity among project sponsors; (ii) restrictive debt-to-equity ratio.	Lack of liquidity in both equity and debt markets.	(i) medium and small scale.	M to H	E+Co CAREC Fund; FIDEME Fund.

Pfms	Description	Financial barriers addressed	Financial market characteristics	Applicable market segment	LP	Example
Guarantee	A risk management tool shares in the credit risk of project loans which CFIs make with their own resources. Typically covers 50-80% of outstanding loan.	(i) high credit risks, particularly perceived risks.	Existence of guarantee institutions and experience with credit enhancements.	(i) large-scale and grid-connected RE; (ii) medium scale RE and EE; (iii) energy access market.	M to H	IFC/GEF Hungary Energy Efficiency co-Financing Programme.
Project loan facilities	Debt facilities organized by entities other than CFIs and providing financing to clean energy project on a project finance basis. Can be combined with commercial financing or can be provided as credit lines to small CFIs for on-lending.	(i) lack of experience with clean energy project finance; (ii) inability or unwillingness to underwrite loans on a project finance basis; (ii) lack of long term lending capacity.	Strong political environment to enforce contractual obligations and enabling laws for special purpose entity.	(i) medium and small scale RE and EE.	L to M	India Renewable Energy Development Agency; Bulgaria Energy Fund.
Soft loan programme	Provides debt capital at concessional interest rate.	(i) financing gap during project development stage.	Lack of liquidity or interest in the target sector.	(i) medium to small scale EE and RE.	L to M	Massachuss. Sustainable Energy Economic Development Initiatives
Equity fund	Equity investment in clean energy companies and/or clean energy projects. Can be targeted at specific market segments, or full range.	(i) lack of long term capital; (ii) restrictive debt-to-equity ratio requirements.	Highly developed capital markets to allow equity investors an exit from investees.	(i) large-scale grid-connected RE; (ii) energy companies	M to H	(i) ADB Clean Energy private equity investment fund; (ii) EE Clean Energy Group.
Venture capital	Equity investment in technology company.	Lack of risk capital for new technology development.	Developed capital markets to allow eventual exits.	Any new technology.	M to H	China Environment Fund; Carbon Trust VC Fund.
Carbon finance	Monetization of future cash flows from the advanced sales of CERs which can be used to finance project investment costs or enhance project revenues. Can also be in the form of carbon delivery guarantee to minimize the risk of under-delivery of carbon credits.	(i) lack of early stage project development capital; (ii) lack of cash flow to provide additional security to project lenders; (iii) uncertainty in the delivery of carbon credits.	Developing countries or emerging markets.	(i) large-scale grid-connected RE; (ii) medium-scale RE and EE; (iii) programme of activities such as in energy access market.	M to H	ADB Asia Pacific Carbon Fund

Pfms	Description	Financial barriers addressed	Financial market characteristics	Applicable market segment	LP	Example
Project Development Grants	Grants that are "loaned" without interest or repayment until projects demonstrate financial viability.	(i) lack of sufficient capital during project development stage; (ii) costly development process.	Developing countries or emerging markets.	(i) large-scale grid-connected RE considered high risk with lengthy project preparation cycle.	M to H	Canadian Green Municipal Funds
Loan Softening Programmes	Grants to help CFIs begin lending their own capital to end-users initially on concessional terms.	(i) lack of FIs interest in lending to new sector; (ii) limited knowledge of market demand.	Competitive local lending markets.	(i) medium to small scale EE and RE.	M	MNRE/IREDA SWH interest subsidy programme; UNEP Indian Solar Loan Programme.
Inducement Prizes	"Ex-Ante Prizes" to stimulate R&D or technology developments. Still needs to be proven in the climate sector.	(i) high and risky technology development costs and spill-over effects.	Sufficient financing availability to deploy winning technologies.	Any technology sector.	M to H	X Prize
Grants for Technical Assistance	Funds aimed at building the capacity of market actors. Technical Assistance programmes include: (i) market research and marketing support; (ii) transaction structuring support and development of new financial products; (iii) staff training and business planning; (iv) establishment of technical standards and engineering due diligence; (v) market aggregation programmes to build deal flow.	(i) lack of investment ready project; (ii) lack of skills and knowledge among market actors.	Developing countries or emerging markets.	(i) all segments in the supply side of the market; (ii) demand side; (iii) FIs.	H	GEF, WB, ADB, UNEP, UNDP TA programmes.

Source: UNEP SEFI "Public Finance Mechanisms to mobilize investment in climate change mitigation", 2008.

3. DFIs and climate mitigation financing

The following is a cursory review of the climate mitigation financing activities of selected Development Finance Institutions (DFIs): ADB, AfDB, AFD, EBRD, EIB, IDB, World Bank Group, as well as the Climate Investment Funds.

Carbon finance (the purchase of carbon credits for the account of third parties), financing granted as implementing agency of the GEF and technical assistance activities are not covered in this appendix, for the sake of brevity. The following focuses on these DFIs' climate mitigation strategy and targets, and achievements in terms of financing commitments and (if available) GHG emission reductions. The financing instruments that DFIs deploy to meet clients' needs are summarised in the table below.

Table III.1: DFIs' Financing Instruments

	Sovereign loan	Non-sovereign loan	Equity	Partial risk guarantee	Partial credit guarantee	Concessional funding
Public sector	ADB, AFD, AfDB, EBRD, IBRD, IDB	ADB, AFD, AfDB, EBRD, EIB		IBRD	AfDB, IBRD, IDB, CTF	ADF, AsDF, AFD, CTF, FSO, IDA, KfW
Private sector		ADB, AFD, EBRD, IFC, IDB, IFC	ADB, AFD, AfDB, EBRD, EIB, IFC, MIF	AfDB, EBRD, IBRD, IFC, MIGA, ADB, IDB	ADB, AFD, AfDB, EBRD, IBRD, IDB, IFC	AFD, CTF

Source: J. Ligot.

The terms and conditions of these financing instruments are not discussed in this appendix. Please refer to the DFIs' websites.

(i) African Development Bank (AfDB)

Established in 1964 and headquartered (temporarily) in Tunis, the AfDB is owned by 77 member countries, including 53 regional (recipient) countries. In 2008 it approved 133 projects for a total commitment of 3.53bn (€3.9bn, $5.4bn) units of account (UA) (non-grant: UA 2.97bn).

• *STRATEGY AND TARGETS*

AfDB Board of Directors approved the Clean Energy Investment Framework (CEIF) in March 2008. The CEIF advocates a three-pronged approach: (i) maximize clean energy options through renewable energy and clean technology; (ii) emphasize energy efficiency; and (iii) enable African countries to participate effectively in carbon credit markets by meeting the requirements of the Clean Development Mechanism (CDM). Apparently, AfDB has set no targets.

• *ACHIEVEMENTS*

Apparently, AfDB does not publish numbers in relation to its climate-related financing and emission reductions.

(ii) Agence Française de Développement (AFD)

Founded in 1941 (as Caisse centrale de la France Libre or Central Fund of Free France) and headquartered in Paris, AFD is a bilateral development bank owned by the French state, which now operates in over 60 countries.

In 2008, AFD's total commitments reached a record €4.5bn (€3.1bn excluding France overseas territories).

• *STRATEGY AND TARGETS*

Preserving "Global Public Goods", especially climate change mitigation and adaptation, is one of the three broad missions given to AFD by the French Government, together with fighting poverty and inequalities and supporting sustainable economic growth. AFD has therefore integrated climate change into all its strategies by supporting low carbon investments and by integrating climate change adaptation in its development actions.

- *ACHIEVEMENTS*

In 2008, AFD has financed 34 projects mitigating GHG emissions, for a total amount of €1.1bn. Cumulative commitments over the period 2005-2008 reached €2.6bn.

The carbon impact of 12 of these 34 projects has been assessed through the AFD Carbon Footprint Tool (Bilan Carbone®), which aims to quantify *ex ante* emission reductions stemming from a project. Overall, these 12 projects will avoid 3.3 MtCO$_2$-equ. p.a.

In common with IFC and EBRD, a significant share of AFD's climate mitigation financing is channelled through dedicated EERE facilities via local banks, e.g. China, India, Mauritius, South Africa, Tunisia, Turkey.

AFD, in collaboration with Japan International Cooperation Agency (JICA), is pioneering a new approach in Indonesia, where it supports the government in transforming its economy with a comprehensive climate strategy, in order to reduce the country's carbon footprint. The "Climate Change Policy Loan" (CCPL) was designed in accordance with Indonesian national strategy on climate change and supports through budgetary aid a wide-ranging three-year action plan (the policy matrix), which may be revised each year. AFD seeks to replicate this experience in other major developing economies.

(iii) Asian Development Bank (ADB)

Established in 1966 and headquartered in Manila, ADB's mission is to help its developing member countries reduce poverty and improve the quality of life of their people. ADB is owned by 67 members, of which 48 are from the Asia-Pacific region.

ADB approved 98 loans (86 projects) valued at $10.5bn in 2008, of which sovereign lending amounted to $8.7bn for 83 loans (72 projects or programs), non-sovereign public sector loans to two state-owned enterprises amounted to $300mln and thirteen non-sovereign loans (12 projects or programs) amounted to $1.5bn. Out of the total amount, $1.8 billion is from the Asian Development Fund (ADF), a concessional window to support equitable and sustainable development for its Developing Member Countries (DMC).

- *STRATEGY AND TARGETS*

Addressing the causes and consequences of climate change is a priority of ADB's broader agenda of environmentally sustainable growth in Asia and the Pacific as stated in its long-term strategic framework Strategy 2020. ADB's new Energy Policy[134] represents a coherent translation of important elements of Strategy 2020. Such elements prioritize energy-related objectives and aim at helping developing member countries provide reliable, adequate and affordable energy for inclusive growth in a socially, economically and environmentally sustainable way.

Under this framework, one of ADB's operational goals is to escalate assistance to support environmentally sustainable development, including efforts to address climate change and greenhouse gas emissions, as a significant share of the lending portfolio. ADB set a target to boost its investments in clean energy to $1 billion per year from 2008 to 2012. ADB's clean energy investments in 2008 surpassed its $1bn target (see Table III.2 for a summary of ADB's clean energy investments from 2003-2008). In response a new target of $2bn by 2013 was set by the new energy policy.

ADB's clean energy program also contributes to its broader climate change initiative which aims to integrate climate change considerations into planning and investment, to ensure continued economic growth and a sustainable future for all in Asia and the Pacific. To do this, ADB has been scaling-up its climate change actions by mainstreaming climate change into its core financing operations to promote the integration of climate change mitigation and adaptation considerations in development activities throughout the region. Working with multiple partners, ADB continues to intensify its efforts to help fill gaps in financing, capacities, and knowledge on this issue.

Table III.2: ADB's clean energy investments (2003-2008)

Year	Approved investments* ($Mln)	Clean energy component of investments135 ($mln)
2003	1,263	226
2004	1,356	306
2005	1,805	757
2006	1,612	657
2007	1,801	668
2008	3,023	1,693**

Source: ADB.
*Total approved investments that have clean energy components.
** Private sector projects accounted for $629mln

ACHIEVEMENTS

ADB provided close to $1.7bn for clean energy investments in 2008, far exceeding the target of $1bn. This investment is expected to result in significant levels of energy savings and avoided CO_2 emissions, with a total of 4,703 MW of installed generating capacity purely from renewable energy resources, an abatement of 30 million tons of CO_2 per year, and 81,074 GWh saved through enhanced efficiency (see figure 10.1).

Figure 10.1: **Clean Energy Activities Toward Outputs, Outcomes and Impacts in 2008**

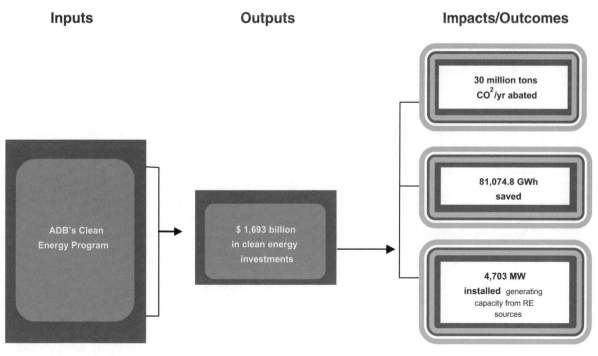

Source: ADB.

(iii) European Bank for Reconstruction and Development

Established in 1991 and headquartered in London, the EBRD supports 29 countries from Central and Eastern Europe, the Caucasus and Central Asia in their transition to fully-fledged market economies primarily through private sector operations.

It financed 302 projects in 2008 for a total commitment amount of €5.1bn supporting investments worth €12.9bn.

- *STRATEGY AND TARGETS*

EBRD's climate strategy is laid down in its Sustainable Energy Initiative (SEI), which originally set a financing target of €1.5bn in new financing commitments for EERE for the three-year period 2006-2008. The recently adopted SEI Phase 2 (2009-11) sets the following targets:
- (i)   Financing target range of €3 to 5bnn for total project value of €9 to 15bn;
- (ii) Carbon emissions reduction range of 25 to 30 million tonnes per annum; and
- (iii) Technical assistance grant funding target of €100mln and investment grant funding target of €250mln.

- *ACHIEVEMENTS*

SEI Phase 1 (2006-2008) financing reached €2.7bn (leveraging ca €14bn worth of investments, not all with an exclusive climate mitigation focus) through 166 projects in 24 countries of operations, enabling EBRD to exceed its three-year target by 77%.

Reflecting the strategic integration and mainstreaming of energy efficiency and climate change into the EBRD operations, the share of SEI activity increased from 15% of total EBRD investment in 2006 to close to 20% in 2008. EE accounted for about 80% of total EBRD investments, reflecting the region's high energy wastage and EBRD's strong focus on the corporate sector. Russia attracted 28% of the total amount. SEI Phase 1 activities are estimated to lead to 21 million tonnes of annual CO_2 emission reductions (equivalent to the total annual emissions of Croatia) and over 8 million tonnes of oil equivalent in annual energy savings (equivalent to over three times the total annual energy consumption of Albania).

Table III.3: SEI Phase 1 results by region, 2006-08

Geography	Amount signed in €mln	% share	Number of operations	% share
East Europe/Caucasus	835	31	49	30
South-eastern Europe	462	17	41	25
Central Asia	170	6	11	7
Central Europe/Baltic	339	13	22	13
Russia	755	28	37	22
Regional	104	4	6	4
Total	2665	100	166	100

Source: EBRD.

Table III.4: SEI Phase 1 results by area of activity, 2006-08

	Amount signed	% share	Number of operations	% share
Industrial EE	679	25	56	34
Credit lines to local banks	362	14	31	19
Power sector EE	1010	38	19	11
RE	227	9	14	8
Municipal EE	388	15	46	28
Total	2665	100	166	100

Source: EBRD.

- *INSTRUMENTS*

EBRD uses the full palette of financing instruments: from sovereign loans to full-risk equity. While a large share of investments in the power and municipal sector involved non-sovereign loans to public entities, financing to the industrial and renewable energy sectors was predominantly private (overall 64% of SEI funds went to the private sector). Credit lines involve commercial loans to local banks, and account for close to 15% of EBRD's overall investment (see item 21 in Section 2.2.8 above).

(iv) Inter-American Development Bank (IDB)

Established in 1959 and headquartered in Washington DC, the IDB is owned by 48 countries, of which 26 are borrowing countries from the region.

In 2008, the IDB approved 136 private and public sector projects for a total investment of $11.4bn in loans and guarantees.

- *STRATEGY AND TARGETS*

IDB's Sustainable Energy and Climate Change Initiative (SECCI) was launched in 2007, in an effort to provide comprehensive sustainability options in areas related to the energy, water, and environmental sectors, in addition to building climate resilience in key priority sectors, which are vulnerable to the impacts of climate change throughout the Latin American and Caribbean countries. SECCI's activities have been supported by two Funds put forward by the IDB and by International Donors. In 2009, SECCI activities were consolidated and the Sustainable Energy and Climate Change Unit (INE/ECC) was established within the Bank's administrative structure.

- *ACHIEVEMENTS*

IDB's investment in projects with a direct impact on climate change mitigation has been steadily growing during the last years.

Table III.5: IDB's low-carbon approved investments

Year	Low-carbon approved investments (in $mln)	Percent of total investment
2003-2006 (average)	62.5	1%
2007	138	2%
2008	638	8%
2009*	1,673	n.a.

Source: IDB.
*Including pipeline

(v) European Investment Bank (EIB)

Established in 1958 by the Treaty of Rome creating the European Community, the European Investment Bank (EIB) is owned by the member states of the European Union. While the main task of the Bank is to contribute towards the integration, balanced development and economic and social cohesion of the EU Member States., it can also operate outside of the EU based on specific mandates decided by the EU, notably in the Enlargement Countries (candidates to EU membership), Neighbour Countries to the South and to the East, Asia and Latin America, the African, Caribbean and Pacific States (ACP and OCT), and the Republic of South Africa.

EIB has become the largest multilateral financier in the world, with €59.3bn worth of projects approved in 2008 (€57.6bn signed), of which €6.1bn outside the EU (also €6.1bn signed).

- *STRATEGY AND TARGETS*

Implementation of the relevant EU legislation and policies and support to the international obligations endorsed by the Union constitute the main pillars for the EIB climate change strategic approach.

Environmental sustainability, including the fight against climate change, is mainstreamed in all EIB operational priorities and objectives both inside and outside the EU.

This is reflected also in all EIB's sectoral policies and strategies (for instance, transport and energy) and in the Bank's Statement on Environmental and Social Principles and Standards –the EIB's policy document on environmental and social sustainability. Mitigation (and adaptation) considerations are consequently integrated in the operational activities of the Bank and systematically included in all EIB project evaluations. Mitigation potential is screened together with the capacity of projects to generate carbon credits.

Lending for renewable energy and energy efficiency has substantially increased in recent years, as, in general, environmental lending.

The EIB has launched initiatives to assess both its corporate carbon footprint and that of the projects that it finances.

Mitigation (and adaptation) financing activities are developed in the framework of the sector lending policies adopted by the EIB including in particular energy, transport, water, waste, and research, development and innovation.

EIB's operational initiatives include:
(i)   Investments to accelerate the development and deployment of cost-effective low carbon technologies (long-term R&D, early-stage commercialization and demonstration; clean transport; carbon capture and storage);
(ii) Support to reduction of emissions from deforestation and degradation (REDD);
(iii) Scaling up lending in sectors particularly vulnerable to climate change and to governments (including local authorities) that need to undertake adaptive action to climate change (e.g. water sector); and
(iv) TA mechanisms.

The EIB has also developed new financial products to facilitate renewable energy and energy efficiency investments such as framework loans (for smaller projects), structured financing and specific investment funds.

The only EIB hard target to date is that at least 20% of its lending for energy in the EU be for RE projects. EIB can finance up to 75% of project costs (against its standard 50%) if the project will yield substantial carbon savings. While coal and lignite plants can still be financed by the EIB, they must replace existing ones and achieve a decrease of at least 20% in carbon intensity.

A reinforced climate change policy is being prepared, which will bring together existing and recent new activities into a consistent comprehensive package, and will include targets.

- *ACHIEVEMENTS*
Since 2004, the share of EERE in total EIB energy lending has risen from 25% to more than 50% of the Bank's total.

In 2008, EIB signed about €8bn worth of projects within the EU which contribute to the combat against climate change (this represent about 15% of its total lending in the region). Outside the EU, in emerging and developing countries, around 30% of total lending, worth around €2bn has had a climate change focus. EIB achieved its hard target for RE lending target in 2008 with €2.2bn, more than 20% of total energy lending.

Loans contributing to projects involving improvements in energy efficiency amounted to € 730 million in 2008, which was the first year when the revised EIB EE project indicators became available

(vi) World Bank Group

Established in 1944, the International Bank for Reconstruction and Development (IBRD) supports development and poverty alleviation in developing countries and countries in transition. It has 186 members.

Today the World Bank Group comprises the International Bank for Reconstruction and Development (IBRD), the International Development Agency (IDA) (the first two constitute the so-called "World Bank"), the International Finance Corporation (IFC), the Multilateral Investment Guarantee Agency (MIGA) and the International Centre for Settlement of Investment Disputes (ICSID).

In Fiscal Year 2009 (ending on 30th June 2009), the World Bank Group committed $59bn, a record high, in support of 767 projects.

Table III.6: World Bank Group Commitments 2008-2009 (in $bn)

World Bank Group	FY09*	FY08
IBRD	32.9	13.5
IDA	14.0	11.2
IFC	10.5+	11.4**
MIGA	1.4	2.1
TOTAL	58.8	38.2

Source: WB Group.
*Unaudited numbers as of July 1.
**Own account only.

- ## *STRATEGY AND TARGETS*

In 2004, at the Bonn International RE conference, the WB Group committed to increase its "new" EE and RE investments[136] by 20% each year over the period 2005-2009, compared to a baseline commitment of $209mln (equal to the average of the previous three years).

In 2008, the WB Group adopted a "Strategic Framework on Development and Climate Change" which sets new, more ambitious, targets of increasing new EE and RE financing by 30% per year between FY 2008-2012.

The framework contains six action areas that are aligned with the Bali Action Plan and aim to:
(i)   Support climate action in country-led development processes;
(ii)   Mobilize additional concessional and innovative finance;
(iii) Facilitate the development of market-based financing mechanisms;
(iv)   Leverage private sector resources;
(v)   Support accelerated development and deployment of new technologies; and
(vi)   Step up policy research, knowledge and capacity building.

- ## *ACHIEVEMENTS*

The WB group recently released numbers for its financing of RE and EE projects over the last five years. It surpassed its "Bonn commitment" by over three times, with cumulative commitments of $7bn in "new" EE and RE, compared to a Bonn target of $1.9bn (see table III.7 below). During this period, the WB Group approved 366 RE and EE projects in 90 countries.

In FY 2009, EE accounted for over 50% of total EERE commitments, similar to FY 2008. However, in FY 2009 the share of large hydro (>10MW) dropped considerably (from $1,007mln to $177mln), while that of new RE increased substantially (from $476 to $1,427mln).

Table III.7: WB Group financing of EERE projects (2005-2009) – in $mln

	FY05	FY06	FY07	FY08	FY09	FY05-FY09
New Re & EE	463	1,105	682	1,665	3,128	7,043
Large hydro	538	250	751	1,007	177	2,724
Target for new RE and EE (Bonn Commitment)	251	301	361	433	520	1,866

Source: WB Group.

Table III.8: World Bank Group financing for RE and EE in FY 2009 – in $mln

Source of funds	Energy efficiency	Hydro > 10mw	New renewable energy	Total
World Bank	1,386	43	840	2,269
IBRD/IDA	1,311	43	804	2,157
Global Environment Facility	68	-	15	83
Carbon Finance	8	-	21	29
IFC Own Funds	315	135	587	1,036
Total	1,701	177	1,427	3,305

Source: WB Group.

(vii) The Climate Investment Funds

The Climate Investment Funds (CIF) aims at reducing the cost of climate actions for developing countries and catalyzing transformational technologies and project approaches for climate change mitigation and adaptation. Approved by the World Bank Group board in July 2008 and supported by $6.1bn in donor funds, the CIF are an interim instrument with specific sunset clauses linked to agreements on the future of the climate change regime.

The CIFs are managed by the World Bank and implemented jointly with the Regional Development Banks (AfDB, ADB, EBRD, and IDB).

The CIF are comprised of two trust funds: the Clean Technology Fund (CTF) and the Strategic Climate Fund (SCF). Each fund has a specific scope and objective as well as a specific governance and administrative structure. The CTF will promote investments in clean technologies and the SCF will serve as an overarching fund that can support targeted programs with dedicated funding to provide financing to pilot new approaches with potential for scaled-up transformational action aimed at a specific climate change challenge or sectoral response. The main focus in this appendix is on the CTF.

The CTF will focus on high abatement opportunities at the country level (but could support sub-regional and regional initiatives) and will be technology-neutral. Financing from the CTF could cover, among other low carbon technologies, one or more of the following proposed transformational investments:

(i) Power Sector

    a. Increase substantially the share of renewable energy (including solar, wind, hydropower, biomass and bio-fuels, geothermal, and waste-to-energy), in the total electricity supply;

    b. Switch to highly efficient gas plants resulting in reduced carbon intensity of power generation;

    c. Achieve significant greenhouse gas reductions by adopting best available coal technologies with substantial improvements in energy efficiency and readiness for implementation of carbon capture and storage;

    d. Promote grid interconnection schemes that support lower carbon energy production and/or significant transmission efficiency improvements;

    e.   Large reductions in transmission and distribution losses (new T&D systems using energy-efficient technologies or retrofits/upgrades); and

    f.   Adopt utility managed demand management programs for retail and wholesale customers.

(ii) Transportation

Modal shift to public transportation in major metropolitan areas, with a substantial change in the number of passenger trips by public transport;
Improve fuel economy standards and fuel switching; and
Energy Efficiency in buildings, industry and agriculture.

(iii) arge-scale adoption of energy efficient technologies that lowers energy consumption per unit of output (by at least 5%) in:
    a.   Building design, insulation, lighting and appliances;

    b.   District heating; and

    c.   Energy-intensive industries and equipment (motors and boilers).

Investment plans and the proposed pipeline of projects and programs will be assessed and prioritized on the basis of the following four sets of criteria:
(i)   Potential for Long-Term GHG Emissions Savings
(ii)   Demonstration Potential
(iii) Development impact
(iv) Implementation potential.

The CTF will be able to provide, through Regional Development Banks, preparation grants, concessional loans and guarantees. The latter can be of the two following kinds:

(i)   Loan Guarantees covering the loss on account of debt service default for lenders up to an agreed portion of the actual loss, with a view to extending maturities of commercial loans for low carbon projects, so that they are competitive with base case technologies or they address specific incremental operating or construction risks that could cause default.
(ii)   Contingent Finance disbursed to the project upon underperformance of a low carbon technology and where such risk is not commercially insurable at reasonable costs or has occurred beyond the period for which commercial insurance is available.

CTF investment plans have been approved for Egypt, Mexico and Turkey, with aggregate CTF funding in excess of $1bn.

4. Legislative and regulatory frameworks by country

Country	Policies (EE&RE)
Albania	Energy Efficiency Law (2005) requiring: (i) National Energy Efficiency Programme to reduce losses to 6%; (ii) Labelling of electrical appliances; (iii) Energy audits; and (iv) Creation of an Energy Efficiency Fund. Kyoto Protocol ratified and entered into force on 01/04/2005 (non-Annex B).
Algeria	Kyoto Protocol ratified on 16/02/2005 (non-Annex B).
Angola	Kyoto Protocol ratified on 8/05/2007 (non-Annex B).
Argentina	There are no laws to specifically promote energy efficiency in Argentina. Two bills were put forward in 2003 and 2005 but expired because they were not passed by the established deadline. Energy efficiency regulations are set out in the following instruments: (i) Programme for the Rational Use of Electrical Energy (PUREE) (2004) and (ii) Programme for the Rational and Efficient Use of Energy (PONUREE). Kyoto Protocol ratified on 28/09/2001 (non-Annex B)
Armenia	Law on Energy Conservation and Renewable Energy (2004). Well-developed framework for ESCOs through international cooperation programmes. Kyoto Protocol ratified on 25/04/2003 (non-Annex B).
Australia	The Building Code of Australia is currently being amended to reflect new provisions on EE in buildings. Mandatory legislation related to EE for selected electrical and electronic products in Australia; regulatory approaches include mandatory approved energy labels and Minimum Energy Performance Standards (MEPS). Kyoto Protocol ratified on 12/12/2007 (Annex B).
Azerbaijan	Law and Presidential Decree on Utilization of Energy Resources (1996). It plans the implementation of EE standards, the grant of subsidies for the rational use of energy, the promotions of FDI and international cooperation in the field of energy efficiency. Kyoto Protocol ratified on 28/09/2000 (non-Annex B).
Bahrain	Kyoto Protocol ratified on 31/1/2006 (non-Annex B).
Bangladesh	Accession to the Kyoto Protocol on 22/10/2001 (non-Annex B)
Barbados	The main mechanisms for promoting energy efficiency are the following: (i) The Government grants companies a tax exemption equal to 150% of the amount invested in energy efficient projects; (ii) The Government allows individuals to seek tax exemptions for money spent on energy audits to assess how to improve the energy efficiency of their business or home; and (iii) The Government allows individuals to seek tax exemptions for money spent on retrofitting their business or home to improve energy efficiency. Kyoto Protocol ratified on 07/08/2000 (non-Annex B).
Belarus	Law on Energy Savings (1998). A plan for 2006-2010 was proposed and adopted by Presidential Decree 399 (2005). Other provisions in specific ministerial plans and industry regulations. Kyoto Protocol ratified on 26/08/2005 (Annex B but no compulsory reduction targets).
Benin	Kyoto Protocol ratified on 25/02/2002 (non-Annex B).
Bhutan	Accession to the Kyoto Protocol on 26/08/2002 (non-Annex B).
Bolivia	Supreme Decree 29272 (September 2007) establishes the National Development Plan "Bolivia: dignified, sovereign, productive and democratic to live well" and strategic guidelines for 2006-2011. The Plan includes alternative energy supply projects aimed at improving the quality of life and the economic income of the rural population. The National Energy Efficiency Programme was approved under Supreme Decree 29466 (March 2008) with a view to establishing policy action and implementing projects to encourage the rational, efficient and effective use of energy. Kyoto Protocol ratified on 30/11/1999 (non-Annex B).
Bosnia and Herzegovina	No specific regulations, targets or incentives. Efficiency is one of the goals of the mid-term development strategy for the energy sector (2004). Kyoto Protocol ratified on 16/04/2007 (non-Annex B).
Botswana	Kyoto Protocol ratified on 8/08/2003 (non-Annex B).

Country	Policies (EE&RE)
Brazil	The Brazilian National Institute of Metrology, Standardization and Quality (INMETRO) instituted a labelling programme in 1984. This includes activities to rate energy equipment and provide information to consumers by labelling a wide range of equipment models, including household appliances, electric engines, stoves, gas water heaters and solar collectors. The National Electricity Conservation Programme (PROCEL) was created in 1985 under the auspices of the Ministry of Energy and Mines and is coordinated by the Brazilian electric power company ELETROBRAS. The Energy Efficiency Programme, run by the National Electricity Regulatory Agency (ANEEL) and set out in Law 9.991/2000, establishes a wire charge whereby a percentage of the utility's revenues are earmarked for energy efficiency, which generates a significant budget for energy efficiency activities. In acknowledgement of similar potential for energy saving in the fuel sector, the Brazilian Ministry of Energy and Mines launched the National Programme for the Rational Use of Oil Derivatives (CONPET) in 1991. This Programme is coordinated by representatives of the Federal Government, the private sector and implemented using technical, administrative and financial resources provided by the Brazilian oil company PETROBRAS. At the federal level, a major step to improve energy efficiency in Brazil was taken with the enactment of Law 10.295 on Energy Efficiency in October 2001, which sets out the National Policy for the Conservation and Rational Use of Energy. Kyoto Protocol ratified on 23/08/2002 (non-Annex B).
Brunei Darussalam	The Brunei Energy Association plays a major role in the development of the energy industry and in disseminating information on energy conservation and efficiency. Accession to the Kyoto Protocol on 20/8/2009 (non-Annex B)
Burkina Faso	Kyoto Protocol ratified on 31/03/2005 (non-Annex B).
Burundi	Kyoto Protocol ratified on 18/10/2001 (non-Annex B)
Cambodia	Energy Centre Cambodia was founded in 2008 as a non-governmental organization established by national and international experts for promoting energy efficiency and conservation (EE&C) and renewable energy (RE) activities Accession to the Kyoto Protocol on 22/08/2002 (non-Annex B).
Cameroon	Kyoto Protocol ratified on 28/08/2002 (non-Annex B).
Canada	Energy Efficiency Act (1995) and periodically revised, provides for: (i) A minimum energy-performance level for a large number of energy-using products, such as appliances, lighting, heating and air-conditioning systems; (ii) Labelling schemes to inform buyers; and (iii) EcoEnergy Initiative which provides capital to boost efficient uses of energy and clean energy supplies. Kyoto Protocol ratified on 17/12/2002 (Annex B, compulsory 6% reduction target).
Cape Verde	Kyoto Protocol ratified on 10/02/2006 (non-Annex B).
Central African Republic	Kyoto Protocol ratified on 18/03/2008 (non-Annex B).
Chile	In 2005, the Government of Chile began to play a leading role in the promotion of energy efficiency, making efficiency a key component of energy policy, and launched the National Energy Efficiency Programme (PPEE). A Commission made up of representatives from national institutions, the private sector, local governments and civil society involved in energy conservation was established and agreements on targets were signed with several public agencies. Kyoto Protocol ratified on 26/08/2002 (non-Annex B).
China	The Energy Conservation Law was promulgated by the 28th Standing Committee Meeting of the 8th National People's Congress on 1 November 1997. The law came into effect on 1 January 1998. In addition to making achievement of energy efficiency goals a component of the performance evaluation of local cadres, the importance of energy conservation as a national policy has been bolstered in the amended law. Approval of the Kyoto Protocol on 30/08/2002 (non-Annex B).
Colombia	One of the most important energy efficiency initiatives in Colombia was the enactment of Law 697 in October 2001, which, inter alia, promotes the efficient and rational use of energy and the use of alternative energies. Article 4 of the Law establishes that the Ministry of Energy and Mines is the entity responsible for promoting, organizing and ensuring the development and monitoring of programmes for the rational and efficient use of energy in accordance with the Law. Article 5 decrees the creation of the Programme for the Rational and Efficient Use of Energy and the Use of Alternative Energy Sources (PROURE). In July 2007, the Office of the President of the Republic issued Decree 2501, promoting practices to further the rational and efficient use of electrical energy. Kyoto Protocol ratified on 10/04/2008 (non-Annex B).
Comoros	Kyoto Protocol ratified on 10/04/2008 (non-Annex B).
Congo	Kyoto Protocol ratified on 12/02/2007 (non-Annex B).
Congo (Democratic Republic)	Kyoto Protocol ratified on 23/03/2005.

Country	Policies (EE&RE)
The Cook Islands	Kyoto Protocol ratified on 27/08/01 (non-Annex B).
Costa Rica	Law 7447 on the Regulation of the Rational Use of Energy has been in force in Costa Rica since 1994 and its Regulations under Decree 25.584 since 1996. Several other decrees and directives have been issued on the rational use of energy resources. Kyoto Protocol ratified on 09/08/2002 (non-Annex B).
Cote d'Ivoire	Kyoto Protocol ratified on 23/04/2007 (non-Annex B).
Croatia	Energy efficiency legislation is based on the Energy Act, which treats EE as a matter of national interest. A National Action Plan was drafted in 2008. An Environmental Protection and Energy Efficiency Fund was established in 2003. Act on Efficient Use of Energy is currently under preparation. Kyoto Protocol ratified on 30/05/2007 (Annex B, compulsory 5% reduction target).
Cuba	Cuba's "energy revolution" generated major changes in how the country produces and uses energy. The basic objective of the process is to radically change electricity generation, distribution and final consumption patterns, mainly by promoting energy efficiency. The programme took off on a large scale in 2005. Given the magnitude of the programme, the National People's Assembly agreed to make 2006 "Year of the Energy Revolution in Cuba". The main objectives are to: (i) Implement standards and a labelling system; (ii) Draw up a legal framework to promote the rational and efficient use of energy in Cuba; (iii) Modify electricity rates; (iv) Strengthen energy service companies and monitoring agencies; (v) Introduce the mandatory application of Quality Standard 220 in new buildings; (vi) Certify the energy efficiency of new projects during the investment process; (vii) Strengthen the energy departments of territorial agencies and governments; and (viii) Introduce the National Electricity Savings Award. Kyoto Protocol ratified on 30/04/2002 (non-Annex B).
Democratic People's Republic of Korea	Accession to the Kyoto Protocol on 27/04/05 (non-Annex B).
Djibouti	Kyoto Protocol ratified on 12/03/2002 (non-Annex B).
Dominican Republic	Law 125-01, modified by Law 186-07 of 6 August 2007, establishes the legal and institutional framework for activities in the electrical, hydrocarbons and alternative energy subsectors and for EE. The National Energy Commission is by law responsible for regulating and creating policies, standards and programmes on EE. In another legal initiative to encourage EE, compact fluorescent lamps have been made exempt from customs duties. Kyoto Protocol ratified on 12/02/2002 (non-Annex B).
Ecuador	In 2007, the Ministry of Energy and Mines was split into two ministries: the Ministry of Mines and Oil and the Ministry of Electricity and Renewable Energy. The latter is responsible for the development and follow-up of EE projects. The Ministry of Electricity and Renewable Energy's objectives include: (i) Returning planning to State control and modifying the energy grid; (ii) Increasing the coverage of electricity services; (iii) Strengthening and restructuring State energy agencies; (iv) Ensuring the reliability and quality of supply, with a view to achieving self-sufficiency in 2012; (v) Promoting the efficient and rational use of energy through EE initiatives in all types of consumption (industrial, residential, commercial and public); and (vi) Furthering the regional integration of energy services. Executive Decree 1681 of May 2009 states that all Government institutions must set up an Energy Efficiency Committee to oversee the introduction of energy-saving measures in coordination with the Energy Efficiency Directorate of the Ministry of Electricity and Renewable Energy. Article 414 states that adequate cross-cutting measures to mitigate climate change by limiting greenhouse gas emissions shall be adopted. Kyoto Protocol ratified on 13/01/2000 (non-Annex B).

Egypt	Plans to produce 20% of electricity from RE till 2020, including a 12% contribution from wind energy (about 7200 MW grid-connected wind farms), with private investment to play a major role in realizing this goal. It is anticipated that about 400 MW/year will be undertaken by the private sector and New & Renewable Energy Authority (NREA) will carry out about 200 MW/year.
	New Electricity Law including RE & EE issues (Section 4, article 45- 49) provides for:
	(i) Establishment of Power plants using RE for electricity generation by:
	    a. Bidding system
	    b. BOO (min 15 years span); and
	(ii) Establishment of a Fund for Developing Electricity Generation from RE to support the electricity market.
	Kyoto Protocol ratified on 12/1/2005 (non-Annex B).

Country	Policies (EE&RE)
El Salvador	In August 2007, the Legislative Assembly of El Salvador issued Legislative Decree 404 on the Law to create the National Energy Council as the senior governing and normative authority on policy and strategy to promote the efficient development of the energy sector. The Council was created to establish strategic policies to promote the efficient development of the energy sector while guaranteeing the provision of basic services to the community and to promote the good use and rational consumption of energy sources. The tasks to be pursued under the National Energy Policy include: (i) The analysis of the long-term trends in energy demand and coverage of that demand; (ii) The promotion of the development of RE sources; (iii) The design of EE programmes; (iv) The harmonization of energy policy at the regional level; and (v) The establishment of subsidy schemes in the energy sector. Kyoto Protocol ratified on 30/11/1998 (non-Annex B).
Equatorial Guinea	Kyoto Protocol ratified on 08/11/2004 (non-Annex B).
Eritrea	Kyoto Protocol ratified on 28/07/2005 (non-Annex B).
Ethiopia	Kyoto Protocol ratified on 14/04/2005 (non-Annex B).
EU-27	The Council Directive 93/76/EEC of 13 September 1993 "to limit carbon dioxide emissions by improving energy efficiency" (SAVE) has urged Member States to draw up and implement programmes in the following fields: (i) Energy certification of buildings; (ii) Billing of heating, air conditioning and hot water costs based on actual consumption; (iii) Third-party financing for EE investments in the public sector; (iv) Thermal insulation of new buildings; (v) Regular inspection of boilers; and (vi) Energy audits. The Parliament and Council Directive 2006/32/EC of 5 April 2006 "on energy end-use efficiency and energy services and repealing Council Directive 93/76/EEC" is aimed at providing incentives to boost the demand for energy savings and it urges Member States to: (i) Set up an energy saving target of 9% by 2015 and take the necessary steps to achieve such goal; (ii) Take an exemplary stance by implementing an EE programme in the public sector; (iii) Ensure the cooperation of local utilities and energy distributors; (iv) Properly exchange and disseminate information; (v) Incentive energy saving through qualification, accreditation and certification schemes, financial instruments and tariff reforms; (vi) Create funds to subsidise the implementation of EE programmes; and (vii) Ensure the availability of energy audits even when they are not commercially viable. Another important directive is the Framework Appliance Energy Labelling Directive (92/75/EEC) adopted in 1992. It was followed by a number of implementing Directives for the following appliances: (i) Cold appliances (Directive 94/2/EC of 21.1.94); (ii) Clothes washers (Directive 95/12/EC of 23.5.95); (iii) Clothes dryers (Directive 95/13/EC of 23.5.95); (iv) Washer-dryers (Directive 96/60/EC of 23.5.95); (v) Dishwashers (Directive 97/17/EC of 7.5.97); (vi) Household lamps (Directive 98/11/EC of 27.1.98); (vii) Air-conditioners (Directive 2002/31/EC of 22.3.2002); (viii) Electric ovens (Directive 2002/40/EC of 8.5.2002); and (ix) Directive 2003/66/EC on refrigerators and freezers (A+/A++). In "An Energy Policy for Europe", a broader strategic document published by the Commission in 2007, the EU enunciates a more ambitious goal by setting the reduction of its primary energy use by 20% by 2020 (equivalent to an annual reduction of 780 million tones of CO_2). The paper also confirms EU commitment to its trading scheme and RE energy targets. The Kyoto Protocol was ratified by all Member States (including the 12 countries that joined the EU later) by the end of 2002 and it entered into force region-wide on 16 February 2005. All EU countries are included in Annex B (Annex I of the UNFCCC) and their emission reduction cap from the 1990 baseline has been distributed between its members.
Gabon	Kyoto Protocol ratified on 12/12/2006 (non-Annex B).
Gambia (The)	Kyoto Protocol ratified on 1/06/2001 (non-Annex B).
Georgia	EE is one of the main priorities in the Parliamentary Resolution on Main Directions of Georgia's State Energy Policy, to be achieved through: (i) A decrease in energy consumption and energy waste; and (ii) The introduction of co-generation systems. An Energy Efficiency Centre has been operative since 1998. Kyoto Protocol ratified on 16/06/1999 (non-Annex B).
Ghana	Kyoto Protocol ratified on 30/05/2003 (non-Annex B).

Country	Policies (EE&RE)
Guatemala	The Ministry of Energy and Mines compiled the 2008-2015 energy and mining policy document which sets out general guidelines for the upgrading and operations of the energy sector in the short and medium terms. The general goal is to contribute to the sustainable development of the country in energy terms while ensuring timely, continuous and quality supply at competitive prices. Guatemala has no government agencies or departments specifically devoted to energy saving. Plans are therefore under way to set up a National Energy Efficiency Council with the technical assistance of the Latin American Energy Organization and the financial support of the Canadian International Development Agency. Draft legislation to prohibit the sale of incandescent lamps in Guatemala is under consideration. In 2006, the clocks were brought forward by one hour between 29 April and 30 September and legislation was proposed to establish a trust fund to finance electrical energy saving measures. Kyoto Protocol ratified on 05/10/1999 (non-Annex B).
Guinea	Kyoto Protocol ratified on 6/09/2000 (non-Annex B).
Guinea Bissau	Kyoto Protocol ratified on 18/11/2005 (non-Annex B).
Guyana	There are no regulations, standards or laws to promote EE in the country. A study on investment strategy and policy for the electrical sector of Guyana is being prepared. Kyoto Protocol ratified on 05/08/2003 (non-Annex B).
Honduras	There have been several isolated initiatives to draft and implement EE policy lines, which have not achieved their purpose, largely due to a lack of political will. All action has involved Government measures implemented by executive decree. A bill on rational energy use has been proposed, the goal of which is to regulate EE programmes and rational energy-use programmes. The bill also provides for the creation of an EE institute, the implementation of policies on the rational use of energy, and the planning, follow-up and evaluation of projects. Kyoto Protocol ratified on 19/07/1999 (non-Annex B).
Iceland	Wide-ranging primary and secondary legislation. Emphasis on regional cooperation with Nordic countries. Governmental priority on the transport sector. Kyoto Protocol ratified on 23/05/2002 (Annex B, but emission cap assigned allows for an increase in GHG emissions).
India	Energy Conservation Act (2001) provides a legal framework, institutional arrangement and regulatory mechanism at the national and state levels to support EE. Various measures under this Act target different sectors. The Act also mandates the setting up of a Bureau of Energy Efficiency that will introduce stringent energy conservation norms for generation, supply and consumption. Accession to the Kyoto Protocol on 26/08/2002 (non-Annex B).
Indonesia	The National Energy Conservation Plan (Rencana Induk Konservasi Energi Nasional (RIKEN), Decree No. 100.K) is the Indonesian framework plan for the implementation of a national energy conservation programme. It outlines the strategies and activities to support the government's energy policy through general policy instruments. It also aims to enhance public awareness and attitude towards energy conservation and to create the appropriate climate that is conducive to energy conservation endeavours. RIKEN as a framework plan for the implementation of a nation wide energy conservation programme not been completely implemented, so the benefits that are expected through the implementation of RIKEN are also not yet fully realized. Kyoto Protocol was ratified on 03/12/2004 (non-Annex B).
Islamic Republic of Iran	Accession to Kyoto Protocol on 22/08/2005 (non-Annex B).
Iraq	New Energy Plan through 2020, including EE & RE: (i) Issuing instructions on the uses of internal lighting and air-conditioning for the governmental sectors; (ii) Limitation for commercial sector lighting levels; (iii) Issuance of the Thermal Insulation Code Buildings to restrict the sectors involved in building designs, permits and execution; and (iv) Using energy saving lamps (watt savers).
Israel	Energy Master Plan (2004) sets the main EE policy directives: (i) Information gathering on international experiences and best practices; (ii) Development of rigorous cost-benefit analysis methods; and (iii) Prioritization of EE as a matter of policy. Secondary legislation in favour of ESCOs since 2004. Kyoto Protocol ratified on 15/03/2004 (non-Annex B).
Jamaica	Apart from the Jamaica Energy Policy (1996), the Ministry of Energy, Mines and Telecommunications has implemented public education programmes over the last few years and is developing an implementation plan supported by a consortium of donor countries. The Ministry has also carried out EE activities in its own organizations. Kyoto Protocol was ratified on 28/06/1999 (non-Annex B).

Country	Policies (EE&RE)
Jordan	Master Strategy of Energy sector in Jordan (2007-2020): (i) Development of a legal framework for promoting RE and to achieve the 10% target for RE in 2020. The law is bound to be passed by Parliament soon. It allows the tariff for RE to be governed by power purchase agreements, following competitive bidding of a project developer. Moreover, a number of investment incentives are suggested, such as exemptions from income tax for facilities (75%) and from custom duties, sales and value added tax for all relevant materials; and (ii) Establishment of Jordan RE/EE Fund (JORDAN REEF). It will form the core of RE development in Jordan and include a RE subsidy window, a EE/RE Guarantee window, a Studies and Technical Cooperation window, a EE/RE Interest Rate Subsidy window and an Equity window. The government committed to provide JD 5 million from the general budget to the JORDAN REEF in its first three years of operation (2008-2010). It has also succeeded in attracting international funding from the French Development Agency (AFD), the French Global Environment Fund (FFEM), the World Bank/GEF and the EU. In 2008, the Jordanian Council of Ministers approved to exempt: (i) Many EE and RE devices and equipment from customs duties and the general sales tax (solar water heaters, energy-saving bulbs, insulation materials for buildings and control systems in heating and cooling, lighting control systems, Wind Turbines for power generation, solar cells and hybrid vehicles); and (ii) Other equipment from custom duties (absorption chillers, cooling towers, air compressors with heat recovery, compressed air control systems, insulation materials that contain ammonia, combustion control systems and high efficiency heat recovery boilers). Kyoto Protocol ratified on 17/1/2003 (non-Annex B).
Kazakhstan	Law on Energy Savings entered into force in 1997 but never effectively implemented. New Law on Energy Savings said to be approved by Parliament at the end of 2009. Kyoto Protocol ratified on 16/06/2009 (non-Annex B).
Kenya	Kyoto Protocol ratified on 25/02/2005 (non-Annex B).
Kiribati	Accession to the Kyoto Protocol on 07/09/2000 (non-Annex B).
Kuwait	Kyoto Protocol ratified on 11/03/2005 (non-Annex B).
Kyrgyzstan	Kyoto Protocol ratified on 13/05/2003 (non-Annex B).
Lao People's Democratic Republic	Accession to Kyoto Protocol on 06/02/2003 (non-Annex B).
Lebanon	Energy Conservation Law was prepared and is awaiting approval by the government before being submitted to Parliament. The Lebanese Centre for Energy Conservation (LCEC) was established with the support of UNDP and GEF. The Country Energy Efficiency and Renewable Energy Demonstration Project for the Recovery of Lebanon (CEDRO) was initiated in 2007, managed by the UNDP in partnership with the Ministry of Energy and Water and the Council for Development and Reconstruction and partially funded by a donation from Spain. Kyoto Protocol ratified on 13/11/2006 (non-Annex B).
Lesotho	Kyoto Protocol ratified on 16/08/2000 (non-Annex B).
Liberia	Kyoto Protocol ratified on 05/11/2002 (non-Annex B).
Libya	Kyoto Protocol ratified on 24/08/2006 (non-Annex B).
Madagascar	Kyoto Protocol ratified on 24/09/2003 (non-Annex B).
Malawi	Kyoto Protocol ratified on 26/10/2001 (non-Annex B).
Malaysia	The Ninth Malaysia Plan 2006-2010 strengthens the initiatives for EE and RE put forth in the Eighth Malaysia Plan that focused on better utilisation of energy resources. An emphasis to further reduce the dependency on petroleum provides for more efforts to integrate alternative fuels. Kyoto Protocol ratified on 04/09/2002 (non-Annex B).
Maldives	Kyoto Protocol ratified on 30/12/1998 (non-Annex B).
Mali	Kyoto Protocol ratified on 28/03/2002 (non-Annex B).
Marshall Islands	Kyoto Protocol ratified on 11/08/2003 (non-Annex B).
Mauritania	Kyoto Protocol ratified on 22/07/2005 (non-Annex B).
Mauritius	Kyoto Protocol ratified on 09/05/2001 (non-Annex B).

Country	Policies (EE&RE)
Mexico	In November 2007, the Government of Dr. Felipe Calderón, through the Secretariat of Energy, published the 2007-2012 Sectoral Energy Programme. Item III. 1 of Chapter III on EE, RE and biofuels establishes the goal of promoting the efficient use and production of energy, and sets electrical energy savings targets (in GW/h) for 2012 that are twice as high as those set for 2006. Eight strategies and their corresponding lines of action are set out: (i) Propose financial mechanisms and policies to accelerate the adoption of EEI technologies in the public and private sectors; (ii) Promote the optimization of energy supply and use by federal government agencies; (iii) Expand coordinated action between the public, social and private sectors to increase efficient energy use among the population; (iv) Promote the reduction of energy consumption in residential areas and buildings; (v) Encourage efficient energy generation through self-supply and cogeneration options; (vi) Draft public policies that encourage the exploitation of the potential of efficient cogeneration; (vii) Propose a set of provisions to enable the Energy Regulatory Commission to expand and strengthen its power to regulate and promote efficient cogeneration; and (viii) Support research aimed at improving the efficiency of electricity generation, distribution and consumption. Since the publication of the Law on Sustainable Energy Use on 28 November 2008, the human and material resources of the National Commission for Energy Saving have been transferred to the new National Commission for Energy Efficiency created under the Law. On 28 October 2008, the instructions of the Energy Commission for the enactment of the Decree to establish the Law on the Use of Renewable energies and the Financing of Energy Transitions were published in the Parliamentary Gazette. Kyoto Protocol ratified on 07/09/2000 (non-Annex B).
Micronesia (the Federated States of)	Kyoto Protocol ratified on 21/06/1999 (non-Annex B).
Moldova	Law on Energy Conservation passed in 2000, currently under revision. Main document on EE is Presidential Decree 1078 (2003). It sets a target of an annual 2-3% decrease in energy intensity and indicates priority areas. Secondary legislation on ESCOs and incentives under development. Kyoto Protocol ratified on 22/04/2003 (non-Annex B).
Mongolia	A draft Energy Efficiency Law exists though has not yet been passed. Accession to Kyoto Protocol on 15/12/1999 (non-Annex B).
Montenegro	Design of an Energy Efficiency Strategy and Action Plan approved in 2005. Kyoto Protocol ratified on 04/06/2007 (non-Annex B).
Morocco	Kyoto Protocol ratified on 25/01/2002 (non-Annex B).
Mozambique	Kyoto Protocol ratified on 18/01/2005 (non-Annex B).
Myanmar	Accession to Kyoto Protocol on 13/08/2003 (non-Annex B).
Namibia	Kyoto Protocol ratified on 04/09/2003 (non-Annex B).
Nauru	Kyoto Protocol ratified on 16/08/2001(non-Annex B).
Nepal	Accession to Kyoto Protocol on 16/09/2005 (non-Annex B).
New Zealand	The Energy Efficiency and Conservation Act (2000) mandated the establishment of an Energy Efficiency and Conservation Authority and Strategy, which is currently being revised. It also provides for mandatory standards for appliances and vehicles, and the provision of information related to EE. Kyoto Protocol ratified on 19/12/2002 (Annex B).
Nicaragua	The legal framework for EE in Nicaragua consists of: (i) The Law on the Electrical Industry No. 72, which establishes the policy guidelines to promote savings and efficient energy use (article 2, paragraph 5); and (ii) Decree 1304 of 2 March 2004. The National Energy Commission drew up the Energy Efficiency Programme in September 2004. This Programme is currently being implemented with the financial and economic support of the Inter-American Development Bank. On 30 January, 2008, the Government published Decree 2-2008 on energy use. This Decree was based on the following fundamental principles: (i) Avoiding whenever possible the prolonged rationing of the supply of electrical energy and fuels; (ii) Minimizing the interruption of economic activities, especially production and employment; and (iii) Promoting the efficient and rational use of different energy forms to contribute to economic competitiveness and improve the quality of life of the population. Kyoto Protocol ratified on 18/11/1999 (non-Annex B).
Niger	Kyoto Protocol ratified on 30/09/2004 (non-Annex B).
Nigeria	Kyoto Protocol ratified on 10/12/2004 (non-Annex B).
Niue	Kyoto Protocol ratified on 06/05/99 (non-Annex B).

Country	Policies (EE&RE)
Norway	Wide ranging network of acts, regulations and measures mainly developed in the 1990s and early 2000s. The policy is based on: (i) Compulsory standards in industry, buildings and vehicles; (ii) Fiscal and economic incentives to reduce consumption; (iii) Establlshment in 2001 of Enova, a state-owned ESCO/EE Fund; (iv) Dissemination of information and education; (v) Implementation of EU directives; and (vi) close cooperation with neighbours (Nordic and Baltic countries). Kyoto Protocol ratified on 30/05/2002 (Annex B, but emission cap assigned even allows for an increase in GHG emissions).
Oman	The sector Law promulgated by Royal Decree 78/2004 to regulate the electricity and related water sector include the following provisions in article 22: (i) A duty to secure and develop the safe, effective and economic operation of the electricity sector(Paragraph 3); and (ii) A duty to afford due consideration to the protection of the environment (Paragraph 11). The Authority for Electricity Regulations invited, towards the end of 2008, the Rural Areas Electricity company (RAEC) to identify possible locations for Diesel system Hybrid Pilot projects and make information available for Potential developers. Kyoto Protocol ratified on 19/1/2005 (non-Annex B).
Palestine	Letter of Sector Policy is prepared. National Targets: a National Master Plan for the development of EE/RE has been set.
Pakistan	The Energy Conservation Act 2008 is Pakistan's first ever National Energy Conservation Policy It provides a broad guideline to promote conservation in all sectors of the economy. Accession to Kyoto Protocol on 11/01/2005 (non-Annex B).
Palau	Accession to Kyoto Protocol on 10/12/1999 (non-Annex B).
Panama	The National Energy Commission was created under Decree 20 of 4 September 1980 as the advisory body to the Executive Branch on the formulation, orientation, coordination and evaluation of national energy policy. In 1998, this body was renamed the Energy Policy Commission (COPE). Article 16 of Law 6 of 3 February 1997 sets out the powers and functions of COPE. Paragraphs 1 and 9 of the article refer to EE: (i) Study and analyse national policy options for electricity, hydrocarbons and rational energy use, and the comprehensive use of all of the country's natural resources and energy sources in keeping with general development plans; (ii) Establish programmes to promote the rational use and saving of energy; (iii) Sign contracts and legalize the corresponding instruments for their administration, as required for the fulfilment of objectives; and (iv) Carry out all the activities and procedures necessary for achieving the objectives of this Law. In light of energy policy and strategic guidelines for the electrical and hydrocarbons sectors and alternative energy sources, a National Energy Plan was drawn up for 2009-2023. This Plan has the following objectives: (i) Diversify the energy grid; (ii) Boost the competitiveness of the energy supply; (iii) Lower the prices of energy for specific low-income sectors; (iv) Increase the use of clean energies; and (v) Promote EE. Kyoto Protocol ratified on 05/03/1999 (non-Annex B).
Papua New Guinea	Kyoto Protocol ratified in 28/03/2002 (non-Annex B).
Paraguay	There is no specific Government programme for EE in Paraguay. Some institutional instruments mention, albeit tangentially, the rational and efficient use of energy. The Strategic Plan for the Energy Sector (2005) provides a framework for the coordination and establishment of activity and deadlines to ensure compliance with the guidelines, specifically regarding the mission, vision, strategic objectives, lines of action and measures for the energy sector in 2005-2013. Objective 3 compares measures on EE and energy saving with those for supply security. Kyoto Protocol ratified on 27/08/1999 (non-Annex B).

Country	Policies (EE&RE)
Peru	{0> Law 27.345 on the Promotion of the Efficient Use of Energy encourages the rational use of energy. The Law was passed in September 2000. In 2006, the Government decided to give higher priority again to EE programmes. A commission was set up in March 2007 to draw up the Law's regulations. On 13 December 2007, through Ministerial Resolution 560-2007-MEM/DM, the Commission for the Compliance of the Transitory Provisions of the Regulations of the Law on the Promotion of Energy Efficiency was established and entrusted with four tasks: (i) The drafting of the reference plan for EE; (ii) The drafting of energy consumption standards; (iii) The methodology for monitoring energy use and energy indicators; and (iv) The implementation of an interactive EE system. The reference plan for EE (2009) was reviewed by an internal commission of the Ministry of Energy and Mines. It is awaiting approval and may still be subject to modification. Kyoto Protocol ratified on 12/09/2002 (non-Annex B).
Philippines	The Republic Act no. 7638 was created in 2002 mandating the Philippines Department of Energy, among other tasks, to develop programmes on EE. Numerous programmes have been implemented under this Act. Kyoto Protocol ratified on 20/11/2003 (non-Annex B).
Qatar	Energy law # 26/2008 on electricity and water consumption conservation. Energy law # 29/2008 on electricity wiring works to regulate the internal electricity wiring works for preventing over loads. Qatar General Electric and Water Corporation (KAHRAMAA) met with representatives of companies specialized in energy savings to study the proper strategy for replacing lamps with watt saver lamps. Kyoto Protocol ratified on 11/1/2005 (non-Annex B).
Republic of Korea (the)	Rational Energy Utilization Act of the Republic of Korea (1998, amended in 2007). The Republic of Korea is pushing to transform its society into one that promotes Green Growth. Some activities being undertaken include encouraging industry to conserve energy, subsidizing the installation of high-efficiency equipment and appliances, along with raising the design criteria for energy saving in buildings and increasing the tax on petroleum fuel. Kyoto Protocol ratified on 08/11/2002 (non-Annex B).
Russian Federation	Law on Energy Efficiency in force since 1996. Repealed by a Presidential Decree in 2008. It provides for: (i) State support for companies investing in EE; (ii) Financial incentive mechanisms for energy saving activities; (iii) Separation of competences between federal, regional and municipal authorities; and (iv) Promotion of production and sales of efficient equipment. Kyoto Protocol ratified on 18/11/2004 (Annex B but no compulsory reduction targets).
Rwanda	Kyoto Protocol ratified on 22/07/2004 (non-Annex B).
Samoa	Kyoto Protocol ratified on 27/11/2000 (non-Annex B).
Sao Tome and Principe	Kyoto Protocol ratified on 24/07/2008 (non-Annex B).
Saudi Arabia	A National Energy Efficiency Programme (NEEP) is being implemented. Its objectives are: (i) Energy audit; (ii) EE information and awareness; (iii) Load management and TOU tariff; (iv) Efficient utilization of oil and gas; (v) Promotion of ESCO industry; (vi) Equipment labels and standards programme; (vii) Building codes for energy efficiency; and (viii) Technical and management training. Kyoto Protocol ratified on 31/1/2005 (non-Annex B).
Senegal	Kyoto Protocol ratified on 20/07/2001 (non-Annex B).
Serbia	No specific EE law, but provisions in the Energy Law. Serbian Energy Efficiency Agency instituted in 2002 in order to: (i) Develop EE projects; (ii) Transfer technology; (iii) Consulting industries and households; and (iv) Organize training and educational programmes. Projected establishment of an Energy Efficiency Fund (to be operational in late 2009). Kyoto Protocol ratified on 19/10/2007 (non-Annex B).
Seychelles	Kyoto Protocol ratified on 07/2002 (non-Annex B).
Sierra Leone	Kyoto Protocol ratified on 10/11/2006 (non-Annex B).

Country	Policies (EE&RE)
Singapore	The National Environment Agency Act (2002 amended in 2003) mandates the Environment Agency to promote EE. In addition, regulations under the Environmental Protection and Management Act provide the legal basis of energy conservation primarily for labels. EE in buildings is also written into the Building and Construction Authority Act (2000). The National Environment Agency chairs the Energy Efficiency Programme Office (E2PO), which is a multi agency committee established to drive EE improvement in Singapore. The Programme undertakes a number of activities, including: Promoting adoption of EE technologies and measures by addressing the market barriers to EE; Building capability to drive and sustain EE efforts and to develop the local knowledge base and expertise in energy management; Raising awareness to reach out to the public and businesses; and Supporting research & development. Accession to Kyoto Protocol on 12/04/2006 (non-Annex B).
Solomon Islands	Kyoto Protocol ratified on 13/03/2003 (non-Annex B).
Sri Lanka	Promoting EE and conservation is mandated in the country's energy policy. This includes supply side and end-use EE through financial and other incentives or disincentives such as appliance energy labelling, building codes and energy audits. The Energy Conservation Fund (ECF) is entrusted to coordinate all the activities relating to energy efficiency. Accession to Kyoto Protocol on 03/09/2002 (non-Annex B).
South Africa	South Africa developed the South African Energy Efficiency Strategy in 2004 and revised it in 2009 with energy reduction targets. The National Energy Regulator of South Africa (NERSA) approved RE targets and feed-in-tariffs (Refit) on 31/03/2009. Kyoto Protocol ratified on 31/07/2002 (non-Annex B).
Sudan	Economic policies, public awareness campaigns and applications of EE technologies. Technology policies related to EE/RE. Setting of environmental measures and legislations. Investment Law providing facilitations for EE/RE investments. Kyoto Protocol ratified on 2/11/2004 (non-Annex B).
Suriname	There are no regulations, laws or standards on nor an official agency responsible for EE. Two public companies and one department of the Ministry of Natural Resources have their own EE programmes approved by the Ministry. Kyoto Protocol ratified on 25/09/2006 (non-Annex B).
Swaziland	Kyoto Protocol ratified on 13/01/2006 (non-Annex B).
Switzerland	Energy policy aligned to the EU as the country is closely interconnected with the Western European power grid. Policy directives focus on the importance of technology and research as a tool to promote EE. The Federal Administration is running programmes in the areas of: (i) Fuel cells; (ii) Cogeneration; (iii) Waste district heating; (iv) Use of accumulators for mobility; (v) Optimization of industrial processes; and (vi) Improvement in storage and transmission of electricity. Kyoto Protocol ratified on 09/07/2003 (Annex B, compulsory 8% reduction target).
Syria	Energy Conservation Law No.3 (2009) aims at reducing electricity consumption and production. Mechanisms for public and private sectors cooperation to enhance RE/EE. Law 18/2008 provides for electrical energy consumption measures for household appliances and Energy Efficiency Labelling. Thermal Insulation Code of 2007 regulates building designs, permits and execution. Draft law for promotion and enhancement of the use of solar water heaters. A new Electricity Law is under preparation. It will encourage private sector (domestic and foreign) investments in RE. Kyoto Protocol ratified on 27/1/2006 (non-Annex B).
Tajikistan	The Law on Energy Saving (2002) describes major strategies and state policy guidelines for ensuring the efficient use of energy. It identifies government bodies and institutions that are responsible for the development and implementation of energy policies and strategies and also introduces the notion of standardization, mandatory energy certification for businesses, institutions, buildings, technological processes and materials, along with the labelling of product production and operation. Kyoto Protocol ratified on 05/01/2009 (non-Annex B).
Tanzania	Kyoto Protocol ratified on 26/08/2002 (non-Annex B).

Country	Policies (EE&RE)
Thailand	The Energy Conservation Promotion Act B.E. 2535 (1992) of Thailand provides the legal foundation and institutional arrangements to encourage EE. Measures included: (i) The introduction of a pilot phase programme for EE in government buildings and the preparation of an action plan for wider dissemination and implementation; (ii) The development of energy conservation building codes; (iii) Set-up a Standards and Labelling Programme to identify EE appliances and equipment; (iv) Assistance to five electric utilities to set up demand side management; (v) The formulation of EE codes and standards; (vi) The introduction of educational programmes to increase awareness regarding efficient use of energy resources; (vii) Establishment of the Energy Conservation Fund; and (viii) The introduction of Energy Conservation Awards to nationally recognize efforts to reduce energy consumption. Kyoto Protocol ratified on 28/08/2002 (non-Annex B).
The Former Yugoslavian Republic of Macedonia	No specific EE law, but special chapter of Energy Law of 2006 includes: (i) Compulsory local EE action plans; (ii) Efficiency standards for new constructions; and (iii) Provisions on energy audits and building certificates. Kyoto Protocol ratified on 18/11/2004 (non-Annex B).
Timor-Leste	Accession to Kyoto Protocol on 14/10/2008 (non-Annex B).
Togo	Kyoto Protocol ratified on 02/07/2004 (non-Annex B).
Tonga	Accession to Kyoto Protocol on 14/01/2008 (non-Annex B).
Turkey	Energy Efficiency Law of 2007 very recently complemented by some secondary legislation. All main sectors (industry, buildings, appliances, power generation, transport) covered. Main provisions of the law include: (i) Data collection and analysis; (ii) Financial support for EE projects; (iii) Audits; (iv) Training and awareness-rising in schools and media; (v) Accreditation and monitoring of ESCOs; and (vi) Traffic control systems. Kyoto Protocol ratified on 28/05/2009 (non-Annex B).
Tunisia	Kyoto Protocol ratified on 22/01/2003 (non-Annex B).
Turkmenistan	Kyoto Protocol ratified on 11/01/1999 (non-Annex B).
Tuvalu	Kyoto Protocol ratified on 16/11/1998 (non-Annex B).
Uganda	Kyoto Protocol ratified on 25/03/2002 (non-Annex B).
Ukraine	Law on Energy Savings of 1994 to be replaced by a new draft developed by the cabinet in early 2009. National Agency for Efficient Use of Energy Resources replaced an older institution in 2005. It is responsible for: (i) Development and implementation of national EE policy; (ii) Monitoring through a network of state inspector; and (iii) Management of the State Energy Conservation Fund. Kyoto Protocol ratified on 12/04/2004 (Annex B but no compulsory reduction targets).
United Arab Emirates	The Government of Abu Dhabi is expected to issue a policy according to which RE sources will account for at least 7% of the Emirate's total power generation capacity by 2020. Abu Dhabi Future Energy Company (MASDAR) promotes and enhances the development of RE. Masdar City will be the first zero emission city. It has been chosen as the interim headquarters of International Renewable Energy Agency (IRENA). Kyoto Protocol ratified on 26/01/2005 (non-Annex B).
United States of America	EE legislation not much developed at the federal level, but all States have their EE regulatory framework, with wide differentiation in scope and provisions. The Department of Energy runs several programmes in the areas of buildings, industrial technology and transport. Kyoto Protocol signed on 12/11/1998 but never ratified (as Annex B party, it should comply with a 7% reduction target).
Uruguay	Since August 2004, the Energy Efficiency Project of Uruguay is officially under way. This project is coordinated by the Vice-Ministry of Energy with financial support from the Global Environment Facility (GEF) and the active participation of the electrical utilities and transmissions body UTE. A draft Energy Efficiency Law was submitted to the Council of Ministers on 16 June 2008 and subsequently presented to the Legislative Branch. It is now being examined by the Senate Industry, Tourism and Energy Commission. The Law will make it possible to consolidate the legal-institutional framework for EE to establish it as a component of the country's energy policy. Kyoto Protocol ratified on 05/02/2001 (non-Annex B).

Country	Policies (EE&RE)
Uzbekistan	EE is one of the priorities of the Energy Strategy. The Law on Efficient Energy Use (1997 amended 2003) establishes an integrated legal foundation to ensure conservation of the national energy sources and efficient energy use. This includes: (i) Establishing efficient and environmentally friendly patterns in production and consumption of energy; (ii) Providing stimulus for development and introduction of energy efficient technologies; (iii) Ensuring accuracy, integrity and unity of measurements for calculation and registration of quantity and quality of produced and consumed energy; and (iv) Providing state control and inspection to ensure efficient production and consumption of energy and its quality, as well as to ensure effective control over technical state of energy equipment, energy supply and energy consumption systems. Kyoto Protocol ratified on 12/10/1999 (non-Annex B).
Vanuatu	Accession to Kyoto Protocol on 17/07/2001 (non-Annex B).
Venezuela (Bolivarian Republic of)	The Government has been working on EE standards and labelling for household appliances since 1995. The main Venezuelan standards refer to: (i) Energy consumption and capacity measuring methods for refrigerators and freezers; (ii) Energy consumption labelling and reporting; (iii) Measuring methods for air-conditioning units installed in windows; (iv) Measuring methods for the cooling capacity, energy consumption and EE of air conditioners; and (v) Labelling and reporting of EE of air-conditioning units installed in windows. The standards are voluntary, but the use of labels informing consumers about energy consumption is mandatory. The Ministry of Energy and Petroleum drew up a draft Law on Energy Efficiency in 2002. The basic objective of this Law is to promote EE to benefit the suppliers and users of energy and energy services of national economic interest, safeguard consumer rights and protect the environment. According to the Law, the Ministry of Energy and Petroleum will be responsible for the promotion of EE nationwide and for the drafting, adoption, coordination, monitoring and evaluation of policies, strategies, programmes and projects on EE in the country. Kyoto Protocol ratified on 18/02/2005 (non-Annex B).
Viet Nam	The Asian Development Bank is currently assisting Viet Nam in drafting its own Energy Efficiency Law. Kyoto Protocol ratified on 25/09/2002 (non-Annex B).
Yemen	Electricity Law issued in 2009. The proposed strategy for EE/RE focuses on: (i) Decreasing the usage of fossil fuels; (ii) Increasing the share of RE (wind farms, geothermal, waste biogas, sewage gas off-grid stand-alone systems) in electricity generation (15% of total generation by 2025); (iii) Supporting decentralization of access to RE technologies; (iv) Enhancing Energy Efficiency and Conservation (15% increase by 2025); and (v) Establishing an electricity market and encouraging investors, through incentives, to produce RE in rural areas (electrification of 110,000 rural households). Kyoto Protocol ratified on 15/9/2004 (non-Annex B).
Zambia	Kyoto Protocol ratified on 07/07/2006 (non-Annex B).
Zimbabwe	Kyoto Protocol ratified on 30/06/2009 (non-Annex B).

References

CHAPTER 1

1. Tanaka. 2009. *Worldwide Implementation Now – The Essential Role of Energy Efficiency*.

2. McKinsey defines energy productivity as the ratio of value added to energy inputs; this currently stands at $79bn of GDP per QBTU of energy inputs globally.

3. Enkvist, Nauclér & Riese. 2008. *What countries can do about cutting carbon emissions*" Farrel & Remes. 2008. *How the world should invest in energy efficiency*; Farrel & Remes. 2009. *Promoting energy efficiency in the developing world*.

4. UNEP SEFI. 2009. *Global Trends in Sustainable Energy Investment 2009*.

5. The total amount invested exceeded $220bn, as it includes *existing money* (i.e. money *already* in the sector, but changing hands via deals such as mergers & acquisitions (M&A) and management buyouts (MBOs)).

6. UNFCCC. 2007. *Investment and financial flows to address climate change*.

7. UFCCC. 2008. *Investment and financial flows to address climate change: an update*.

8. UNEP SEFI. 2009. *The global financial crisis and its impact on renewable energy finance*.

9. REN21. 2009. *Renewables: Global Status Report. 2009 Update*.

CHAPTER 2

10. UNFCCC. 2008. *Investment and financial flows to address climate change: an update*; Doornbosch & Knight. 2008. *What role for public finance in international climate change mitigation*.

11. As any selection, this one is to an extent arbitrary. At least it does not purport to be a selection of the best mechanisms. As this paper indeed argues, the term "best" is highly relative, and the lack of proper evaluations makes this best even harder to pinpoint.

12. Robert Taylor. 2009. *Creating an ESCO Industry in Developing Markets*. Presentation at EE Global Conference, Paris 28th April 2009.

13. The California Solar Initiative is part of the Go Solar California campaign and builds on 10 years of state solar rebates offered to customers in California's investor-owned utility territories: Pacific Gas & Electric (PG&E), Southern California Edison (SCE), and San Diego Gas & Electric (SDG&E.) The California Solar Initiative is overseen by the California Public Utilities Commission.

14. A good overview is in McLean, John. 2008. *Mainstreaming Environmental Finance Markets (I): Small-Scale Energy Efficiency and Renewable Energy Finance*.

15. Taylor, Robert et al. 2008. *Financing Energy Efficiency: Lessons from Brazil China, India and beyond*.

16. http://lnweb90.worldbank.org/oed/oeddoclib.nsf/DocUNIDViewForJavaSearch/BF056AB0D696393185256DD7005A5C9A/$file/PPAR_India_C2449.pdf.

17. "Green Investment Schemes" may blur the difference between projects (offset)-based mechanisms and IET in the Kyoto system: these are fundamentally IET deals that require a minimum volume of GHG emission reductions through projects or policies in the host country. They are most likely to happen in countries in transition.

18. Capoor & Ambrosi. 2009. *State and trends of the carbon market 2009*.

19. The Carbon Trust. 2008. *Global Carbon Mechanisms: Emerging lessons and implications*.

20. Based from UNEP Risoe database.

21. Zoellick, Robert B. 2008. *Carbon Markets for Development*. Presentation at the Bali Breakfast/Development Committee Series.

22. Au Yong. 2009. *Investment additionality in the CDM*.

23. WWF Hong Kong/Beijing Office. 2008. *The value of carbon in China*.

CHAPTER 3

24. SourceOECD.

25. GEF. 2007. *Focal Area Strategies and Strategic Programming for GEF-4*.

26. http://esa.un.org/un-energy/pdf/un_energy_overview.pdf.

27. http://www.sefi.unep.org/.

28. UNFCCC. 2008. *Investment and financial flows to address climate change: an update*.

29. Bonzanni. 2009. *Regional Perspectives on Major Projects to Overcome Barriers to Energy Efficiency Investments*.

30. http://www.undp.org/energy.

31. http://www.unido.org/index.php?id=o18258.

32. http://africa-toolkit.reeep.org.

33. http://www.ted.reegle.info/.

34. http://www.gtz.de/en/themen/umwelt-infrastruktur/energie/20726.htm.

35. http://www.managenergy.net/progs.html (EERE only) and http://ec.europa.eu/grants/index_en.htm#policy (overview of EU funding programmes).

36. http://www.managenergy.net/index.html.

37. Taylor *et al*. 2008. *Financing Energy Efficiency: Lessons from Brazil China, India and Beyond*.

CHAPTER 4

38. Taylor *et al*. 2008. *Financing Energy Efficiency: Lessons from Brazil China, India and Beyond*.

39. http://www.odyssee-indicators.org/index.php.

40. McKinsey & C. 2009. *Pathways to a Low-Carbon Economy*. For the industrial sector, see for example Vattenfall. 2007. *Global Mapping of Greenhouse Gas Abatement Opportunities up to 2030. Industry Sector Deep-Dive*.

41. UNEP SEFI. 2009. *Global trends*.

42. The Economist. 2009. *Fossilised policy*. 1 Oct 2009. www.economist.com/world/international/displaystory.cfm?story_id=14540043.

43. Taylor *et al*. 2008. *Financing Energy Efficiency: Lessons from Brazil China, India and Beyond*.

44. For definitions, see Bertoldi, Boza-Kiss & Rezessy. 2007. *Latest Developments of Energy Service Companies across Europe*.

45. Taylor *et al*. 2008. *Financing Energy Efficiency: Lessons from Brazil China, India and Beyond*.

46. Definition from US Energy Information Administration.

47. www.eva.ac.at/publ/pdf/ewc_brochure.pdf.

48. Stern, Nicholas. 2006. *Stern Review: The Economics of Climate Change. Summary of Conclusions*.

49. The total cost per tonne avoided is an even better indicator, as it takes into account the revenues (RE) or avoided operating costs (EE) generated by the investment. This is equal to the Net Present Value (with a minus sign) of the project divided by emission reductions over the economic life of the project. This "cost" is negative (positive NPV) for most EE measures. For RE projects selling electricity at Feed-in Tariffs, the revenues that are discounted should be calculated using wholesale electricity prices, otherwise the true cost is masked.

CHAPTER 5

50. The United Nations Economic Commission for Europe comprises the following 56 countries: Albania, Andorra, Armenia, Austria, Azerbaijan, Belarus, Belgium, Bosnia and Herzegovina, Bulgaria, Canada, Croatia, Cyprus, Czech Republic, Denmark, Estonia, Finland, France, Georgia, Germany, Greece, Hungary, Iceland, Ireland, Israel, Italy, Kazakhstan, Kyrgyzstan, Latvia, Liechtenstein, Lithuania, Luxembourg, FYR Macedonia, Malta, Moldova, Monaco, Montenegro, Netherlands, Norway, Poland, Portugal, Romania, Russian Federation, San Marino, Serbia, Slovakia, Slovenia, Spain, Sweden, Switzerland, Tajikistan, Turkey, Turkmenistan, Ukraine, United Kingdom, United States of America, Uzbekistan. The smaller countries of Andorra, Liechtenstein, Monaco and San Marino are not take into consideration in this report.

51. Based on IEA data, 2008.

52. Particularly important with respect to energy market liberalization is the Directive 96/92/EC of 19 December 1996 concerning "common rules for the internal market in electricity".

53. Data on prices tend to be based on a large number of assumptions which make comparisons problematic. The graphical representation is not exempt from uncertainties.

54. Based on IEA data, 2008.

55. Figures for Ireland refer to 2001-2004, figures for Serbia refer to 1998-2001.

56. The Global Corruption Index (CPI) is meant to "rank the countries by their perceived levels of corruption, as determined by expert assessments and opinion surveys". Originally calculated on a 0-6 scale, it has been transformed to a 0-10 scale.

57. The Global Competitiveness Index "measures the set of institutions, policies, and factors that set the sustainable current and medium-term levels of economic prosperity".

58. See in particular: Directive 93/76/EEC to limit C_2O emissions by improving energy efficiency (SAVE), Directive 2006/32/EC on energy end-use efficiency and energy services, the 2005 Green Paper 'Doing More with Less' and the 2006 'Energy Efficiency Action Plan'.

59. Bertoldi, Atanasiu & Rezessy. 2009. *EU Energy Efficiency Policies and JRC Activities*.

60. See for additional information: IEA. 2008. *In Support of the G8 Plan of Action: Energy Efficiency Policy Recommendations*.

61. IEA. 2009. *Progress with Implementing Energy Efficiency Policies in the G8*.

62. The targets are calculated as a percentage reduction relative to the baseline of 1990 emission levels, to be achieved by 2012. Hence, some Annex I countries do not need to reduce emissions in absolute terms in order to comply with the targets.

63. Bonzanni. 2009. *Regional Perspectives on Major Projects to Overcome Barriers to Energy Efficiency Investments*.

64. Sambucini. 2007. *Sustainable Development needs Energy Efficiency. New Approaches to International Partnership and Governance in Europe*.

65. FEEI participating countries are: Albania, Belarus, Bosnia and Herzegovina, Bulgaria, Croatia, Kazakhstan, Republic of Moldova, Romania, Russian Federation, Serbia, The former Yugoslav Republic of Macedonia and Ukraine.

66. RENEUER participating countries are: Albania, Bosnia and Herzegovina, Bulgaria, Croatia, Montenegro, Republic of Moldova, Romania, Serbia and The former Yugoslav Republic of Macedonia.

67. The Energy Efficiency Market Formation in South-Eastern Europe Project participating countries are: Albania, Bosnia and Herzegovina, Bulgaria, Croatia, Romania, Serbia, The former Yugoslav Republic of Macedonia, Turkey and the United Nations Interim Administration in Kosovo (UNMIK).

CHAPTER 6

68. ESCAP member states are: Afghanistan, Armenia, Australia, Azerbaijan, Bangladesh, Bhutan, Brunei Darussalam, Cambodia, China, Fiji, France, Georgia, India, Indonesia, Iran (the Islamic Republic of), Japan, Kazakhstan, Kiribati, Korea (Democratic People's Republic of), Korea (Republic of), Kyrgyzstan, Loa People's Democratic Republic, Malaysia, Maldives, Marshall Islands (the), Micronesia (the Federated States of), Mongolia, Myanmar, Nauru, Nepal, Netherlands (the), New Zealand, Pakistan, Palau, Papua New Guinea, Philippines (the), Russian Federation (the), Samoa, Singapore, Solomon Islands, Sri Lanka, Tajikistan, Thailand, Timor-Leste, Tonga, Turkey, Turkmenistan, Tuvalu, United Kingdom of Great Britain and Northern Ireland (the), United States of America (the), Uzbekistan, Vanuatu, Viet Nam. Associate members: American Samoa, Cook Islands (the), French Polynesia, Guam, Hong Kong (China), Macao (China), New Caledonia, Niue, Northern Mariana Islands (the).

69. ESCAP. 2008. *Statistical Yearbook for Asia and the Pacific 2008*.

70. IEA. 2006. *World Energy Outlook 2006*.

71. IEA. 2006. *World Energy Outlook 2006*.

72. BP, *Statistical Review of World Energy June 2009*.

73. IEA. 2009. *Energy Balances of Non-OECD Countries*.

74. ESCAP. 2008. *Statistical Yearbook for Asia and the Pacific 2008*.

75. IEA. 2009. *Energy Balances of Non-OECD Countries – Indicators Vol 2009 release 01*.

76. BP. 2009. *Statistical Review of World Energy June 2009*.

77. ESCAP, *Energy Security and Sustainable Development in Asia and the Pacific*.

78. Korea Energy Economics Institute, Energy Policy and Statistics in Northeast Asia.

79. International Geothermal Association, "Contribution of geothermal energy to sustainable development", submission to the Commission on Sustainable Development at its ninth session, 28 March 2001.

80. IEA, *World Energy Outlook 2006*.

81. IEA. 2008. *CO_2 Emissions from Fuel Combustion*.

82. ESCAP 2008 *Key messages from the theme study Energy Security and Sustainable development in Asia and the Pacific*.

83. ESCAP. 2008 *Energy Security and Sustainable development in Asia and the Pacific*.

84. Julio Lumbreras. 2005. *Official development assistance for energy activities: a perspective from the NGOs*, a presentation made at the Conference on Investment for Sustainability organized by the Sustainable Energy Society of Southern Africa, Madrid, 19-20 May 2005.

85. UNCTAD, *World Investment Report 2009:Transnational Corporations,Agricultural Production and Development*.

86. UNCTAD. 2009. *World Investment Report 2009: Transnational Corporations, Agricultural Production and Development*.

87. UNCTAD. 2008. *World Investment Report 2008: Transnational Corporations, Agricultural Production and Development.*

88. ASEAN Energy website, ASEAN Plan of Action for Energy Cooperation 2004 – 2009, accessed in October 2009 from <www.aseanenergy.org/ace/work_programme.htm>.

89. Xinhua News Agency article 10 October 2009 accessed from <http://news.xinhuanet.com/english/2009-10/10/content_12206684.htm>.

90. UNPFA. *State of the World Population Report.*

91. ADB, accessed in September 2009 from <http://www.adb.org/Documents/Periodicals/Clean-Energy/EEI-Update-Issue8.pdf>.

92. Zhang, Y. (2006), Special Quick Report. China's "11th Five-Year Guidelines" with a Focus on Energy Policy. http://www.nautilus.org/aesnet/2006/MAY1006/IEEJ_PRC_fiveyear.pdf.

93. Greenlaw website (http://www.greenlaw.org.cn/files/laws/energy-conservation-law.pdf).

94. GTZ. 2008. *GTZ International Fuel Prices 6th Edition – Data Preview.*

95. OECD. 2006. *OECD Environmental Performance Reviews Korea.*

96. World Bank Group Global Environmental Facility. 2006. *World Bank GEF Post Implementation Impact Assessment - Thailand Promotion of Electrical Energy Efficiency Project.*

97. National Energy Efficiency and Conservation Program website (http://www.doe.gov.ph/neecp/).

CHAPTER 7

98. The United Nations Economic Commission for Latin America and the Pacific includes the following 44 countries: Antigua and Barbuda, Argentina, Bahamas, Barbados, Belize, Bolivia, Brazil, Canada, Chile, Colombia, Costa Rica, Cuba, Dominica, Dominican Republic, Ecuador, El Salvador, France, Germany, Grenada, Guatemala, Guyana, Haiti, Honduras, Italy, Jamaica, Japan, Mexico, Netherlands, Nicaragua, Panama, Paraguay, Peru, Portugal, Republic of Korea, Saint Kitts and Nevis, Saint Lucia, Saint Vincent and the Grenadines, Spain, Suriname, Trinidad and Tobago, United Kingdom of Great Britain and Northern Ireland, United States of America, Uruguay, Venezuela. It also has 9 associated members: Anguilla, Aruba, British Virgin Islands, Cayman Islands, Montserrat, Netherlands Antilles, Puerto Rico, Turks and Caicos Islands, United States Virgin Islands.

99. OLADE. 2009. *Energy-Economic Information System (SIEE).*

100. OLADE. 2009. *Energy-Economic Information System (SIEE).*

101. Based on OLADE and IEA data.

102. ECLAC.

103. Documents available online at www.cepal.org.

104. The results can be viewed online at www.eficiencianeergetica.gub.uy/documentos.asp in the PAEE folder. The reports on the 2006 and 2008 plans and the evaluation of the results are posted on the same website.

CHAPTER 8

105. ECA member countries are: Algeria, Angola, Benin, Botswana, Burkina Faso, Burundi, Cameroon, Cape Verde, Central African Republic (CAR), Chad, Comoros, Congo, Democratic Republic of the Congo (DRC), Cote d'Ivoire, Djibouti, Egypt, Equatorial Guinea, Eritrea, Ethiopia, Gabon, Gambia (The), Ghana, Guinea, Guinea-Bissau, Kenya, Lesotho, Liberia, Libya, Madagascar, Malawi, Mali, Mauritania, Morocco, Mozambique, Namibia, Niger, Nigeria, Rwanda, Sao Tome and Principe, Senegal, Seychelles, Sierra Leone, Somalia, South Africa, Sudan, Swaziland, Tanzania, Togo, Tunisia, Uganda, Zambia and Zimbabwe.

106. IEA. 2006. *World Energy Outlook 2006.*

107. WEC. 2009. *World Energy Council Survey of Energy Resources Interim Update 2009.*

108. WEC. 2009. *World Energy Council Survey of Energy Resources Interim Update 2009.*

109. BP. 2009. *BP Statistical Review of World Energy 2009.*

110. IEA. 2008. *World Energy Outlook 2008.*

111. IEA 2009. *Key Energy Indicators 2009.*

112. Based on IEA data, 2009.

113. Based on IEA data, 2009.

114. Based on IEA data, 2009.

115. ECA. 2009. *Economic Report on Africa 2009.*

116. ECA. 2009. *Economic Report on Africa 2009.*

117. OECD/AfDB. 2009. *Economic Outlook 2009.*

CHAPTER 9

118. The United Nations Economic and Social Commission for Western Asia includes the following 14 countries: Bahrain, Egypt, Iraq, Jordan, Kuwait, Lebanon, Oman, Palestine, Qatar, Saudi Arabia, Sudan, Syria, United Arab Emirates, Yemen.

119. UNESCWA. 2009. *9th Sectoral Meeting between the League of Arab States (LAS) and the United Nations (UN) and their Specialized Organizations, Climate Change Mitigation Actions and Potentials, the UN – LAS Cooperation.*

120. UNESCWA. 2009. *9th Sectoral Meeting between the League of Arab States (LAS) and the United Nations (UN) and their Specialized Organizations, Climate Change Mitigation actions and Potentials, the UN – LAS Cooperation.*

121. Arab Union of Producers, Transporters and Distributors of Electricity (AUPTDE), *Statistical Bulletin, 2008, 17th Issue.*

122. Organization of Arab Petroleum Exporting Countries (OAPEC), *Annual Statistical Report 2008.*

123. UNESCWA. 2009. *Survey of Economic and Social Developments in the ESCWA Region 2008-2009.*

124. UNESCWA. 2009. *Survey of Economic and Social Developments in the ESCWA Region 2008-2009.*

125. UNESCWA. 2009. *Survey of Economic and Social Developments in the ESCWA Region 2008-2009.*

126. Organization of Arab Petroleum Exporting Countries (OAPEC), *Annual Statistical Report 2008.*

127. Heritage Foundation. The Economic Freedom Index is a series of 10 economic measurements developed by the Heritage Foundation and Wall Street Journal. Its stated objective is to measure the degree of economic freedom in the world's nations.

128. UNESCWA. 2009. *Document E/ESCWA/SDPD/2009/IG.1/5 (Part II).*

129. Country's response to inquiries issued by ESCWA Sustainable Development and Production Division (SDPD), 2009.

130. Country's response to inquiries issued by ESCWA Sustainable Development and Production Division (SDPD), 2009.

131. Country's response to inquiries issued by ESCWA Sustainable Development and Production Division (SDPD), 2009.

132. Country's response to inquiries issued by ESCWA Sustainable Development and Production Division (SDPD), 2009.

133. Country's response to inquiries issued by ESCWA Sustainable Development and Production Division (SDPD), 2009.

134. Country's response to inquiries issued by ESCWA Sustainable Development and Production Division (SDPD), 2009.

ANNEXES

135. http://www.adb.org/Clean-Energy/policy.asp.

136. ADB's accounting methodology can be found at http://www.adb.org/Documents/Clean-Energy/Guidelines-Estimating-ADB-Investments.pdf. Full list of projects available at http://www.adb.org/Documents/Clean-Energy/Summary-Table-2003-Q1-2008.pdf#page=20).

137. These definitions given by the WB Group are important and worth quoting in full:

138. *New Renewable Energy:* solar energy for heat and power, wind energy for mechanical and electrical power generation, geothermal and biomass energy for power generation and heat, and hydropower of 10 MW or less per installation.

139. *Energy Efficiency:* supply side and end-use thermal and electricity efficiency improvement activities. Examples include efficiency improvements in industry, transport, buildings, and appliances; power generation rehabilitation, loss reduction in transmission and distribution, and improvements in the efficiency of heating systems. Hydropower rehabilitation projects are classified as energy efficiency when energy output is increased as a result of the investment with no increase in rated capacity of the installation.

140. *Hydropower Greater Than 10 MW:* The World Bank considers hydropower, regardless of scale, to be renewable energy. For reporting purposes, hydropower projects in which the installed capacity at a single facility exceeds 10 MW are reported separately. Run-of-river hydropower, and hydropower projects with dams are included here if the capacity exceeds 10 MW."

141. (http://web.worldbank.org/WBSITE/EXTERNAL/NEWS/0,,contentMDK:22308139~menuPK:34463~pagePK:34370~piPK:34424~theSitePK:4607,00.html).

Bibliography

Papers, Reports & Presentations

Arab Union of Producers (2008), *Transporters and Distributors of Electricity*, Statistical Bulletin 2008, 17th Issue.

Au Yong, H.W. (2009), *Investment additionality in the CDM*. Econometrica Technical Paper. http://www.ecometrica.co.uk/wp-content/uploads/Technical_Paper_-_Investment_Additionality_in_the_CDM.pdf

Bertoldi, Paolo, Boza-Kiss, Benigna and Rezessy, Sylvia (2007), *Latest Developments of Energy Service Companies across Europe*. Institute for Environment and Sustainability, JRC Scientific and Technical Report. http://www.energy.eu/publications/LBNA22927ENC_002.pdf

Bertoldi, Paolo, Atanasiu, Bogdan and Rezessy, Silvia (2009), *EU Energy Efficiency Policies and JRC Activities*. Presentation at the JRC Workshop in Istanbul, 29 September.

Bonzanni, Andrea (2009), *Regional Perspectives on Major Projects to Overcome Barriers to Energy Efficiency Investments*. UNECE Draft Paper.

BP (2009), *Statistical Review of World Energy June 2009*.

Capoor, Karan and Ambrosi, Philippe (2009), *State and Trends of the Carbon Market 2009*. World Bank Report. http://wbcarbonfinance.org/docs/State___Trends_of_the_Carbon_Market_2009-FINAL_26_May09.pdf

Doornbosch, Richard and Knight, Eric (2008), *What Role for Public Finance in International Climate Change Mitigation*. Discussion Paper, Round Table on Sustainable Development. http://www.oecd.org/dataoecd/20/26/41564226.pdf

Ellis, J. and Kamel, S. (2007), Analysis on Barriers to CDM Projects. OECD/IEA/UNEP Risoe

Enkvist, Peter-Anders, Nauclér, Tomas and Riese, Jens (2008), *What countries can do about cutting carbon emissions*. The McKinsey Quarterly. http://www.mckinseyquarterly.com/What_countries_can_do_about_cutting_carbon_emissions_2128

ESCAP (2008), *Statistical Yearbook for Asia and the Pacific 2008*.

ESCAP (2008), *Energy Security and Sustainable Development in Asia and the Pacific*.

ESCWA (2009), *Report on 9th Sectoral Meeting between the League of Arab States (LAS) and the United Nations (UN) and their Specialized Organizations, Climate Change Mitigation actions and Potentials*. The UN – LAS Cooperation. Cairo, June 17-18, 2009.

ESCWA (2009), *Survey of Economic and Social Developments in the ESCWA Region 2008-2009*. E/ESCWA/EDGD/2009/2.

ESCWA (2009), *Parliamentary Document E/ESCWA/SDPD/2009/IG.1/5 (Part II)*.

Farrel, Diana and Remes, Jaana K. (2008), *How the world should invest in energy efficiency*. The McKinsey Quarterly. http://www.mckinseyquarterly.com/How_the_world_should_invest_in_energy_efficiency_2165

Farrel, Diana and Remes, Jaana K. (2009), *Promoting energy efficiency in the developing world*. The McKinsey Quarterly. http://www.juccce.com/documents/Perspectives/Consultancies/Promoting%20Energy%20Efficiency%20 in%20Developing%20Countries.pdf

GEF (2007), Focal Area Strategies and Strategic Programming for GEF-4. GEF/C.31/10. http://www.thegef.org/ uploadedFiles/Documents/Council_Documents__(PDF_DOC)/GEF_31/C.31.10%20Focal%20Area%20Strategies. pdf

GTZ (2008), *GTZ International Fuel Prices, 6th edition – Data Preview*.

IEA (2006), *World Energy Outlook 2006*.

IEA (2008), *World Energy Outlook 2008*.

IEA (2008), *In Support of the G8 Plan of Action: Energy Efficiency Policy Recommendations*. http://www.iea.org/ G8/2008/G8_EE_recommendations.pdf

IEA (2009), *Progress with Implementing Energy Efficiency Policies in the G8*. http://www.iea.org/G8/docs/Efficiency_ progress_g8july09.pdf

Korea Energy Economics Institute (2006), *Energy Policy and Statistics in Northeast Asia*.

Murphy, Deborah, Drexhage, John and Wooders, Peter (2009), *International Carbon Market Mechanisms in a Post-2012 Climate Change Agreement*. International Institute for Sustainable Development.

McLean, John (2008), *Mainstreaming Environmental Finance Markets (I): Small-Scale Energy Efficiency and Renewable Energy Finance*. http://www.kfw.de/EN_home/Topics/Financial_Sector/Events/Symposium_2008/Pdf_ documents_-_symposium_2008/Session_3_Expert_Paper_Final_Version.pdf

McKinsey & Company (2009), *Pathways to a Low-Carbon Economy*. http://www.mckinsey.com/clientservice/ccsi/ pathways_low_carbon_economy.asp

Organization of Arab Petroleum Exporting Countries (2008), *Annual Statistical Report 2008*.

REN21 (2009), *Renewables: Global Status Report. 2009 Update*. http://www.ren21.net/pdf/RE_GSR_2009_Update. pdf

Sambucini, Gianluca (2007), *Sustainable Development needs Energy Efficiency. New Approaches to International Partnership and Governance in Europe*. Unpublished Doctoral Dissertation, University of Bologna.

Stern, Nicholas (2006), *Stern Review: The Economics of Climate Change. Summary of Conclusions*. http://www.hm-treasury.gov.uk/d/CLOSED_SHORT_executive_summary.pdf

Tanaka, Nobuo (2009), *Worldwide Implementation Now – The Essential Role of Energy Efficiency. Presentation for Energy Efficiency Global Forum and Exposition*. http://www.iea.org/Textbase/speech/2009/Tanaka/EE_Global.pdf

Taylor, Robert *et al.* (2008), *Financing Energy Efficiency: Lessons from Brazil, China, India and Beyond*. http:// www.wds.worldbank.org/external/default/WDSContentServer/WDSP/IB/2008/02/18/000333037_20080218015226/ Rendered/PDF/425290PUB0ISBN11OFFICIAL0USE0ONLY10.pdf

Taylor, Robert (2009), *Creating an ESCO industry in developing markets*. Presentation at EE Global Conference, Paris 28th April 2009

The Carbon Trust (2008), *Global Carbon Mechanisms: Emerging Lessons and Implications*. http://www.carbontrust. co.uk/publications/publicationdetail.htm?productid=CTC747

The Economist (2009), *Fossilised policy*. 1 Oct 2009.

The World Bank (2008), *Development and climate change: a strategic framework for the World Bank Group*. http://siteresources.worldbank.org/EXTCC/Resources/40786312193392233881/DCCSFReporttoDevelopmentCommitteeOct122008.pdf

UNCTAD (2008), *World Investment Report 2008: Transnational Corporations, Agricultural Production and Development*.

UNCTAD (2009), *World Investment Report 2009: Transnational Corporation, Agricultural Production and Development*.

UNEP SEFI (2009), *The global financial crisis and its impact on renewable energy finance*. http://sefi.unep.org/fileadmin/media/sefi/docs/publications/Study_Financial_Crisis_impact_on_RE_.pdf

UNEP SEFI (2009), *Global Trends in Sustainable Energy Investment 2009. Analysis of Trends and Issues in the Financing of Renewable Energy and Energy Efficiency*. http://sefi.unep.org/fileadmin/media/sefi/docs/publications/Executive_Summary_2009_EN.pdf

UNFCCC (2007), *Investment and Financial Flows to Address Climate Change*. http://unfccc.int/files/cooperation_and_support/financial_mechanism/application/pdf/background_paper.pdf

UNFCCC (2008), *Investment and Financial Flows to Address Climate Change: an Update*. http://unfccc.int/resource/docs/2008/tp/07.pdf

Vattenfall (2007), *Global Mapping of Greenhouse Gas Abatement Opportunities up to 2030. Industry Sector Deep-Dive*. http://www.vattenfall.com/www/ccc/ccc/Gemeinsame_Inhalte/DOCUMENT/567263vattenfall/P0272863.pdf

WWF Hong Kong/Beijing Office (2008), *The value of carbon in China*. http://www.wwf.org.hk/eng/pdf/references/pressreleases_hongkong/WWFcarbon_report_FINAL_20080630_ENG.pdf

Zoellick, Robert B. (2008), Carbon Markets for Development. Presentation at the Bali Breakfast/Development Committee Series. http://siteresources.worldbank.org/INTCARBONFINANCE/Resources/Development_Committee_Bali_Breakfast_Series_Carbon_Markets_4_Development_10-08_final.pdf

Databases

Heritage Foundation, Index of Economic Freedom (http://www.heritage.org/Index/).

ECE, Statistics (http://www.unece.org/stats/links.htm)

Ecofys Azure International

OECD/IEA, SourceOECD statistical database, (http://www.sourceoecd.org/)

OLADE, Energy-Economic Information System (SIEE) (http://www.olade.org.ec/sieeEn.html)

Transparency International, Corruption Perception Index (http://www.transparency.org/policy_research/surveys_indices/cpi/2008)

UNCTAD, Division on Investment and Enterprise, FDI statistics (http://www.unctad.org/Templates/Page.asp?intItemID=4979)

UNEP, Risoe (http://cdmpipeline.org/)

World Bank, World Development Indicators (http://web.worldbank.org/WBSITE/EXTERNAL/DATASTATISTICS/0,,contentMDK:21725423~pagePK:64133150~piPK:64133175~theSitePK:239419,00.html)

World Economic Forum, Global Competitiveness Index (http://www.weforum.org/en/initiatives/gcp/Global%20Competitiveness%20Report/index.htm)